Research Methods in Indigenous Contexts

Arnold Groh

Research Methods in Indigenous Contexts

 Springer

Arnold Groh
Technical University of Berlin
Berlin, Germany

ISBN 978-3-319-72774-5   ISBN 978-3-319-72776-9   (eBook)
https://doi.org/10.1007/978-3-319-72776-9

Library of Congress Control Number: 2017964502

Printed on acid-free paper

This Springer imprint is published by Springer Nature
The registered company is Springer International Publishing AG
The registered company address is: Gewerbestrasse 11, 6330 Cham, Switzerland

"O brave new world that has such people in it."

Contents

Chapter 1
Introduction

Abstract Defining indigenous contexts is challenging, as attempts to define indigeneity even at UN level have had only limited success. However, we can describe perspectives that are essential with regard to our topic. The cultural approach is seen as necessary, because research in indigenous contexts inevitably implies trans- and intercultural aspects. Due to the different backgrounds of persons involved in such field research, effects of transgenerational traumata need to be taken into consideration, since this burden might play a role for indigenous persons when encountering globalised persons. To gain more insight into the mechanisms, some relevant cultural theories are addressed. Several theorists have used the metaphor of a cultural spectrum, with "cold", traditional, archaic or indigenous culture at one end and "hot", modern, fast-changing culture at the other end. When we model cultural change according to cultural theories, synthesis of different cultures leads to "heating up" in the sense that the resulting culture, as compared to the predecessor cultures, is located in a "warmer" part of the spectrum, further away from the traditional end and closer to the end representing "hot", modern, fast-changing culture. As another consequence, cultural dominance can be explained as resulting from the relative positions of cultures within the spectrum, because during the process of synthesis, those cultural elements are chosen to be kept that are expected to be advantageous, while those that are seen as less effective are given up. Thus, "hot" culture is dominant – and eventually destructive – towards "cold" culture. These perspectives clarify the constellation of roles, when globalised researchers are situated in indigenous contexts.

Keywords Indigenous · Transgenerational traumata · Cultural theories · Cultural dominance · Spectrum of cultures · Cultural change

Doing research in indigenous contexts calls for a particular attention regarding the methodology applied. To understand why this is so, and how research in indigenous contexts should be done in the best way, we need to have a sound conceptualisation of culture. This is a precondition for explaining the difference between indigenous and other research contexts.

The definition of indigeneity is an issue that has not been finally clarified; probably it is not definable in the customary sense. However, there are some points upon which at least the UN bodies in charge have agreed, as we shall see in more detail

© Springer International Publishing AG 2018
A. Groh, *Research Methods in Indigenous Contexts*,
https://doi.org/10.1007/978-3-319-72776-9_1

in Chapter 2. What we mean by indigenous contexts in this book is based on relevant conceptualisations of culture. We shall have a look at some noteworthy cultural theories later on in this chapter. An indigenous context is not given per se by the fact that someone there has indigenous ancestry. Nor is it given just due to the legal circumstance of a territory belonging to an indigenous group, if that group has decided to live the global industrial way of life. Rather, a context is considered indigenous if traditional culture is alive in it. And when we talk about culture being lived, then we do not mean folklore that is presented on festivals and celebrations or that is on display in museums. Argyle (1972) put it this way:

> "By the culture of a group of people is meant their whole way of life - their language, ways of perceiving, categorizing and thinking about the world, forms of nonverbal communication and social interaction, rules and conventions about behaviour, moral values and ideas, technology and material culture, art, science, literature and history". (p. 139f.)

As long as we do not investigate the particular culture's members' cognitions, the semiotic aspects are those that matter. This includes everything directly perceivable, the visual culture, behaviour patterns, food and language. Culture is a communication space, and if that space is our research context, then we should be very much aware of any effects that result from our own presence within that space. We are the intruders, and everything perceivable of us interferes with that context. Ourselves, in particular our visual or otherwise perceivable self-presentation, as well as the material culture that we carry as artefacts, and our behaviour are all units or acts of communication. As these two communication systems, the hosts' and our own, contact and pervade each other, we should take care to minimise the interference effects and make sure that no destabilisation of the indigenous culture results from our presence.

The research that takes place in indigenous contexts is, by nature, field research. There are, of course, situations in which indigenous persons might participate in research outside their traditional context. This would be the case, for example, when indigenous persons leave their group to participate in a conference dealing with indigenous affairs and, while being there, take part in a survey or in a research interview or answer the items of a questionnaire.

The necessity of doing research in indigenous contexts is increasing, as we tend to forget about the way of life that is specific to our species. The more traditional an indigenous way of life is, the more it differs from our globalised lifestyle. This generally means that it is closer to the way that *Homo sapiens* has lived on this planet throughout the millennia. With regard to the effects of globalisation, such as CO_2 emissions, the rapid increase of the extinction of species, the poisoning of the oceans, the destruction of the ozone layer or the population explosion, things have gone out of hand relatively recently in the history of humankind. There is no orientation in looking ahead, as the figures of global change are not very promising. We do not really have any effective remedies to cure the planet from desertification, and with regard to global warming, all we have come up with so far are mitigating measures to slow down the temperature increase. When we talk about man-made problems, we should be somewhat more precise and say that it is predominantly the industrial culture that is responsible. Labelling these problems anthropogenic does not mean that we can generally blame them on humans. Rather, we have to blame a particular lifestyle. Humans have lived here for thousands of years without bringing about such global harm. And there are our fellow humans, in other cultures, who also live in a more environmentally friendly way. Among the options that we have regarding our approach towards them, infecting them with our destructive lifestyle is the worst, though the most practised. The best option would be to learn from their ways.

But that is only possible as long as these indigenous cultures exist. Our culture's incompetence to live on earth without destroying it is reason enough to do research in indigenous contexts. But it would be very irrational if we did that research in a way that would bring about an end to indigenous cultures. Research in indigenous contexts needs to be done in a minimally invasive way, and if our culture has already started to destroy a particular indigenous culture, we should do our best to restabilise it. That is what this book is about: doing research in indigenous contexts in a way that conforms with indigenous rights and other legal requirements, with methodological standards and with ethical norms.

Of course, the global ecological problems are not the only motivation for doing research with indigenous peoples. Psychologists, who want to understand the functions of the human being, often need to do cross-cultural research, in order to contrast behaviour patterns that are prevalent in the industrial culture, with the corresponding behaviour in non-industrial cultures, so that they can filter out culturally specific from universally human behaviour. Similarly, sociologists, anthropologists and ethnologists are interested in social structures and their relation to the status of a culture. Architects might want to find some down-to-earth inspirations for new designs. Botanists could be interested in plants as yet unknown to them and therefore ask indigenous peoples about the species that they know and their uses. It is not uncommon that indigenous peoples can tell you some usage for up to 98 percent of the plants in their area.

The necessity to behave in a culturally sustainable way concerns anyone who comes into contact with indigenous peoples. Even if botanists are not directly interested in the indigenous culture, or if linguists are only interested in the flections of particular adjectives, and not in the rest of the culture, or if geologists only want to investigate the rock strata of a certain cliff in an indigenous territory, they all are seen and otherwise taken notice of by the indigenous peoples. This transcultural input cannot be avoided, because the researchers exist, they are present and they cannot make themselves invisible. Once the research takes place, it is no longer the question *if* it should happen at all, but what matters is *how* it is carried out.

If the transfer of cultural elements that is to say of certain behaviour specific to the dominant, global industrial culture is the source of risk to delete the last, most valuable indigenous cultures of the world, then we need to understand these mechanisms and functions that pose the hazard. In these indigenous cultures, information is stored of human behaviour that is compatible with the natural environment. Apparently, our culture is not able any more to make use of nature without destroying it. If we would now destroy the indigenous cultures, too, no one would be left, who knows how to live the natural way. Indigenous cultures are often destroyed with the best intentions, claiming that they need "development". If this planet is still inhabited in, say, 500 years, then it is likely that the industrial culture does not exist anymore. It is not based on stability, but on fluctuation, on the consumption of resources and on profit maximisation. If things go on as they do now, then a small chance is left for humankind to survive due to indigenous peoples, especially those, who live in voluntary isolation in remote regions, deep inside areas that are difficult to penetrate. These are the niches, where *Homo sapiens* could survive. The industrial culture is the opposite of that.

When we link theory to indigenous contexts, then our attention should be directed to cultural theories that are of explanatory value regarding the transcultural mechanisms within the relation of the global culture and indigenous peoples. Furthermore, in the linkage of theory to the concrete settings, those indigenous contexts are of particular interest to our considerations that are most prototypical for non-globalised, non-industrial ways of living.

The research methods pertinent to indigenous contexts are those which do not push forward the destruction of indigenous cultures. Apart from the fact that destroying cultures is a violation of various international and national human rights and indigenous rights articles, researchers should meet indigenous peoples with respect. They should not rate the global culture better or rank it higher than other cultures. Methodologically, such a feeling of superiority would cloud the objective view, anyway, because it would constitute an undue premise, which would then influence the outcome. We shall discuss methodological applications under the aspect of their cultural sustainability in Chapter 3.

About This Book This book aims at equipping researchers and researchers-to-be with the methodological knowledge necessary to conduct fieldwork with indigenous peoples in a way that is acceptable from both cultures' perspectives, whereby the acceptability from the globalised point of view should be given with regard to legal, methodological and ethical requirements. At the same time, by stimulating the culture-related discourse, decision-makers, stakeholders and others in charge of defining policies are provided with information that should serve as a basis for bringing about positive changes, as well as for averting further destabilising impulses.

By doing so, this book shall try to avoid the presentation of commonplaces. Since it primarily addresses advanced readers, many of the basics of already existing student textbooks are not repeated here. Various things, which can be assumed as known, or which you can easily look up at Wikipedia or other readily accessible sources, shall not be reiterated here. Whereas such things are skipped, this book points out aspects that other books circumvent, and it focuses on aspects that others ignore. In that way, this book directs the attention very much towards those indigenous cultures, which are least affected by the dominant culture. There are countless publications about hybrid cultures that are positioned somewhere in the transition zone between the previous indigenous state and the globalised culture. They are often proudly presented as indigenous cultures, although in these cases, the indigenous cultural elements have already been given up for the most part and replaced by elements of the globalised culture. Adducing such societies as paradigms for indigenous cultures is problematic under the aspect of conceptualisation, epistemology, methodology and application. For exactly these reasons, and furthermore under human rights aspects, disregarding indigenous peoples close to nature is inadequate, although it is a phenomenon on its own, and it would certainly be worthwhile to investigate it under a socio-cognitive perspective. However, this book tries to counterbalance such biases, which exist in the perception and interest of the dominant culture, of which scientific research is an originary part.

Serving the functions of a textbook as well as of a handbook, it is a complement to the classical standard literature, where you can look up things like how to build a design, how to select samples, how to conduct interviews or how to present the data (e.g. Ritchie & Lewis, 2003), as most readers are probably familiar with this, and it would be boring to recapitulate it. Therefore, this book rather explains how to apply field research methods in an appropriate way to indigenous contexts, and it directs the attention to peculiarities to be mindful of. You might find some rhetorical resemblances to Girtler's (2001) book on methods of field research, but actually, the present book starts where Girtler ends, and it does not follow the stipulation of confining oneself to a very limited qualitative approach, but by all means, it also appreciates quantitative approaches, as long as they are compatible with the requirements of the indigenous setting. Generally, researchers should be encouraged by this book to work trans- and interdisciplinarily and to bring together various approaches, so that the strength of one approach will compensate the weakness of another approach and they complement each other. Therefore, it is useful to likewise resort to psychological studies, theoretical treatise from the humanities, legal debates and so forth, if they help us to answer the research question. The psychological perspective, which is taken consistently here, is regarded as essential for any studies that have to do with humans. As for field research in indigenous contexts, this pertains to both sides: those who are researching and those who are being researched. The necessity to examine the researchers' perceptions, cognitions, motivations, decisions, emotions and behaviour is often underestimated, although their reasonable functioning is the precondition for any useful research.

The reasons for the perspectives taken in this book are given by the learning processes that I had to go through myself, and during which I had to give up some positions, perspectives and aspects that I had previously taken for granted. I did not give them up in a sweeping way, though, like some ideologists and dogmatists do, by condemning one culture altogether, while idealising others. The globalised culture and indigenous cultures all consist of humans, with virtues and shortcomings. I appreciate very much the tools of the trade, with which the various sciences have equipped us as researchers. It is the consistent application of these tools, based on logic, which helps us to realise where the interpretive schemes, which we have internalised due to our socialisation in our own culture of origin, hinder us from understanding phenomena in an objective, unbiased way.

Although I have been doing research and have stayed with indigenous peoples in Asia, Australia, Africa and the Americas since the 1980s, I definitely am a globalised person. No doubt about it. This does not mean that indigenous cultures did not have any impact on me. The experiences gained with indigenous peoples certainly have enabled me to see and reflect about the world in ways that would not have been possible otherwise. But being raised in Europe, the fact is that my formative socialisation took place within the industrial culture. By the way, this book resorts to a number of non-English resources, which the English-speaking audience will hopefully find to be an enrichment.

The impact of indigenous culture on a globalised but eager-to-learn researcher is an asset rather than something that would erase the initial socialisation and undo it. This is a premise, under which this book addresses the academic audience – researchers and researchers-to-be. We have to bear in mind, though, that the concept of a "researcher", as applied here, is something genuinely European, as is the idea of science. These concepts have originated in Europe, even if it is translated into action in non-European places nowadays. Globalisation is, in fact, the worldwide implementation of basically European culture. For us scientists, being able to analyse, as well as to criticise, globalisation should imply the honesty to admit that we are part of this culture, if we like it or not. At the same time, we should be able to separate our personal feelings towards whatsoever culture from scientific work. From the perspective of the philosophy of science, we can say that science only *takes place within* the world. This is comparable to football: it takes place on a defined field, and it has to be played within that field according to defined rules. When the ball crosses the line, it goes into touch, meaning it is out of game then. The whole, big rest of the world is outside the playing field. Likewise, there is life and there is the world outside of science, which is only the application of procedures in order to gain knowledge. The procedures have been defined by ourselves. We could have defined them differently, and in fact, when we look at the history of science, the rules are changing over time. Writing this book with regard to our understanding of science does not mean that I ignore indigenous voices calling for indigenous research (e.g. Rigney, 1997) with foci analogous to the globalised disciplines, such as indigenous psychologies, indigenous sociologies and so forth. These indigenous approaches are often termed as plurals, to highlight the fact that, different from globalised standardisation, there are at least as many different indigenous approaches per discipline as there are indigenous peoples involved in it. Anyway, it would be presumptuous for a globalised author to claim expertise for such an indigenous approach. This is not only true for the author of this book but also for anyone socialised in and educated by global standards. This is largely independent of a person's family background. The colour of the skin does not matter; that would actually be racist. There are so many scientists in the world with indigenous backgrounds, but once they primarily have internalised global patterns of thinking and acting, it would be racist, too, if they would claim to be indigenous experts with reference to their genes, when their cognitive and behavioural patterns are, like those of researchers with European family history, globalised. In that sense, this book is written by a globalised researcher for other globalised researchers.

1.1   Indigenous Contexts

According to Article 33 of the United Nations Declaration on the Rights of Indigenous Peoples, it is the indigenous peoples themselves, who have the right to define their indigeneity. At first sight, this article looks somewhat problematic. By referring to this, there might be groups or single persons, who claim to be "indigenous", even though all renowned experts on this issue would agree that they were not. In fact, there was a French lady, who participated over years in sessions of the UN Working Group on Indigenous Populations,[1] claiming to be a representative of the Celts. And there were self-declared representatives of the "Washita" participating in these sessions as well. The latter were black people from the south of the USA. It would be difficult to call them Afro-Americans, because they claim to have been in their place before Columbus and that they had founded all great empires on earth, like Ancient Egypt, Ancient China and so forth. As we can see from these two examples, there are uncommon people around, and at least at UN session on indigenous issues, we have become used to live with that.

Article 33 of the UN Declaration on the Rights of Indigenous Peoples is a reaction to the lengthy discussion about indigeneity, which did not come to a final conclusion and thus did not reach any agreement about a definition of the term. There had been many suggestions, of course, some of which also are reflected by particular articles of the declaration, like the territorial aspect or the aspect of knowledge systems, which has also been pointed out by Purcell (1998). Other authors criticised the attempt to define indigeneity at all, pointing out that any categorisation of that kind was subject to certain interests, especially with regard to political power. These interests should be seen as being in the tradition of former colonial constellations; they therefore include strong economic aspects, and the perception of the other culture takes place in relation to the own culture, which implicitly serves as valuing measure and orientation (cf. Zaumseil, 2006).

Although we have not come up with any final definition of indigeneity, there have been conceptualisations in two prominent United Nations working papers, one by José Martínez Cobo (United Nations, 1981–1983) and another one by Erica Daes (United Nations, 1996), which gave direction to the perspectives taken in the United Nations Declaration on the Rights of Indigenous Peoples. We shall go into more detail in the next chapter of this book and only touch the international law aspects rather briefly here.

Claiming Acknowledgement   The conceptual context, in which the term "indigenous" is used, needs some differentiation. There are persons who claim to be indigenous by quite rightly referring to their genealogical descent from an indigenous people. But sometimes, that is about all. They might live in New York, work as a lawyer and hardly differ in their lifestyle from their non-indigenous neighbours. Apart from tiny genetic particularities, it is the consciousness that they have indigenous ancestry, which matters to them. They might therefore be interested in folkloric

---

[1] Then renamed "United Nations Working Group on Indigenous Peoples".

cultural elements, which then serve as semiotic reference to their forefathers and foremothers. As we can derive from studies on symbolic self-completion, the more the person feels deficient with regard to the claimed identity, the stronger is the use of such signs (Wicklund & Gollwitzer, 1982; Gollwitzer et al., 2009). However, their wish of being seen as someone with a certain identity should be respected, and it should be noted that such a psychosocial situation is nothing static. Rather, Article 11 of the United Nations Declaration on the Rights of Indigenous Peoples grants the right of revitalisation, so that one day, such persons or their descendants might indeed live the traditional way.

From a philosophy of law perspective, this brings us into a slight dilemma. There are other people out there without that particular gene segment but with the same or similar passion for First Nations or one certain people thereof. They might engage in activities related to this culture; might even learn the language, learn their dances and learn how to prepare typical food; and perhaps be the proud owner of a feather headdress. Not accepting their indigeneity would, at first sight, be problematic because in the constitutions of many countries, it is clarified that no one may be discriminated on the basis of descent or "race". A solution to this problem was pointed out in Erica Daes' (United Nations, 1996) UN Working Paper: the self-identification as being indigenous by an individual is not enough; there also needs to be acceptance of that claim by the group concerned.[2] This could lead to special cases of persons being indigenous even without any such genes. For example, I know a First Nations enthusiast from Geneva, Switzerland, with a big eagle tattoo across his chest, who has been adopted by a North American indigenous group.

Again, determining indigeneity merely on the basis of genealogy or ethnicity would actually be equivalent to a racist position (cf. Harris et al., 2013). It is not the genes that make up a person to be indigenous. Seen from another perspective, persons, who have been born into an indigenous culture and raised there, have the right to change over to the globalised culture. Indeed, many of such persons do so. But as equal rights should be afforded to all, the same switching of sides should then also be possible from the globalised into an indigenous culture. When we take an even more abstract view by speaking of culture A and culture B or X, Y and Z, then it becomes clear that changes *between different* indigenous cultures have to be equally accepted.

Unfortunately, persons' changes between cultures are not always an involuntary act. Even until the second half of the twentieth century, indigenous children have been systematically removed from their parents and given to non-indigenous foster parents or to special boarding schools, in order to prevent them from internalising indigenous culture but instead make them part of the global culture. The governments responsible for this were actually aiming at cultural genocide, or ethnocide, not striving for the physical elimination of the indigenous peoples but rather for the deletion of the indigenous cultures. Some features of these actions had their parallels

---

[2]Cf. section G 35, quotation from Mr. M. Dodson, Aboriginal and Torres Strait Islander Social Justice Commissioner.

in the Nazis' plans of the Germanisation ("Eindeutschung") of those eastern Europeans, who they would consider life-worthy (Heiber, 1958). Depending on the age of the children, separation from their families can cause lifelong suffering. In this context, we should not fail to mention that child theft is part of some indigenous cultures. Whereas throughout their history such abductions primarily took place in the form that indigenous peoples took away children from other indigenous peoples, it also happened, though rarely, that they took non-indigenous children. Child theft committed by indigenous peoples, though, is by far outnumbered by the cases of indigenous children, who have been forcibly removed from their parents by dominant government authorities. However, the one aspect doesn't make the other any better.

When any of these persons, who have changed over to another culture in their early childhood, voluntarily or involuntarily, then have grown up in that other culture, they have been socialised in that context. There, they have implemented culture-specific behaviour patterns, including cognitive styles. It could then hardly be maintained that these persons are still part of the cultural context, in which they had been before their abduction. Such a cultural belonging would imply knowledge of the language, dietary customs and many other cultural techniques and skills, which are characteristic to a particular society. Furthermore, when those persons are not told about their origin, and if they do not come to wonder about it, because their ethnic features do not differ significantly from those of their present cultural context, then their social and cultural identity would be equivalent to the identity of anyone of the society they are living in. However, if these persons are told where they come from, they might either become interested to find out more about their biological background, or they might block it out, because they find the issue burdensome, as they do not want to destabilise their present social system. When their ethnic features are strikingly different from the social context, they might feel a need for clarification and thus become more involved in the issue of their origin. Yet, when they start to become acquainted with the culture, from which they had been abducted, by learning the language and acquiring knowledge about that culture, then they can only do that from a position like other persons from their context culture, who have not been abducted but have been born into it. What is important for the question of indigeneity is the point that persons do not belong to a culture because of their genes but rather because of the memes they share. The term "meme" describes units of cognitive content referring to behaviour patterns that are culturally transmitted. While some theorists have preferred approaches parallel to genetics – hence the phonetic resemblance of genes and memes – others have pointed out the differences of these two conceptualisations (Boyd & Richerson, 2000).

Indigenous Cultures   The usage of the term "indigenous", referring to the belief of single persons regarding their indigeneity, is hardly of any relevance for our topic, as such a belief can take place in a globalised, industrialised context, which by no means can be called an indigenous context. But when we speak of an "indigenous culture", things are quite different. "Culture" by itself is a context. Therefore, by using the term "indigenous culture", we mean a context that has been subject to relatively little influence from globalisation or perhaps one that even has not had any such influence. The less globalised influence it has had, the more authentic it is. Or the more globalised influence such a culture has had, the less authentic it is. At a certain point, it would cease to exist as an indigenous culture. That does not mean that it would not be a culture any more. It might be a hybrid culture, such as the creole cultures. It might still have some vivid folklore but otherwise live a more modern lifestyle. By the way, there is no social system without culture, though not all cultures are indigenous.

Indigenous cultures differ very much from each other. This is not only due to environmental conditions. For outsiders, indigenous peoples of a certain region of the world might look more or less the same, so that they sweepingly refer to them as "Indians of Brazil" or "Australian Aborigines". But in fact, indigenous peoples generally contrast themselves from neighbouring groups. One aspect under which this makes sense is ecology. When each group has dietary preferences different from the other groups, then no species is overused – no animal species is over-hunted and no type of fruit is over-collected, so that enough seeds are left and the plant species can continue growing. For example, when one group would like to hunt and eat toucan birds, then it would abominate to eat ant bears. But a neighbouring group would love to eat ant bears and abominate to eat toucans. This is comparable to the fact that in the European culture, the idea of eating cats or dogs would be abhorrent, but people keep these animals as pets. These dietary preferences are part of indigenous peoples' identities (Gibbons, 1992). With regard to linguistics, the dialects or even languages spoken can vary enormously. Even when languages of indigenous groups living a few kilometres apart belong to the same language family, they can differ considerably. For example, the linguistic differences from one indigenous camp in North Australian Arnhem Land to the next indigenous camp are such that only very few of the everyday life expressions resemble each other (Brinke, 1977). This is comparable to Spanish, German, English and Russian, which all are Indo-European languages, but the speakers cannot understand each other properly, unless they have learnt the other speaker's language. Interestingly, indigenous peoples often are proficient in several languages, but usually, this does not have the effect that they give up their mother tongue and agree upon one lingua franca. Only where dominance effects take place, such as globalisation, the indigenous persons of the cultures concerned adopt official languages or creole languages. Persons from families that have been urbanised since generations are often even monolingual in the colonial language, although they assign themselves to a precolonial local culture. As these persons live in cities, which are manifestations of imported cultural elements, it is evident that language use goes along with lifestyle.

With regard to their culture-environment relation, indigenous peoples also differ a lot. If we consider a scale from total compatibility with the natural environment to total incompatibility with the natural environment, then the modern industrial culture can be found at the incompatible extreme. For millennia, there had been humans at the other extreme of total compatibility with the natural environment. Like other species, they lived in, with and from nature without destroying it. The last known people living in such total immersion in nature were the so-called Tasman Aborigines (Halfmann, 1998). Generally, the use of fire is said to make humans distinct from other species. But the Tasmanians probably did not use fire and therefore were non-destructive, only living from what nature provided. They could have been our teachers of sustainable management. But by the mid-nineteenth century, they were killed in the course of British colonisation. It is said that when the last male Tasmanian had died in 1869, a tobacco pouch was made out of his scrotum. The extinction of the Tasmanians was one of the many genocides of the European expansion, which is still going on. We call it globalisation now. Europeans apparently have a problem with accepting other cultures' lifestyles.

As far as known, none of the indigenous peoples left alive live in such total immersion in nature as the Tasmanians did. Slash-and-burn agriculture is widely practised (Moran, 1995). On the scale of compatibility with the natural environment, indigenous cultures gradually differ from each other, although they are generally positioned within the more compatible section. However, we should be eager to see things objectively. It would be a misconception if someone would think that indigenous peoples and their cultures were to be glorified. Their compatibility with nature is often an effect of the lack of means to interfere with nature. If they had these means, their behaviour would probably not be that different from industrial people's behaviour. As a result of globalising influence, many indigenous persons would nowadays be happy to have a chainsaw, because then, they could quickly and easily make money by selling timber. And they know best, where the valuable trees can be found. Environmental destruction is not unique to the European culture, and it has been practised by indigenous peoples before receiving European influence. For example, there is evidence that there is a connection between pre-Columbian deforestation by indigenous peoples in the southwest of North America and the desertification, which led to the present arid situation of that region (Kohler & Matthews, 1988). In a much larger scale and other than their Tasmanian neighbours, Australian indigenous peoples have burnt down forests for thousands of years prior to European colonisation (Bliege Bird et al., 2008), giving shape to what is now a desert continent.

Earth must have been a nice green planet in former times. There is this popular joke about two planets, one asking the other, "How do you do?" – "Not too good, I am very ill." – "What is it?" – "Homo sapiens".[3]

Some indigenous contexts still preserve the last remnants of the formerly intact functional interaction of human culture with nature. There is a correlation of traditional indigenous life with the intactness of culture. Rich ecosystems with a high density of species can especially be found in the territories of tropical hunter-gatherer societies.

Since cultures are located in a wide range, from those living in intimate relationship with nature to the industrialised culture, which is most distant to nature by seeing it as an object to manage, with many possible locations along this range, in

---

[3] Some sceptics carry on: "Don't worry, it'll soon be over".

between the two extremes, indigeneity can only be conceptualised as something relative. The most indigenous cultures are those which still live in intense closeness to culture, like hunter-gatherers, followed by those who already practice some slash-and-burn agriculture and then by those who live in even further distance from nature. In practice, further distance from nature nowadays means further involvement with globalisation. Earlier in history, the equivalents to globalisation were present in the regional ancient civilisations. The point we can make here is that indigeneity dwindles with distance from nature.

Indigenous Peoples' Relations with Their External Contexts In today's world, indigenous peoples always live in a socio-political context, formally. But how about those living in voluntary isolation? It is a matter of definition if one could say that indigenous peoples have lived in a socio-political context at any time in history. Yet, one could probably say so, when internal, as well as inter-tribal, regulations are seen as equivalent to modern world politics. What is relevant for our concerns is the relation of today's indigenous peoples to the government and official authorities of the country within the borders of which they live. Usually, they have not been involved when borders had been defined. Neither have they been asked in which country they wanted to live or if they would be fond of the idea of any nation at all. Nevertheless, states are a reality now, and indigenous peoples are affected by this reality to different degrees. A few of them can still enjoy a remoteness, in which they rarely are disturbed. If they are disturbed, this commonly does not happen by government officials but by settlers, loggers or backpackers, which government policies fail to keep away, in the case that the indigenous territory lies in a protected area. Other indigenous peoples might be concerned by the states borders themselves, which are dissecting their land and their community, or the area, in which they formally used to lead a nomadic life. The more an indigenous people's habitat is accessed by a globalised infrastructure, the more involved is this people with the industrial culture. The degree of this involvement implicates a likewise gradual involvement with the economy of the country, so that we also have to take the relativity of an integration into the economic context into consideration. As a general rule, the globalised economic context is not compatible with the indigenous culture and with its social structures. Consequently, many indigenous peoples are challenged to cope with this incompatibility. Some of them try to evade this challenge, either by withdrawal, if that is possible, to areas less affected by globalisation or by predominantly staying in their village and avoiding to go to town. In certain cases, attitudes towards globalisation split indigenous communities, and elders are not respected by the young ones any more, as tradition requires and as it used to be in former times and for ages. Usually, it is the elders who wish to maintain the cultural and social structures, but their authority vanishes under the globalising influences. There is a dilemma, which, to a certain extent, is also reflected in the United Nations Declaration on the Rights of Indigenous Peoples, in which precautions are installed to prevent that indigenous peoples are refused to have access to healthcare, sanitation and the industrial culture's amenities in general (Article 21). Theoretically, the younger ones, who leave the indigenous village and go to town could refer to these promises of the UN declaration, and theoretically again, it could be expected that the dominant culture's representatives in charge would follow such claims, without taking into consideration the position of the elders back in the village. However, ignoring their position would collide with quite a number of rights granted in the UN declaration, such as the right to self-government, the right to own legal systems or the right to maintain traditions and customs. One basic aspect throughout the United Nations Declaration on the Rights of Indigenous Peoples is that indigenous peoples are to be seen as collectives, and it seems that the decay of indigenous communities has not sufficiently been taken into consideration. Nevertheless, there is a tenor of the UN declaration that traditional legal norms be respected, and since in most indigenous societies, the elders traditionally are the legal authorities, rather their wish to maintain their culture has to be respected, than young indigenous individual's appreciation of globalisation. But we have to further differentiate even on the individual level. Of course, not all younger indigenous individuals prefer the globalised lifestyle. An indigenous lady from a relatively traditional village in Panama, only about 2 h away from the capital, once told me that she had never been to the city and that she had no intention of going there, because it was so nice in the village. There are other indigenous persons, who only stay away temporarily, for example, when they go to market, and again others are globalised on workdays, when they have a job in town, and they are indigenous on the weekends, when they live in their village.

However, indigenous persons, when taking part in the economic system, are often short-changed, be it on the market or be it as employees, although the United Nations Declaration on the Rights of Indigenous Peoples seeks to take precautions against this (Article 17). In some Australian age groups, for example, non-indigenous persons earn 3.4 times as much as indigenous persons (Biddle, 2013). Similarly, indigenous peoples are disadvantaged regarding educational attainment, like in Bangladesh, where there is a lack of teachers in the peripheries and instruction does not take place in the indigenous languages (Hossain, 2013). Indigenous peoples generally have less access to healthcare than non-indigenous persons. In Latin American countries, indigenous infant mortality is three to four times higher than the national averages, indigenous maternal mortality is estimated several times higher in remote areas, and generally, morbidity rates are higher in indigenous populations than in the non-indigenous population; for instance, the prevalence of tuberculosis among the Guaraní of Bolivia is five to eight times as high as the national average (Montenegro & Stephens, 2006). Indigenous persons' life expectancy at birth is significantly lower as compared to the non-indigenous population. These gaps have been estimated, for example, for Australian Aboriginal peoples as 12.5 years for males and 12.0 years for females and as 7.3 years for male and 6.8 years for female New Zealand Māoris (Phillips et al., 2017). At the same time, indigenous peoples generally have higher birth rates than globalised societies. To give an Australian example again, estimated figures are 2.1 babies per Aboriginal and Torres Strait Islander mother, as compared to 1.8 babies per non-indigenous mother (Smylie et al., 2010). It has to be taken into consideration, though, that it is very difficult to obtain reliable birth rate data regarding indigenous populations

(Johnstone, 2009). An excellent global overview on indigenous health issues is given by Silburn et al. (2016).

Official assessments of the situation of indigenous peoples, who are participating in the economic context, usually fail to take sufficient account of indigenous perspectives as how to meet their requirements, standards and expectations. The indigenous peoples' position regarding their relation to the economy and politics of the state in which they live is seen as subordinate to the goals of the globalising economies. This becomes particularly evident in the formulation of the so-called Millennium Development Goals (MDGs) as presented by the United Nations member states at the Millennium Summit in 2000. The eight goals defined are (1) the eradication of extreme hunger and poverty; (2) universal primary education; (3) gender equality and women's empowerment; (4) the reduction of child mortality; (5) the improvement of maternal health; (6) the combat against HIV/AIDS, malaria and other diseases, (7) ensuring environmental sustainability; and (8) the development of a global partnership for development (UN Millennium Project, 2005). These goals sound very positive and appreciable to globalised ears. Yet, this is only the very narrow perspective of the dominant culture. Surprisingly, the United Nations Department of Economic and Social Affairs puts it straight in its 2009 report on the State of the World's Indigenous Peoples:

"By advancing the dominant paradigms of health and development rather than an approach based on individual and collective human rights, the MDGs also promote projects that are potentially detrimental to indigenous peoples, and which violate their rights to their collective land, territories and natural resources. Moreover, because the cultures and worldviews of indigenous peoples are not taken into account in the formulation of the MDGs, the goals do not consider the indigenous concept of health, which extends beyond the physical and mental well-being of an individual to the spiritual balance and well-being of the community as a whole". (p. 156).

The treatment which indigenous peoples receive in many countries of the world is actually not targeted at the well-being of their communities as a whole. Globalised pragmatics are rather functional and often dehumanised. Strategies of governments that are directed against indigenous life include coerced abortions (Frohmader, 2013) and forced sterilisations. "Coercive sterilization policies and practices against indigenous peoples and ethnic minorities, particularly girls and women, have a long history across the globe" (WHO, 2014, p. 4). This is not just a dark chapter of the colonial past, as "indigenous peoples and ethnic minorities (…) continue to be sterilized without their full, free and informed consent" (ibid., p. 1). As we can see, many indigenous peoples are not just socially or economically disadvantaged. Ethnic cleansing continues in many parts of the world to an extent that even the relevant Wikipedia lists need regular updates.[4] At the 2017 session of the United Nations Expert Mechanism on the Rights of Indigenous Peoples, I attended a panel

---

[4]<https://en.wikipedia.org/wiki/List_of_ethnic_cleansing_campaigns#21st_century>

discussion[5] on a markedly disgusting aspect, which is ongoing cannibalism based on the belief among some Bantu that not only sexual intercourse with a Pygmy woman would heal any illness, including HIV, but that eating Pygmy flesh would make them invulnerable, even against bullets. Other practices directed against indigenous peoples have been the deportations of indigenous children, as mentioned above, in connection with government initiatives such as the American Indian boarding schools in the USA, the Canadian Indian residential schools or the official removal of Aboriginal children in Australia (Tatz, 1999). It is perfectly clear that indigenous persons who remember that they have been torn away from their families, who have experienced sexual or any other physical violence or who have been subject to any other of these forcible measures are severely traumatised. Such traumatisations have been practised throughout centuries, with devastating effects over generations.

1.1.1 Transgenerational Traumata

When doing research in indigenous contexts, not only the present situation with its constellation of cultures matters, but there is also the burden of the past. We know that people from our culture have committed atrocities against indigenous peoples, and indigenous peoples also know that. Whereas for us this is a rather abstract issue, indigenous persons often are affected by the ongoing European expansion, or globalisation, themselves, and they are familiar with first-hand information. They experience logging and the destruction of their habitats, and they might have clan members, who report of eviction and maltreatment. Psychologically, there are profound differences between the notion of being part of the culprits' culture and the notion of being part of a victimised culture. Research on the effects of such a consciousness has primarily been carried out with regard to descendants of Holocaust survivors. The general findings are that effects can still be found, even in the second and third generation.

The mechanisms behind that have been discussed within several lines of research relating to the Holocaust that try to explain the transgenerational passing on of trauma effects. Those mechanisms that have been claimed, or for which even evidence has been found, are of relevance not only for persons with Holocaust-related family histories but for anyone with traumatised ancestry.

The epigenetic model has gained some prominence. It says that external factors can cause changes in the genes of a person and that these changes are then passed on to the next generation. Actually, everybody's DNA is modified by influences of

---

[5] United Nations, Geneva, side event, 10 July 2017, "Monitoring, reporting and advocacy for human rights and the prevention of genocide", organised by the Indigenous Peoples of Africa Coordinating Committee, with panelists Diel Mochire (DRC), Vital Bambanze (Burundi), Albert Barume (President / African Expert to EMRIP), Victoria Tauli Corpuz (UN Special Rapporteur on Indigenous Peoples) and OHCHR representatives.

the environment by chemical tags, which switch certain parts of the genes on or off. Usually, these tags attached to the genes only affect the respective person, but not the offspring, because the DNA is cleaned during the fertilisation process. But apparently, some particular tags manage to be excluded from the cleaning, thus being transmitted to the child. One of the studies supporting this has been carried out by Yehuda et al. (2015), who found that not only Holocaust survivors themselves but also their children have lower levels of cortisol. This hormone restabilises the bodily functions after traumatisation. These findings are in line with earlier studies showing that animals, which had been trained to fear certain stimuli, can pass this fear on to their descendants, although that offspring never encountered those stimuli themselves (Callaway, 2013).

Other approaches manage to explain the transgenerational passing on of trauma effects without taking genes into consideration. In the model of learning theory (Bandura, 1962), children perceive others', especially their parents', behaviour patterns and copy them. From the perspective of behaviour theory, particular behaviour is conditioned through reinforcement (Skinner, 1948; Miltenberger, 2012). More complex approaches consider family dynamics and disturbed communication, which cause children to internalise certain trauma-related perspectives, although it was their parents, but not them, who had experienced the trauma.

Social-cognitive models (Lewin, 1951), too, can explain traumatised behaviour by proxy, even when the children do not receive any trauma-related input by their parents. Knowing that "I belong to a group that has suffered" is enough for the person to identify with the trauma-related perspectives, which then unfold their psychological and social, cognitive and behavioural, effects.

All these models of passing on trauma effects across generations underline the aspect that we, as researchers in indigenous contexts, have to take into consideration that indigenous peoples, who me meet, might carry such a load. In a generalising way, they might project the reasons of the trauma onto us, as we are representatives of the dominant culture. Therefore, we should do our best by ensuring them by ways of our behaviour that we distance ourselves from all evil and that we have no destructive intentions. With our behaviour and self-presentation, we should rather communicate acceptance and respect towards the indigenous peoples.

1.2   Cultural Theories and Cultural Dominance

There are various theories on culture that have been presented, especially during the twentieth century. Some of them had a lasting effect on academic conceptualisations, some have been refuted by later investigations, and others have been refined to follow up theories that are more precise. Among the various approaches, two general perspectives stand out – one that sees cultures as information pools and another that understands cultures as sign inventories. However, both ideas do not need to be in conflict with each other. Rather, they can be integrated by the cognitive approach, because any perceived cultural element needs to be cognitively represented, so that it is rather irrelevant if it is considered a unit of information or a sign. These recent approaches, in combination with the idea that cultures can be located within a spectrum from traditional to progressive, have yielded the conceptualisation of cultural syntheses over time, which now has high explanatory value for cultural change and for the emergence of cultural dominance. Though from quite different aspects, the various theoretical approaches shed light on the roles and positions of researchers on the one hand and indigenous persons on the other hand. It is these roles that come into play during actual field studies.

There are several reasons for us to take a look at cultural theories. We want to understand their role with regard to cultural dominance. This implies, on the one hand, the question: To what extent were cultural theories – and thus cultural theorists – involved in the emergence of dominant positions, which we find in nowadays culture(s)? This is an important issue for our topic, because identifying sources of dominant thinking could help us to avoid mistakes when we plan and carry out research in indigenous contexts. But on the other hand, we also want to look at cultural theories hoping to understand the intra-, inter- and transcultural mechanisms. So, we shall focus in the remaining sections of this chapter on those theories that enable us to formulate practical strategies for culturally sustainable research methods, and in doing so, we shall also try to understand them in their scientific context. Theories always arise within a particular historical situation, and they are characterised by their unidirectional sequentiality. They can build upon anteceding theories. They cannot know which approaches will follow, but further along the historical timeline, they can influence subsequent theories.

In Search for a Definition of Culture   So, what is culture at all? The following paragraphs shall give a brief synopsis of cultural theories. To put it in an abstract, yet simple way, cultures consist of persons. A large number of socially interconnected persons are also called a society. What, then, is culture? We should be careful not to separate the concepts just mentioned too much. As Ralph Linton (1945) has pointed out, individuals, society and culture are so closely integrated into each other that any attempt to focus on one of these aspects while ignoring the others will sooner or later be locked in stalemate.

Any outlining of a concept of culture needs to take account of the particular situation or the issue in question. Kroeber and Kluckhohn (1952) have compiled about 120 different approaches that try to define culture; each of them has come to a very own idea, what culture is, from their respective point of view. Kroeber and Kluckhohn (1952) came to the conclusion that:

> "Culture consists of patterns, explicit and implicit, of and for behaviour acquired and transmitted by symbols, constituting the distinctive achievement of human groups, including their embodiments in artefacts; the essential core of culture consists of traditional (i.e., historically derived and selected) ideas and especially their attached values; culture systems may, on the one hand, be considered as products of action, on the other as conditioning elements of further action".[6]

---

[6] Kroeber & Kluckhohn (1952), p. 357; parentheses in original.

Argyle (1972) put it a bit handier, as already mentioned above, by referring to social, cognitive and communicational aspects, as well as to artefacts. And we can simplify this even further. Culture can be described as the effect of behaviour of humans living together or otherwise affecting each other collectively. So, culture is the effect of human interactions. Eco (1968) took the semiotic perspective that culture basically consisted of communication.

The theoretical discourse about culture boomed in the twentieth century. There had been earlier approaches on the topic, but from about 1900 onward, scientists tackled the concept of culture and analysed it in a more and more systematic way. And along the timeline, conceptual influences occurred. Each theorist could draw on earlier works that already were available, so that by and by, over decades, the ideas about culture became more complex and elaborated. As this happened, schools with particular lines of thought were established. Whereas some theorists were rather loyal to their personal academic background, ignoring others that did not have the right pedigree, there also were researchers who understood that it makes sense to work inter- and transdisciplinarily when dealing with such a sophisticated issue as culture. Towards the end of the twentieth century, interest in cultural theories seemed to wane, only to return in the second decade of the twenty-first century. This revival was predominantly fuelled by the circumstances brought along by globalisation, which inevitably is associated with more and more contact between cultures.

In the following, some theories are highlighted that are relevant to our subject – either directly or in a sense that the upcoming of certain perspectives could hardly be understood without knowing predecessor theories. Although we cannot fully cover all aspects of the theories presented, we shall outline those points that reveal the line of thoughts, which have led to our present-day understanding of cross-cultural issues and which clarify the necessities of specific research strategies in indigenous contexts.

Endeavours from the Desk Especially in the beginning of the twentieth century, some theories took their views on other cultures from quite a distance. This could have had different reasons. First of all, these theorists simply lacked the opportunity of immediate contact with other cultures. They either did not have the means or the chances to go to places far away, or they were academically socialised to work only in a theoretical way, so that it did not come to their mind to work away from desk. But there also were very intentional views from a distance that authors took as a stylistic device, even when they were familiar with different cultures. And yet another reason was that the theorist, although being transculturally experienced to a certain degree by having visited another culture, preferred not to have too much contact with these other people. Let us have a look at some examples of theories taking views from a distance.

Sigmund Freud was one of those, who worked on culture from their desk. Nevertheless, his *Totem and Taboo* (1913) had a long-lasting effect on culture-related discourses. Freud made the attempt to set up a comprehensive theory on the origin of culture without visiting other cultures. Indeed, *Totem and Taboo* is all but austere; it is rather written in quite a vivid style. Among the authors Freud refers to, two stand out in particular – Charles Darwin, who in fact had seen other cultures, and James George Frazer, who, with regard to indigenous cultures, relied on reports that he had collected from missionaries and other travellers. When Freud wrote *Totem and Taboo*, Darwin's *Origin of Species* (1859) was ubiquitous in the academic world as a matter of intense discussions, and similar was the reception of Frazer's *The Golden Bough* (1890) and *Totemism and Exogamy* (1910). Frazer, on his part, had been influenced by Darwin. He wanted to apply the evolutionary perspective to culture, postulating the sequence of magic followed by religion followed by science, and he tried to put cultural phenomena in a systemic coherence, similar to what Lévi-Strauss (1958) later did in his structural anthropology. Freud amalgamated Darwin's, Frazer's and other perspectives. It is also evident that he was very much influenced by Haeckel's (1866) Recapitulation Theory, which claimed that the embryonical development reflected evolutionary stages.[7] Freud applied this, with a psychoanalytic perspective, to human history, which he claimed to be paralleled in the psychosocial development of humans. The key episode of *Totem and Taboo* is about the "primal horde"[8] of early humans. This "horde" consists of a male with a harem of females and their offspring. One day, when the old male has become quite feeble and the sons have become young men, the old man is killed by his sons. But the young men soon repent what they have done and decide two consequences as compensation: they deny themselves the horde' females, thus declaring them *taboo*, and they define an animal as commemorative *totem* that is seen as sacred and may not be killed. In a way, it symbolises the father, and the prohibition of killing it counterbalances the murder they have committed. Freud warped some essential aspects of the sources he referred to, in order to make them fit into his theory. What he claimed to be "Darwin's primal horde"[9] of early humans is actually based on Darwin's description of certain behaviour found among mountain gorillas. But this is one of the less problematic aspects. Much more serious are the conclusions Freud draws from this alleged episode. Although it is a very fanciful story, he explains this incident as the foundation and reason that humans have religion and that there is the worldwide phenomenon of exogamy in human cultures. As many scholars of his time, Freud – like Frazer, to whom he referred – took up Darwin's evolutionary perspective and generalised it, integrating it into his particular academic field. Unquestioned, therefore, he understood himself as being part of the highest of all cultures, with all other, contemporary, and all previous cultures being on lower stages. The subtitle of *Totem and Taboo* is programmatic: *Some Points of Agreement between the Mental Lives of Savages and Neurotics*. It suggests that being "savage" was something like an illness or, at any rate, an imperfection. Although slavery had been abolished, at least in Europe and in the Americas, scientists were still reluctant to acknowledge the equality of non-European cultures to their own culture. It seems that Freud did not have a high opinion of the "savages". In contrast to the reality of

---

[7] Haeckel's Recapitulation Theory was later refuted (e.g. Blechschmidt 2004).

[8] Freud (1913), *Totem and Taboo,* translation by James Strachey, London, 1950, p. 146.

[9] ibid., p. 146.

indigenous cultures, he held that "We should certainly not expect that the sexual life of these poor, naked cannibals would be moral in our sense or that their sexual instincts would be subjected to any great degree of restriction",[10] and when it comes to slaying the father in the *Totem and Taboo* key story, Freud assures the reader that "Cannibal savages as they were, it goes without saying that they devoured their victim as well as killing him".[11] The history of perceiving indigenous cultures might have taken a different path if Freud had visited non-European societies himself, contacting them in a respectful way, integrating into their culture and trying to understand their ways on an equal footing.

Changing Perspectives   That is, in a way, what Hans Paasche did. Nevertheless, he chose to take a distant view, although quite a different one than Freud's. Paasche and his wife had spent some time in Africa. Hans Paasche, a senior lieutenant of the German colonial army, changed his mind and became a pacifist. He knew Swahili, and he was not only very interested in African cultures, but he tried to arouse interest in those other societies' ways of living by publications and by giving public lectures. Paasche was then persecuted because of his writings, in which he was very critical against militarism, exploitation and civilisation with all its inequalities. He was eventually killed by a nationalist death squad in 1920. One of his critical writings was a fictitious series of letters by an African, describing the European way of life. Paasche chose an unusual way of publishing – these letters were first printed in the journal *Der Vortrupp* in the years 1912–1913 and later published as a compilation titled *Lukanga Mukara* (1921). Hans Paasche was inspired to invent this character by a person he and his wife met when they lived at Victoria Lake in 1909 and 1910. Paasche's wife Ellen, by the way, was the first European woman to reach the sources of the White Nile. The character Lukanga from Ukara Island in southern Victoria Lake – hence the name Lukanga Mukara, meaning "Lukanga from Ukara" – was sent to Europe by his king and then describes what he sees in the letters he is sending home. What Paasche presented was a radical critique of contemporary civilisation. He managed to cast off the perception he was socialised with, including the values, norms and standards, and described European, and in particular German, culture as seen through the eyes of a person from a very different background. At least for parts of his readership, this must have been quite confusing, and on the emotional level, it might have contributed to the hatred that then led to his killing. The letters are still eye-opening today, for example, when Lukanga Mukara describes that each day, he sees a lorry full of bread driving from A to B, and at the same time, another lorry full of bread is going from B to A. Both lorries even pass each other halfway, and Lukanga wonders, why are the *Wasungu* (white people) always moving things back and forth, why don't they leave them where they are? Likewise, he gives account of a number of irrational things, be it that Wasungu keep wrapping their bodies or that they light little rolls to make smoke, which they then inhale. Paasche chose the pseudo-external perspective as a stylistic device to convey his message in a much more effective way than a theoretical treatise would have done.

---

[10] ibid., p. 2.
[11] ibid., p. 164.

Fictional Romanticism And an example of the third kind of taking a distant view would be the depiction of Samoa by Margaret Mead (1928, *Coming of Age in Samoa*), who preferred not to be in too much contact with traditional Samoan culture. Mead's work had an immense influence on the twentieth-century pedagogics, sociology and neighbouring sciences. Her impact on society can hardly be overestimated. The concept of anti-authoritarianism, counter-culture and the Hippie movement is directly related to her ideas. Her work was scrutinised very late, after decades, by Derek Freeman's (1983) critical book *Margaret Mead and Samoa: The Making and Unmaking of an Anthropological Myth*, causing dismay across disciplines. Freeman had checked sources thoroughly, and he came to the conclusion that the picture of Samoan culture as drawn by Mead had little to do with reality. Margaret Mead had been sent to Samoa by her mentor Franz Boas, whom she and her colleague Ruth Benedict, both former students of Boas, called "Papa Franz" in their correspondence,[12] to find supporting evidence for his idea of cultural relativism. Young Mead had little knowledge of field research, and after her arrival in Samoa, she could not cope with local culture. Irritated by chicken, pigs, noise and the lack of American comfort, she took shelter on the island of Ta'ū with the family of a US Navy pharmacist, where she could enjoy the kind of accommodation and food that she was used to from home. In her letters, she clearly expressed her disgust for the indigenous population's lifestyle and food.[13] To fulfil her mission however, she interviewed some girls of the island, although she hardly had knowledge of the Samoan language. But the linguistic aspect is not the only problematic one. The way in which she collected data was not very sensitive. She asked the girls about their menstruation and even more private things, such as "masturbation, homosexual and heterosexual experience".[14] Mead herself would probably have refused to answer those questions and been upset, had someone insisted. The results presented in her study *Coming of Age in Samoa* lack validity, as they are not based upon an appropriate research design and they contrast sharply with anthropological findings. Samoan culture of that time was very reserved against speaking frankly about intimate issues. This is quite typical for traditional societies. But Mead's (1928) claim of Samoa being a place of sexual freedom and promiscuity conformed to the idea of a "tropical paradise" and thus further fuelled this projection. *Coming of Age in Samoa* was generally rejected by Samoans themselves. But the book apparently was what the readership of the "civilised" world wanted. This does not only apply to English-speaking readers. When we compare Freud (1913) and Mead (1928), the similarities of style and thematic aspects addressed are quite surprising. Both wrote best-selling books for their audience, and in a way, both remained in their culture. From her room in the pharmacist's house, which also was her workplace, Margaret Mead could look over a part of the village, thus taking a distant view in the literal sense.

---

[12] Mead (1977), Letters from the Field.
[13] ibid.
[14] Mead (1928), p. 283.

Cultures on the Move While some authors took distanced perspectives in the early twentieth century – for whatsoever reason – others were preoccupied with the aspects of cultural change. We shall look at two prominent theories that are of importance for our topic, as they prepared the ground for the idea that cultures are always and more or less constantly changing. Although ethnological data show that indigenous cultures can persevere in their state over long periods, the concept that cultures were always dynamic is all too often taken as an excuse for destabilising interferences, alleging that the societies concerned would change anyway or even declaring that the intervention would be for their own good.

Most notably, it was Oswald Spengler,[15] who promoted the idea that cultures were beings, each going through childhood, youth and adulthood. Like plants, their growth was determined by the soil; therefore, cultures in forests, in the mountains or in deserts were different from each other. Spengler allotted 1000 years to each culture. To bring his theory into accordance with history, he pruned, stretched, split and merged cultures on the timeline, from the Egyptian Early Dynastic Period of 3400 B.C. until present time. However, he did not suggest that cultures, at the end of their life, simply ceased to exist. A very interesting aspect of his approach is his distinction of culture and civilisation. At the end of such a cycle, according to Spengler, a culture dries out and becomes a mummy. That state is then what he called civilisation. And Spengler was very pessimistic about that: "Culture and Civilization – the living body of a soul and the mummy of it".[16] He saw civilisation as characterised by bureaucracy, administration and official machineries. Although some of his critique of civilisation deserves some approval, Spengler's ideas of discrete cultures, each with limited lifespan, cannot be sustained against historical evidence and the results of other disciplines' research. As long as societies are not isolated, there is a continuity of cultural elements being passed on to successive cultural systems. For example, some central aspects of the legal systems of modern states can be traced back to the Roman empire, and likewise, architectural, linguistic and other elements of our culture have their roots in preceding cultural systems.

Another theorist, who focussed on change, was Norbert Elias. But his concept of civilisation was very different from Spengler's. As a sociologist, he directed his attention to social processes. He was wondering how and when did our society become civilised. In investigating historical sources, Elias put particular emphasis on the Middle Ages. Largely ignored when it was first published in 1939, Elias' *The Civilizing Process* was received almost enthusiastically after it was published again in 1969.[17] Norbert Elias not only compiled a considerable number of passages, but he also analysed pictorial representations in order to describe what happened in medieval times, when major transitions took place in Europe. He was especially interested in norms, standards and the setting of rules with regard to behaviour patterns, and many of the examples he had collected relate to table manners, to private

---

[15] *The decline of the West*, English translations 1926 (vol. I) and 1928 (vol. II).
[16] Spengler (1926), p. 353.
[17] Engl.: Vol. I, 1969; Vol. II, 1982.

habits concerning aspects such as sleep and defecation as well as to public principles of nudity or body covering. All these examples indicate that rules of behaving properly emerged in the courtly society, from where these rules then were imposed on the common people. Notable critique of Elias' propositions only came up in the late 1980s, mainly with regard to anthropological aspects. One thing to be noticed is that *The Civilizing Process* does not have much explanatory value: Even if we assume that things happened the way Elias tells us, it does not explain why it was so. Why did people at European courts all of a sudden have the idea of defining decency? What was the origin of these new concepts? What caused the courtly society to dress and to use handkerchiefs, knife and fork?

We won't find the answers in Elias' approach, but from a more recent perspective of cultural psychology, we can now analyse the situation at the medieval European courts, where people from various cultural backgrounds came together. The cultural landscape of that time was quite heterogeneous, similar to what we find in indigenous contexts. The more a cultural system has been able to consolidate itself over time without much external influence, the more the elements it consists of are culturally endemic. In other words, the cultural elements that become established are locally specific and adapted to that particular context. Their appearance differs from equivalent elements in neighbouring cultures or subcultures. Even in today's Europe, we find architectural variations from region to region. Language is a fine paradigm for culture, and here we find not only a certain language per country but dialectal differences from village to village. Several centuries ago, these disparities were much stronger. In the Middle Ages, people in each region had their particular language, bodily appearance, food, architecture and behaviour styles in general. At the European courts, people from various parts of the respective kingdom, duchy or principality came together. And they all had their own behavioural rules – ways of greeting, table manners, passing compliments and many more. This could lead to confusions and to grave misunderstandings. People at the courts had to cope with that and make definitions of what was to be considered correct. In general, when different social systems have to come to an agreement of rules, the stricter one is chosen if regulations differ in their strictness, or a new regulation is defined, which is even more strict than any of the previous ones, just to be on the safe side. In the course of time, the more social systems go into synthesis, the resulting interconnected system becomes more and more rigid with regard to rules of decency – what has to be said in which situation, which parts of the body have to be covered when and how and which physical actions, like handshakes, have to be performed. After people at the medieval courts came to agreements, what was to be considered *courteous*, this was not only established as standards of correctness at the courts themselves. In the social hierarchy, aristocracy ranked high above the common people, and therefore, the nobility's behaviour style was seen as exemplary, so that people from the courts were role models for the lower social strata. The written codes of conduct from which Elias quotes were targeted at implementing behaviour that was considered correct. Although Elias himself did not provide cultural-psychological explanations of the factors that triggered the sociological phenomena, which he described, his *The Civilizing Process* gave substantial impulses to discourses on history and culture.

One aspect that we have to bear in mind with regard to field research in indigenous contexts is the normative function emerging from a person's behaviour, when the situation is marked by an imbalance of dominance between those taking part in it. Humans function today as they did in the Middle Ages. Dominant persons are role models for those who are dominated by them. That mechanism worked within the hierarchical social structure at the medieval courts, it worked between the courts and the people ruled by the aristocracy, and it works between representatives of the global culture and indigenous peoples. This implies some responsibility for globalised persons, who are contacting indigenous peoples, which can hardly be overestimated.

The standardising influence of the courts, first within its internal hierarchy and then on the common people, led to a reduction of cultural endemicity. Cultural systems that are adapted to their particular contexts are highly endemic, with high variations even between neighbouring places. As an effect of cultural standardisation, cultural elements are aligned towards the standards set by the ruling social entity. Practically speaking, one has to travel longer distances to find differences between certain elements. In Europe, we can find this process going on with the vanishing of dialects and local customs. With regard to the impact of globalisation on indigenous culture, the mechanism is the same. The global standardisation leads to the loss of cultural specificities, of cultural elements and of information stored in indigenous cultures. We are not talking about a single event or about one single culture affected. There are thousands of indigenous cultures prone to be deleted.

Para-semiotic Approaches Having mentioned the geographical distribution of cultural elements, we cannot leave Leo Frobenius out of consideration. During his research in Africa, he noticed structures regarding the local occurrence of cultural elements, and he had the idea to cartographically represent these distributions. Actually, Frobenius tried to do something that was much more applicable to our multimedia techniques, but he managed to do it with the means available at his time and eventually published *Atlas Africanus* in 1921. Such a deep going into detail and elaborating particularities of indigenous cultures has also been realised by the anthropologist Claude Lévi-Strauss, though not on a graphical, but on a descriptive level. Both, Frobenius and Lévi-Strauss, without especially pointing it out, actually worked semiotically. They analysed signs and sign processes in the sense that they not only had an eye on the meaning of cultural elements but also on the structures that resulted from the interconnections of these signs. Claude Lévi-Strauss can be seen as the initiator of French Structuralism, which soon spread beyond the boundaries of anthropology. For him, cultural elements were not only signs, which meant or symbolised something; much more important were the structures, within which the signs are active. People read these signs and attribute symbolical content to them. People behave by producing signs, exchanging them and thus communicating. Signs are effective on the conscious, as well as on the subconscious level. Social rules structure the processes that happen with the cultural elements of and within the particular society. In a different way than Freud in his theories of culture, Lévi-Strauss (1949) payed special attention to kinship, which he saw as the central manifestation of social structures. Besides in a number of monographs, his engagement in culture-specific structures of human interactions found expression in three collections of essays in 1958, 1973 and 1983 on *Anthropologie structurale*, the third of which he decided to name differently, *Le Regard Eloigné (The View from Afar)*. However, this should not be understood in any way of the distant views described above in this chapter.[18] Rather, emphasis is put on discussing aspects of indigenous societies that have implications for our industrial culture, so that comparative perspectives emerge.

System Theory The description of structures does not primarily have processes in mind but rather relations between entities. In that sense, they are snapshots of interconnections and constellations of entities. Whereas structures are something static, the concept of a system includes the factor time as added value. A mere structure, without considering time, would not be a system. Only then can it be called a system if something happens within it. Life not only exists within systems, but it also actively forms systems, so that we can say that a key feature of life is that animate matter interferes with inanimate matter, structuring it, restructuring it and yielding new structures that did not exist before. As long as there is only inanimate matter, we have systems that are confined to the natural laws. Its chemical and electrical processes can be described by the laws of physics. Life violates these principles, in a way. When there is life in a grain that is put in the ground, it will grow, if the circumstances allow. But that would never happen when the grain is dead. When humans interact and communicate, they modify the existing structures of matter. When we speak, we structure air molecules into soundwaves. When we write, we structure ink on paper, the light emission patterns of the monitor's liquid crystals, chalk on a blackboard or some other physical structure. These interferences with existing structures would not take place if we were not alive. As living creatures, we always have a behaviour, and as long as this can be perceived, there is communication that takes place within a system. And communication is the basis of culture.

Actually, this has just been a short introduction into system theory. There are some prominent protagonists of the systemic approach, among them Paul Watzlawick – his main concern was communication as seen from a psychotherapist's point of view – and Niklas Luhmann, who had enormous influence on other theorists and on further theories that have to do with human coexistence. In his major work, Luhmann (1984) presented a new approach to *social systems*. It is somewhat difficult to read, as it is formulated in quite an idiosyncratic way, with a number of neologisms. Among the innovations that we can find in his application of system theory is his further elaboration of former classifications. One central matter

---

[18] Almost as if to apologize, Lévi-Strauss (1983) explains in the preface that with the second volume's title, he wanted to show his loyalty to principles but that with the third volume's title, he did not want to give the impression of not making any progress.

of dispute with regard to systems is their relation to the environment in which they exist. Hardly any system, let alone organic systems, can be considered to be truly closed. As Watzlawick et al. (1967) have pointed out, there is always some correspondence between the system and the outside. If somebody would claim a can of tinned food to be a closed system, we can simply disprove that by heating it. When the food inside is warmed up, it receives energy from the outside, and therefore, it cannot be a closed system. Unless we discuss the theological implications of the existence of the universe, we can say that all systems are in some way related to their context, and thus, they cannot be totally closed. But if they correspond with their context, shouldn't they be considered subsystems of their context, which is the superordinate system? Well, but then, the context of the context would be the next superordinate system and so forth. Each system contains subsystems, which also contain subsystems, which also contain subsystems, and the end of that chain seems to be only determined by the state of the art of elementary physics. On the other hand, systems are subsystems of superordinate systems, which are subsystems of superordinate systems, and no one on earth can tell us with all certainty how far this goes on and if it is limited at all.

All consideration of systems, therefore, is a deliberate reduction, in order to make things understandable. When we call something a system, we do so to highlight particular processes, mechanisms and functions. By doing so, we neglect, of course, many other processes, mechanisms and functions of the system, because they are irrelevant to the issue we are dealing with. For example, when we talk about communication systems of humans, we usually do not mention the fact that those participants of systemic interaction need to breathe, they eat and drink or go to sleep at night. Although all these behavioural aspects are important for the persons constituting a communication system, they are outside the focus of the question we are dealing with. System theory is a very formal approach. It can help us to reduce complex phenomena, such as cultures or groups, to the aspects that we consider essential. Depending on the subject of interest, we can include subsystems or superordinate systems into our modelling.

With regard to research in indigenous contexts, the systemic approach is an option that we can also combine with or integrate into other approaches. We could elaborate particular aspects of a semiotic analysis by drawing up a system, or we could illustrate some socio-cognitive mechanisms. This applies not only to the evaluation and interpretation of data gathered in the field. Even before we start the research, the systemic perspective can help us to become clear about pivotal social constellations or to figure out possible investigation strategies and weigh them against each other. Applying Watzlawick et al. (1967) to field research situations, we can say that by being in an indigenous context, the researchers are then part of particular interpersonal systems, which have emerged simply because the researchers are there.

As it is impossible to have no behaviour, we always communicate, as long as our behaviour is perceived by someone. Within communication systems, the participants always play roles. It is actually impossible not to play a role, and therefore, by communicating, the participants define their relations within the system. Hence, the research design should ensure that the visit does not destabilise the indigenous social system, to which the visitors become linked temporarily. For theoretical modelling, it might be helpful to include the aspect of what Watzlawick et al. (1967) have called "homeostasis", which means a state of equilibrium of the system. All the interactions taking place, as well as all the roles that are defined, are then balanced in a way that the system is running smoothly. When that equilibrium is disturbed, the system reacts, at the best, with strategies that establish a new equilibrium. At the worst, it collapses. If its members survive, they will have to reorganise themselves and their roles within the new situation, which might mean to connect themselves to other systems. Whether a system, after having been disturbed, manages to establish a new equilibrium, depends on the availability of suitable strategies, which its members have acquired by experience so far.

1.3   Transcultural Perspectives and Conceptualisations

As researchers, we want to understand things neutrally and from an objective point of view. Physicists or chemists can control potentially influencing factors in their laboratories much easier than social scientists can do that in the fields. However, full neutrality is not even possible in the natural sciences. The choice of the equipment, for example, has an influence on the results of an experiment and so has the handling of the equipment, the ways of analysing the data obtained, as well as social and psychological factors of the staff (Knorr-Cetina, 1981).

When such factors already come to bear in the very structured settings of laboratories, then this is much more the case in the complex, multifactorial settings of real-life social systems. A further dimension of uncertainty is added, when we carry out research not only within one culture but across cultures. From the beginning, young researchers do not have the competence of taking a meta-perspective, by which they are looking at different cultures, weighing each of them equally, except for those few, who have grown up in several cultures and thus have a multicultural background. But even then, it would be unlikely that they really perceive cultures in a fully equal way. Transcultural competence needs to be acquired, in order to obtain a less subjective and more objective perspective. However, we should not deceive ourselves, but rather remain self-critical and bear in mind that we might be able to reduce subjectivity but that this does not mean that we reach full objectivity.

So, what is the problem? The point is that we have a cultural background ourselves and that we, when we do field research in the context of another culture, look into that culture from our perspective. While doing so, we want to avoid misconceptions. Yet, misconceptions are unavoidable, as long as we do not identify possible sources of error and try to neutralise them as far as possible. With regard to transcultural perspectives, it is our own point of view that needs to be scrutinised. A priori, our perceptions and interpretations of the other culture are biased. What we can do against it is, on the one hand, to reflect about it, trying to understand the mechanisms and our own role, and, on the other hand, to become acquainted with the other culture. Of course, when we are going to visit a particular culture for the first time, then we could practically not become acquainted with it beforehand. Nevertheless, being aware that cultures are located within a spectrum, reaching from those very close to nature, to the industrial culture, and perhaps also being experienced with cultures that are similar, we have a certain basis for the interpretation of our perceptions regarding the other culture. Although this is not perfect, it is better than nothing. In transcultural research, we often have to live with provisional arrangements, trying to make the best out of it.

Becoming acquainted with indigenous culture will change your way of thinking. But it will do so for the good. It will widen the base upon which you can build your reflections. By this, it also offers you a wider variety of choices for your decisions. This is especially true with regard to your theorising and formation of hypotheses, as by becoming experienced with other cultures, you are trained in seeing things from different perspectives. You will generally start to question things that you have taken for granted and take into consideration other possibilities. At least, you will be less prone to exclude other possibilities beforehand. Take, for example, our concept of time (Groh, 2008). We generally assume that time is linear. But people in different cultures might have other conceptions. What if time is not just one line, but rather a decision tree with many branchings? Time could just as well be multifold, in the sense that at each decision made, alternative decisions divert to other directions, where courses of time likewise exist, make further branchings and so on. From our respective present point of view, we can only look back along the line of decisions that have brought us here, as we do not know about the other possible courses of events. However, independent of any such exotic concepts of time, identity is built on your past. You have been moulded by the path your life has taken so far.

Already at the planning stage, even before we have been to the indigenous context, where we want to do our research, we have some attitudes and positions concerning the particular culture that we want to see. We do well if we call these premises thoroughly into question. Where, when and how did we obtain these ideas? In which ways do we draw our conclusions from the information that we have, and are these conclusions appropriate? Apart from academic teaching, the main mechanism to convey images of other cultures nowadays is the media – the Internet, as well as other not-so-new media, such as television, radio, books, journals and other print media. And even the academic teaching is subject to a cultural bias, as our academic world consists of people, who are part of the industrial culture and thus exposed to and involved in its communication structures, standards and mechanisms.

Biasing Accounts Herman and Chomsky (1988) included intercultural perspectives into their considerations when they investigated what they called "manufacturing consent" in our media-dominated culture. These perspectives come to bear as these authors explicate how attitudes about incidents in various parts of the world are created. Parameters, such as the size of the report, the frequency and rate of reporting or figures, for example, of victims, implicitly convey a judging, which may be appreciation or contempt. While these authors focussed on political and economic aspects, Bartlett (1932) had already investigated the mechanisms of transcultural perception from a psychological perspective. He could show that information about a culture that people are not familiar with becomes distorted as it is passed on along the communication chain. There are typical modifications, such as a levelling down by omitting particularities on the one hand while accentuating other details by exaggerating them. In his famous study, Bartlett (1932) found that unfamiliar information was rationalised, passages were made more compact and tailored by the sender according to the expectations attributed to the receiver of the message.[19] The implications of culturally biased perspectives find their expression especially in racism. Frantz Fanon (1986) was one of those who brought critical aspects on post-colonial discriminations into the intellectual discourse. However, culturally biased perspectives do not only become evident in their extremes. Rather, there are gradual differences, starting with very subtle prejudices. Some of these perspectives are taken for granted, and they are conveyed within the industrialised world without being questioned and without any feeling of guilt. People living in non-industrialised societies are referred to as "backward", "underdeveloped", "not as advanced" or as being "at a lower stage". Wicklund (1990) critically analyses such categorisations, pledging for taking different views, which take into consideration the particular backgrounds of the behaviour of the persons described. Thereby, he strongly takes position against perspectives that generalise others. To avoid misunderstandings, it has to be pointed out that this has to be distinguished from George Herbert Mead's (1934) conceptualisation of "the generalised other", which has a controlling function on the self. A controlling function, if there is any at all, with regard to the generalising of others that Wicklund (1990) criticises, would work just the other way around, as those who are generalising would rather control the others than be controlled by them.

Classifying Cultures   This brings us to the problem of categorising cultures. On the one hand, it is unacceptable when outgroups are regarded in an undifferentiated way, as an ideological bias can be assumed, especially when there is a derogatory overtone. But if then, on the other hand, we would avoid any categorisation, this would be ideologically motivated as well. It would not reflect reality, and it would actually restrict science. Human cognition is based on categorisation to a large extent. Humans are of equal worth, but they are all different, like the cultures formed by humans. And they have the right to be different. Treating humans and their cultures as equal in the sense of all the same would mean to deny some basic rights. The right to be different is highlighted in the various articles of the United Nations Declaration on the Rights of Indigenous Peoples.

Claude Lévi-Strauss (1962) defined a framework for classifying cultures, which since then has been adopted by other social scientists. It consists of a simple metaphor that conveys the idea of a continuum. He used the terms *cold* and *hot* in a neutral way to differentiate between peoples close to nature, who are disposed to

---

[19] Overview: Mayer (1979/1977).

maintain their culture, and our modern society, which is disposed to cultural change. This responds to the reality of many parallels that can be found in traditional indigenous societies. Those who are closest to nature live on hunting and gathering, regardless of region and climatic conditions. Indigenous peoples hunt and gather in polar regions, in rainforests, mountains and deserts. Next to them in the spectrum would be pastoralists, who intervene in nature to a certain extent. When we proceed within this continuum, we find cultures that are warmer and warmer, until we reach the hot end, which is our global, industrial culture. Along the way from cold to hot, there are systematic changes. There are, for example, architectural differences regarding the type of housing when we compare hunter-gatherer cultures with those in warmer parts of the continuum. We also find that the warmer the cultures are, the more predecessor cultures they have from which they have emerged.

Lévi-Strauss (1962) found that in the social systems of peoples close to nature, there are behavioural rules and mechanisms to prevent changes and to ensure the continuation of lifestyles that have proven their functionality. The metaphor that he introduced not only expounds categories quickly, but it can also easily be visualised by the colour spectrum from blue to red, which is especially helpful for teaching purposes. This is then a meta-metaphor, because the colour spectrum metaphorically stands for the continuum from cold to hot, which, on its part, metaphorically stands for the different cultural states. Thus, a particular culture could be located on the corresponding spot within the spectrum. Mario Erdheim (1988) applied the cold vs. hot concept even to subcultures; for example, he described the military as a cooling unit within a culture. Whereas Erdheim (1988) took a psychoanalytic approach on culture, Jan Assmann (1992), who also integrated Lévi-Strauss's (1962) concept of a metaphorical continuum from cold to hot, into his theory, did so from the perspective of historical science. All of these approaches, which draw on this metaphor, illustrate the regularity of the heating-up processes that take place during cultural change. Neither the *if* nor the *how* of cultural change is a matter of chance. But where do new features come from?

Cultural Information Especially from an information theory perspective, the idea of spontaneous generation of information would be unacceptable. Due to this, cultural change may be explained by the recombination of units of information and integration of contingent new findings. By the way, although Assmann (1992) does not explicitly call it that way, his approach on *Cultural Memory* is an information-theoretical one. His model describes cultures as storages of information, which implies that cultures are characterised by the information upon which they are constituted. Assmann (1992) had picked up and elaborated Halbwachs's (1925, 1939) concept of *collective memory*, which also corresponds to Eco's (1968) notion that culture basically consists of communication. It seems that these authors want to express something very similar, but each of them does so from his own perspective. The common denominator inherent in these approaches could be summarised as follows: cultures are made up of cultural elements. These elements constitute the particularities of a culture. Also, these elements are typical for each culture, so that we can discern cultures by their architectural styles, by their languages, by their food preferences and so forth. Basically, these elements are results of human behaviour. Applied to practice, this means that even when children with different ethnic features would be adopted by foster parents in a culture different from the biological parents, they would internalise the behavioural styles of the foster parents' culture, where they are socialised.

Cultural elements can be looked at under various aspects. They can be analysed, as signs, from a semiotic perspective or they can be studied, as units of information, from the perspective of information theory, to take up a consideration from the beginning of the previous section: as cultural elements are cognitively represented within and by the members of a culture, they can be seen, from a psychological perspective, as cognitive units. Each culture forms a pool of cultural elements that are characteristic for that culture. At the same time, these elements represent the present state of the culture, which can be, metaphorically, any temperature within the continuum from cold to hot.

1.4 Synthesis and Dominance: The Mechanisms of Change

If peoples close to nature are in the cold state, how come that our culture is so hot? Along the historical way that has brought us here, our ancestors have gradually left nature, so that we now live relatively distant to it. If there is something that we call "nature" within our sphere of influence, we keep it under control. The process of distancing ourselves from nature – or rather distancing nature from ourselves – went along with the heating-up. But how does this actually happen? Can't we zoom any closer to a historical situation where heating-up takes place?

The Initial Spark This is exactly what Roman Herzog (1988) did. He looked at early human civilisation and the origin of what we could call a state in the political sense. Herzog (1988) provides evidence based on archaeological and geological data that a cultural quantum leap took place in Mesopotamia after immigrants had settled there and mixed with the earlier inhabitants around 3200 B.C. Apparently, the immigrants were not familiar with marshlands, so they erected huge artificial hills and plateaus, which probably were reminiscent of their former mountainous or hilly homeland. Out of the cultural synthesis, which is also reflected linguistically, emerged Sumer as an urban civilisation with writing, economy and administration. Herzog (1988) gives us a hint as to why the new arrivals came to Mesopotamia at all. A profound climate change took place during these centuries, as geological data, especially from seafloor sediments, clearly indicate. There is always a reason, a trigger for human behaviour.

We are a step further now, as we see that a new culture that has emerged from the synthesis of different preceding cultures has new features, which reflect a higher temperature, to put it in that popular metaphor. This happened in many places and at many times. Assmann (1992) points out that Dynastic Egypt emerged from the synthesis of Lower with Upper Egypt. But cultural synthesis also happens right now. We call it globalisation. Cultural synthesis is the driving force of progress. When people from different cultural backgrounds come to live together, they become acquainted with the others' cultural elements in addition to their own. And when they can choose, they pick the element that they consider to be the most useful for the situation at hand. Thus, the synthesis culture accumulates the effective elements, while the less effective cultural elements become forgotten, as they are not practised any more. In that sense, a hot culture generally has more power, and therefore, it is dominant towards a cold culture.

Transfer of Cultural Elements The cultural elements that we have in modern cultures have their origins in predecessor cultures. Our pool of cultural elements consists of those elements that have survived in the sense that they have been passed on from generation to generation. Those elements, which have become out of use, have not been handed down to us. They have become forgotten, and thus, they have been deleted from the pool of cultural elements. But one might ask, where do airplanes come from? Our ancestors did not have them. And computers? And cars, and rockets? To explain this metaphorically, let us take a look at chemistry. All molecules are composed of chemical elements that are listed in the periodic table. This table is limited, but a virtually infinite number of molecules can be created by plugging together different elements. All natural molecules are created that way, and beyond, modern technology allows for additional, non-natural molecules. These synthetic materials are produced by making other combinations than those found in nature. But they all rely on the natural elements, which are precisely defined and listed in the periodic table. The molecules can have characteristics that are entirely different from those of the elements they consist of. And by exchanging a single element of a molecule, it might then again have totally different properties.

If we look at airplanes and cars not as single cultural elements but understand each of them as a combination of many cultural elements, then we can see that these single elements have been passed down to us. Any particular combination then has distinct qualities, in the sense of the *Gestalt* effect. A central aspect of *Gestalt* psychology is the notion that the whole is not just the sum of its parts but that the combination of the parts yields the properties of the whole.

But not all of our modern cultural elements exist within complex combinations with other elements, thus forming new "molecules" or clusters with new properties. Firstly, when we work with theoretical models on culture, we have to make arbitrary decisions regarding the classification of what is an element. This actually depends on the question. For example, when we make certain considerations about housing, then we might define the hut of a certain culture as a cultural element, which we can compare to the hut of a different culture, which would be another cultural element. When we deal with questions regarding the building of huts, then we might define the different materials as discrete cultural elements, the design of the walls or the roof could be seen as specific cultural elements. From a particular cognitive perspective, the availability of the materials and the effort, as well as the speed of building the hut, the extent to which the hut can host persons or the durability of the hut, can all be defined as cultural elements.

Secondly, there are cultural elements that have been passed down as a whole, such as the books of the Bible. Assmann (1992) analysed three classical cultures in search for the question, why Judaism continues to live, whereas ancient Egypt and ancient Greece have ceased to exist as cultural systems. All three have been located around central religious conceptualisations. But in ancient Egypt, there was no exegetical tradition that managed to function as a connecting link to interpret the religious concepts in an adaptive way, so as to keep pace with changing times. In ancient Greece, there was a very fruitful philosophical tradition, but that was undocked from the religious concepts, so that they had no common values to convey. Only in Judaism – and, one must add, in consecutive Christianity – there are various mechanisms to relate the central canonical biblical texts to the reality of everyday life throughout changing times.

Interestingly, there are archaic cultural elements, which have been relabelled and integrated into a new context. Already Anrich (1894) described the influence of the ancient mystery cult on Christianity. Meanwhile, it is commonly accepted that the ancient depiction of Isis with the Horus child was the model for later images of Mary with the infant Jesus. Likewise, the ancient fertility cult in springtime with the hare as a fertile animal and eggs as symbols of fertility survived within the Easter traditions. Even the name of this feast is apparently derived from the ancient concept of a spring goddess, Eostre.

There are some novelties in Assmann's (1992) cultural theory, which are significant for explaining the emergence of cultural dominance. He elaborated the predecessor theory of the collective memory by Halbwachs (1925, 1939) by differentiating between the communicative and the cultural memory. The communicative memory refers to the information stored in and communicated between the living members of a culture. The cultural memory also comprises a culture's information stored in artefacts and texts. A phenomenon typical for nonliterate cultures is the "floating gap": as the communicative memory is linked to the living members of a culture, it reaches back for about 80 years. As long as witnesses are alive, they can report events. Beyond that, things become forgotten soon. But there are tales in nonliterate cultures about things in the very distant past, such as myths of primeval times. Instead of looking at the collective memory as a snapshot, Assmann (1992) examines the information of a society on the timeline. While the culture is moved on the trajectory of time, new members are born into it on the one side, and old members expire on the other side. And as long as artefacts or texts exist, the culture carries them on, so that they are available as sources of information, too. However, the communicative memory is alive. Things can be discussed; witnesses can contradict. The artefacts and texts of the cultural memory, by contrast, are dead. If information is transferred from the communicative into the cultural memory, it sclerotises. Due to this differentiation, the significance of a subculture in charge of interpretation or exegesis with regard to relating old texts to the living becomes clear. This subculture moves along the timeline as part of the living culture, maintaining by its interpretation the connection to the extracorporeally stored cultural memory.

So, what is of use for us from the cultural theories? What do they contribute that helps us to understand the constellation of researchers and indigenous peoples? Of globalised versus non-globalised culture? And to understand the functions of the cultural gradient with the dominant on the one side and the dominated on the other?

Cultural Synthesis If we put the pieces together, the picture becomes evident, and the different cultural theories make sense in their interplay. As we remember, Herzog (1988) has shown that mutual influence of cultures is the starting point for innovation and change and that the synthesis of two cultures can even lead to a quantum leap in progress. Theorists such as Erdheim (1988) and Assmann (1992) have picked up the metaphorical allocation of cultures within a spectrum, as supposed by Lévi-Strauss (1962). These are two crucial aspects of cultural theory, namely, the ranking of cultures according to their state of elaboration and the explication of what is the prerequisite for a culture to progress within this spectrum. In the model that inevitably emerges, cultures go into synthesis with each other and then make progress. What we still need to know now is, what progress more precisely means, and what that has to do with cultural dominance.

Each culture is characterised by a discrete set of cultural elements. When two cultures go into synthesis with each other, they both bring their cultural elements along to share them. Therefore, in the beginning of the synthesis, when both have just started to overlap, the number of shared cultural elements has doubled with regard to each of the two cultures before they merged: if each culture came with n cultural elements, the synthesis culture initially has $2n$ elements. This means that for each task in life, the synthesis culture initially has two answers or strategies. These corresponding cultural elements form so-called equivalence classes.[20]

In the time to follow the merge, the participants of the synthesis, that is, the members of both predecessor cultures, have the choice which of the two alternative cultural elements they are going to apply. This pertains to every area of life, because for every aspect to decide upon, each of the two cultures contributes a strategy. Seen from another perspective, such a pair of strategies represents two alternative, equivalent cultural elements. And the people of this joint culture will have to make a choice each time, so that sooner or later, it will become apparent in each case which of the two alternative elements is usually favoured over the other. In the long run, this has the consequence that the non-favoured element becomes forgotten. As it is not applied any more, the transgenerational passing on ceases, and when the last person has died, who had known that particular element, it will be extinct from the collective memory. In our model, this means that the pool of cultural elements, which had been inflated at the merge in the sense of $n + n = 2n$, will then have shrunken back to just n elements again.

But the new culture's pool of elements, although these elements appear comparable in quantity to those in the pools of each of the predecessor cultures, differs considerably with regard to the quality of the cultural elements. This has to do with the choices that had been made during the time, when the process of synthesis was in full swing. It is unlikely that the two alternative elements were always equal in their effectiveness. Actually, such a case of equal effectiveness might be rather a

---

[20] I have described these processes and mechanisms in more detail e.g. in Groh (2006).

rare exception. Therefore, people make their choices from the binary equivalence classes in a way that they apply the cultural element, which they assume to be more effective, and forget about the other element. When the process of synthesis has come to an end, those cultural elements that had been supposed to be less effective will have vanished. The pool of cultural elements will then exist of those elements that have been considered the more effective ones. In this simplified model, there are no more binary classes of equivalent elements any more after the synthesis. However, such abstract models are necessary to clarify the principal mechanisms within complex systems.

One aspect that has to be pointed out here is that effectiveness is not an objective measure but is a subjective assessment. You certainly remember the example given above (Sect. 1.1) of the chainsaw passed to an indigenous person. Cutting trees quickly and selling them might seem to this person to be something effective. But for the overall system, it is not good to cut down rainforests.

There are several consequences resulting from the course of cultural synthesis. Given that at t_1, a relatively early point in time in human history, there were x discrete cultures, which (in this very simplified model) all went into synthesis pairwise, then there will only be $\frac{x}{2}$ cultures at t_2. If they again go into synthesis pairwise, there will only be $\frac{x}{4}$ cultures at t_3 and so on. Due to the merging of cultures, the number of cultures shrinks.

At the same time, assumed effective cultural elements are accumulated, while assumed less effective elements are discarded. In the end, there will be one global culture, which has collected all the cultural elements deemed effective along the way of history. However, as already said, this is only a simplified model. If we elaborate it a bit more, we shall be happy that in reality, things are not quite so facile.

Firstly, as you might have derived from the chainsaw example, we have to call the choices into question. Persons make choices that are convenient with regard to the particular situation. This choice, made at that moment, might have no relevance for other situations. Or, seen from another perspective, the alternative element of the binary equivalence class, which is rejected, might be needed in future situations. Yet, it might then not be available and lost.

Secondly, another reason for calling those choices into question is given by the results that we see as caused by the accumulation of effective strategies. We have diminished nature so effectively that large parts of the earth are now desert, where there had been lush green (and thus, CO_2 sinks) before. We have accumulated very effective strategies of warfare, regardless of the provenance of the pertaining cultural elements. Rockets and missiles, nuclear bombs and even stealth aircrafts were all sick ideas of the Nazis but are now cultivated worldwide. Actually, effectiveness has become a maxim of globalisation. We become more and more effective to keep humans alive, and at the same time, we become more and more effective to kill human lives, in whatever ways.

Thirdly, from a system theory point of view, an overall system (in this case: humankind) is the more stable, the more functioning subsystems (in this case: cultures) it has. It is like a building standing on many pillars. If one subsystem collapses, the overall system can continue to exist, as it still rests on enough other subsystems. But if all the subsystems are interconnected in a way that they are all merged into one system, without distinct subsystems, then instabilities can affect the whole system, and when it collapses, nothing is left. Systems in space and time tend to become unstable sooner or later. Therefore, it is wise to have many subsystems. But what we do in our course of action called globalisation is just the contrary.

Fourthly, along the historical course of cultural syntheses, there are subjective perceptions of an increase of effectiveness, of convenient strategies and of available information. But that is quite deceptive. Yes, strategies are more effective now, in the sense that we have just examined, and yes, information is more easily accessible now for the globalised individual. But while reaching this accumulation, along the historical way, much more information has been deleted. When at each synthesis, the $2n$ elements shrink back to n, then half of the information is being deleted. Both sides have contributed their elements and then, they decide upon in each case upon which one of the two equivalent elements they are going to keep and which one they dismiss. And the same thing happens then again at the next stage, when that culture, which has emerged out of the synthesis, goes into the next synthesis with another culture and so on. In the long run, most of the information units that had existed in autonomous cultures are being deleted. Or, in other words, humankind has lost most of its cultural elements during the processes of cultural synthesis. That is why the feeling of gaining information is deceptive. And this process is going on. Again, we call it globalisation.

Although our reflections have now reached a point, where it has become evident, why Europe is the origin of globalisation, as there was a migration period for centuries with very intense cultural exchange and syntheses, we cannot leave these considerations without extending the model to aspects that are closer to the reality of intra-, inter- and transcultural processes. Let us start with adding some more specificity to the last point addressed, the one about the loss of information. And we can link this with an important argument to push the model more towards reality. In the simplified model, the syntheses come to pass *inter pares*, which means that two cultures go into synthesis with each other, with each of them having emerged out of the same number of syntheses. At t_1, the starting point of the level, cultures go into synthesis that have been autonomous for such a long time that we consider them not synthesised. At t_2, those cultures go into synthesis that have emerged out of that primary synthesis and so forth. In the simple model, cultures go into synthesis in pairs, and both partners of such a pair are of the same degree of synthesis. But what if these partners are of different degrees? If one of them has emerged from more syntheses than the other? Then, the one with a larger record of previous syntheses has accumulated more effective strategies in its pool of cultural elements than the other. And when they decide about their equivalent cultural elements, more elements are kept of that culture, which has brought more effective elements into the synthesis, and less elements are kept of the other culture, which has brought in less effective elements. So here, we have a measure for cultural dominance!

Cultures become the more dominant, the more syntheses they have emerged from. This is because at each synthesis, effective elements are kept, while those that are considered less effective are being discarded. But mind out – the concept of dominance is always a relative one. A culture, a person, a state, a plant or an animal species behaves or is dominant towards or with regard to another entity or several others. The term dominance specifies a relation. A single entity without relations cannot be dominant. Or it cannot be dominant anymore, because it has destroyed or absorbed all other entities, which had been dominated by it.

If we look now at the synthesis of two unequal cultures, we can see that the process of information loss is going on to the same extent as during syntheses inter pares, yet the proportions of what is lost are different between the cultures. When the partners were equal, each of them can be expected to lose 50% of its cultural elements and to keep the other 50%. From another perspective, we can say that when these equal cultures meet, each one brings along its 100% elements, so that for a transitory time, there are 200%, and when each side has lost 50%, what is left are the twice 50%, and these are the 100% of the emerging culture. In the case of the unequal partners, the dominant one will keep, say, 80% of its elements and lose only 20%, whereas the dominated one will keep only 20% and lose 80%. So, the 80% kept from the one side and the 20% kept from the other side will also sum up to the 100% of the emerging culture. But again, 20% of the one and 80% of the other culture are deleted. As we see, at the synthesis of unequal cultures, too, an amount of cultural elements is lost, which equates the number of elements that make up a whole culture.

The more different the cultures are regarding their previous numbers of syntheses and thus their effectiveness, the more dominant one will be over the other. In the extreme case, the dominant culture keeps all of its cultural elements, while the dominated culture loses all.

To further align theory to practice, it has to be mentioned that of course, in reality there can be more than two cultures that go into synthesis. In those cases, the model has to be made more complex accordingly. When we apply the model to concrete intercultural processes, we also find that there is some relativity of cultures, especially with regard to their boundaries. Not always can it be determined exactly, where one culture ends, and where the other begins. There are transitory zones, which, on the interpersonal level, are represented by intermarriages. For social researchers, this is a very interesting field, as the inter- and transcultural processes then take place within the families. Another thing to mention is that there are subcultures within cultures. Here, too, boundaries are not always clear to see, and the categorisation depends on the parameters and criteria set by the researcher. As so often, language and dialects exemplify the structure of culture very well. To understand the difficulties of determining what a culture is, what a subculture is and where their boundaries are, we can look at a language map in a region, where lifestyles have established themselves over longer historical periods. For example, German, the language with the second-largest number of speakers in Europe (after Russian), is spoken in several countries. But if we take a closer look, the categorisation is not that easy. The German spoken in Switzerland has, from a linguistic perspective, approximately the same distance from High German as Dutch has. Yet, the Dutch claim that they don't speak a German dialect but a language of their own. At the same time, the Swiss claim that they speak a German dialect. The question if a particular tongue is a distinct language or a dialect of another idiom is certainly often politically biased. Yiddish also has a similar linguistic distance to High German, as Dutch and Swiss German have. The majority of its words shares historical roots with other German dialects. Yet, it is clear that for reasons to be found in the twentieth-century history, it is favoured to speak of it as a distinct language and not of a German dialect. If we zoom a little closer to the language map, we can see that what is spoken changes gradually from place to place. The people of a town can tell you that they use some expressions, which are different from the corresponding ones of a neighbouring town. Such differences can not only be found in rural areas. In large cities like Berlin, there are variations of pronunciation between the different parts of the city. Villages certainly are not the lowest threshold. Within the villages, people might be aware of words and speech preferences according to the different families, and within families, we can find personal preferences.[21] On a linguistic map, dialectal varieties are operationalised by isoglosses. Their fine-tuning is decided upon by the scholars in charge. They take samples in different places by asking locals to say particular sentences or pronounce the words of given lists. Then, the differences are determined by raters.[22] On the map, isoglosses can then indicate where there are less than 10 differences between places, or between 10 and 30 differences, or more than 30, and so on.

The point here is that there are no regions, where all people speak the same, or are all the same according to any other culture-related parameters. If there were such regions, then there would be sharp borders, and one could visualise that with monochrome spaces like on a political map. Indeed, standardisations are forced upon people by political systems on a large scale, whereas in indigenous contexts, comparable processes work on a face-to-face basis.

Whereas in indigenous contexts the high density of cultural information parallels, especially in rainforests, the genetic density of the highly endemic natural environment, density also plays an important role within globalisation. In immigrant societies, there is a fine-grained distribution of cultural backgrounds. In places like New York, families of various origin live next to each other. When you go from one apartment to the other, you could find people of Polish, German, English, Spanish, Italian and many more backgrounds living in the same building. Each immigrant is a bearer of specific cultural information. Try to visualise for yourself each specific background as a dot of particular colour, then zoom out, and you can imagine a very colourful picture, similar to a puzzle that consists of many, many pieces. In their respective countries of origin, you won't find diversity to such an extent, but the

---

[21] Even within persons, there are differences of language use across situations. Additionally, physiological factors can be assumed that lead to such intrapersonal differences (cf. Abrams et al., 2008).

[22] Problematically, inter-rater reliability of dialect transcribers is very low due to psycho-physiological processes that lead to very early interpretation of auditory information (cf. Groh, 1996).

picture, to stay with the metaphor, would be more or less unicoloured. And if you go back on the timeline, then you can see that today's multicultural situation existed earlier in the New World than in the European motherlands. In a way, the culturally heterogeneous situation of the New World resembles the situation at the medieval European courts, only that participants of modern multiculturality outnumber the aristocracy of the Middle Ages by far and that the modern situation is much less characterised by hierarchy.

To explain what happens in the multicultural situation, we can again use a metaphor from the natural sciences. These many different cultural backgrounds are like many different molecules, their exchange of information leads to friction, and thus, the whole mixture heats up, like a blend of many different chemical substances that react with each other. This metaphor is the equivalent to the theoretical modelling, in which the emerging cultural system shifts further into the warmer part of the spectrum.

On the interpersonal level, the participants of such multicultural situations have access to the many different information pools of the other participants, so that the processes of picking the most effective cultural elements take place to a very enhanced extent. While, under the circumstances of only two cultures overlapping and going into synthesis, the exchange and evaluation of cultural elements of both information pools might take one to three generations, many of such processes occur simultaneously in multicultural situations, and they become self-dynamic in the way that targeted search for effective information takes place. Whereas indigenous peoples, the further their culture is in the "cold" part of the spectrum, seem to be almost frozen in time over centuries or even millennia, we, in the globalised culture, experience changes of increasing rapidity (Baudrillard, 1986).

Many authors have criticised the processes of cultural change as destructive or as destabilisations of social systems. For example, Kohr (1977), taking an economic perspective, warned that oversized societies would collapse, arguing in certain analogy to nuclear physics. Like there is a critical mass, at which radioactive material starts to have uncontrollable reactions, societies would have a critical size according to the concept of Kohr. Höhn (1988) analysed sociological and demographical changes within the industrial society, with particular focus on family size, which has shrunk remarkably during the twentieth century. Weeber (1990) took an ecological approach by showing that the destruction of the environment is not a modern phenomenon but that it already took place to a large extent in ancient times, especially in ancient Rome. While these critical authors highlighted particular aspects of cultural change, either rather abstract or with a focus on certain phenomena, Erler (1987) presented a critical study on prototypical transcultural destabilisations, which continues to be highly relevant with regard to practical transcultural policies, as it goes into details of the so-called developmental aid, presenting a number of examples of projects that failed and made situations worse than they had been before.

Other authors have substantially contributed to our understanding of the role of the individual within the processes of changing culture. Individuals live in interaction with their social context. Their self-presentation within this context has the function of defining their social role. At the same time, however, the social context influences the individual. In each society, there are cultural standards and subcultural styles of bodily self-presentation, which the individual adopts. This adoption is not a simple process, in which a person consciously takes up a certain look that seems to be fashionable. The perception of social stimuli in general causes cognitive as well as bodily states, and the perception of others' bodily states, in turn, causes a person to mimic that bodily state. This usually happens in a rather subtle and unconscious way. Nevertheless, it causes corresponding affective states in the perceiving person (Barsalou et al., 2003; Niedenthal et al., 2005; Meier et al., 2012). These interdependencies are investigated by the research area of social embodiment, which had predecessors in the approaches of disciplines as different as humanities (Zahavi, 2010) or physiology (Blascovich & Mendes, 2010). Already, before the effect of the body on the psychological state was studied, Roland Barthes (1967) laid the ground for systematically analysing self-presentations in cultural contexts. He came up with his somewhat provocative postulate that fashion was a language, but he could show in a convincing manner that fashion fulfilled the requirements for being a language, as it can be claimed that it has semantics, pragmatics and syntax. In a historical approach of investigating body semiotics, the sociologist Eric Hobsbawm (1978) showed that placing the female breast under a taboo is only a modern phenomenon, which is linked to the changed perspectives of the industrial culture.

Hobsbawm (1978) investigated processes, which took place in our own culture. But due to the mechanisms of cultural dominance, it is also other cultures that are influenced by our behaviour. In consequence of the influence from the dominant culture, behaviour standards are implemented in those other cultures. These standards, which are transferred, include the bodily taboos of the dominant culture. They are even transferred primarily, as they are perceived in the most obvious way. Once these taboos have been internalised by the recipients, they unfold their psychological effects in terms of affective and cognitive modifications. To put it more simply, our culture is dominant, and due to our influence, the other cultures change their behaviour, especially the way they present their bodies, and because of that, they also change their way of thinking and feeling, in the direction towards the way we think and feel.

The theory of symbolic self-completion by Wicklund and Gollwitzer (1982) pertains to a general socio-cognitive process, and it is a key to understand what happens to the individual under the influence of cultural dominance. Under this influence, individuals feel inferior. Consequently, they want to escape that situation and reduce their feeling of inferiority. When they see a chance of such a change, they abandon their old identity, which is linked to that negative feeling, and strive for the other identity, with which they expect to be more respected. Yet, as long as they have not yet reached the new identity – what perhaps they never will – there is a gap between the fact of their cultural background and the new identity they are striving for. This gap is bridged by symbols, hence the name of the theory. The individual feels deficient and incomplete, and as long as this perceived incompleteness persists, it is symbolically completed in the literal sense, by using symbols. Practically, indigenous peoples worldwide, when they are under the pressure of cultural dominance, submit to the global culture and dress up according to the dominant standards. While the breast taboo in particular deletes positive connotations of femininity and motherhood by replacing it with sexual aspects, the overall modified presentation of the body in general leads to identification with the global culture. With regard to cultural identity, the abstract term of destabilisation describes these processes only in very rough outlines. Women lose their dignity, and collectively, the indigenous cultures are motivated to leave their stable systemic relation with their environment and to replace it by the industrial culture's ideals of economic growth, progress and other non-stable principles, which do not really have a final goal except for the consumption of resources. The fact of being treated as the inferiors in most countries of the world has the paradoxical effect that indigenous peoples make advances to the global culture, as they try to escape from their role of being the underdogs. Once they have undergone the step of cultural change by abandoning their traditional culture and adopting the globalised culture in the towns and cities of their respective countries, then they are furthermore exposed to media input, which globally portrays Europe and other industrialised countries as attractive and thus, implicitly, as being worth striving for. It is very understandable that these people, although they are already attached to the globalised culture in terms of infrastructure, try, in another step, to concretely leave their countries and go to places which they are convincingly told to be better. In addition to often arbitrary governments, precarious life conditions, experience of violence and deficient supply, media play a pivotal role as triggers of mass migrations. Intervention would be much more effective if this would be clearly understood, and measures would be taken to enhance the self-confidence of the peoples concerned by acknowledging and endorsing their cultural backgrounds. These people are stuck between a rock and a hard place, between traditional indigenous culture, which is, by the way, better for the planet in the sense of sustainability, and the industrial world, which is destroying ecosystems and climate. Migrants are acting rationally in the sense of Max Weber's (1922) conception of chance.[23]

The mechanisms of cultural synthesis are furthermore accelerated by the eviction of indigenous peoples from their traditional land. This regularly happens with the installations of national parks and nature reserves, in violation of Article 10 of the United Nations Declaration on the Rights of Indigenous Peoples, which clearly says that "Indigenous peoples shall not be forcibly removed from their lands or territories".[24] Often, conservationism is only the pretext, while the real reason is the commercial exploitation of the respective area by the tourism industry. Once the indigenous peoples have been forced to leave the shelter of their forest, they are much more exposed to dominant groups than they had been before.[25] Sexual violence

---

[23] Wirtschaft und Gesellschaft. Grundriss der verstehenden Soziologie. Erster Teil: Die Wirtschaft und die gesellschaftlichen Ordnungen und Mächte. I. Soziologische Grundbegriffe. § 16: Macht und Herrschaft.

[24] United Nations General Assembly (2007).

[25] See various reports at <https://s-a-c-s.net/uno/papers-and-reports-to-the-un/>

against indigenous women is very common (United Nations Inter-Agency Support Group on Indigenous Peoples' Issues, 2014). For example, a high percentage of Batwa women suffer rape (Deela, 2013). The Batwa pygmies have been evicted from the national parks in eastern Uganda. They have been denied to pursue their traditional subsistence of hunting and gathering. A programme, financed by the European Union, aiming at re-educating them to earn their living from dancing for tourists and selling handicrafts, has failed and left the Batwa in misery. Batwa men are but helpless witnesses of their women's situation and resort to alcohol and marijuana. A great number of indigenous women and girls have slipped into prostitution, either due to force (US Office on Colombia, ABColombia and Sisma Mujer 2013) or due to the destabilisation of their culture (Gomes Garcia & Souza Nascimento, 2014).

In view of the concrete effects of cultural synthesis on indigenous peoples, it is interesting to analyse the reaction of the dominant culture with regard to the indigenous peoples' suffering. There hardly is any reaction. Official institutions that are in charge of indigenous issues either do lip service or print nice words on paper. Year by year, we are having UN sessions pertaining to indigenous peoples, but they remain largely unnoticed by the public, and improvements, if any, are very slow and are often shattered by setbacks. Dominant individuals do not like to see the sufferings of indigenous peoples and prefer to suggest that they should be "developed" and integrated into the globalised culture, ignoring the problems associated with the loss of indigenous cultures and their ecosystems. Indigenous persons, as long as they are not subject to cultural dominance, prefer to maintain their cognitive constructs and behaviour styles. It is quite eye-opening to analyse such perseverance in the light of Frey's (1981) study, who has investigated the determinants of perspective changing. Taking these cognitive mechanisms into consideration would be helpful in the discourse on best practices, as it is necessary and seems long overdue to overcome the dominant culture's irrational rigidity, which is contradictory to pretended human rights standards.

When we examine the processes of cultural synthesis in order to consolidate the theoretical basis that is necessary for research in indigenous contexts, we have to remain factual without blocking the ethical aspects of indigenous rights. And then, we should ask ourselves, what do we do with the findings? What are the consequences?

One of the perspectives that we have taken in this first chapter is a phenomenological one, relating to the question, what are the semiotic processes that take place in the interactions between persons. After these considerations, the next question might arise, if the mechanisms of power and dominance are automatisms. Or is there any way that we could intervene? At least, when the effects of dominance become destructive, researchers should feel compelled to contribute to the amelioration of the situation. Preferably, we should try to prevent such effects. Before we go into details of these substantial points in Chapter 3, we first have to prepare the ground by giving thoughts to the legal perspectives that advise us, apart from our ethical and methodological considerations, not to exert any dominance upon indigenous peoples and not to destabilise their cultures.

References

Abrams, D. A., Nicol, T., Zecker, S., & Kraus, N. (2008). Right–hemisphere auditory cortex is dominant for coding syllable patterns in speech. *The Journal of Neuroscience, 28*(15), 3958–3965.

Anrich, G. (1894). *Das antike Mysterienwesen in seinem Einfluß auf das Christentum.* (Original Göttingen: Vandenhoeck & Ruprecht). Reprint: Hildesheim: Olms, 1990.

Argyle, M. (1972). The psychology of interpersonal behaviour. 2nd reprint of the 2nd edition, 1974, Harmondsworth: Penguin Books.

Assmann, J. (1992). *Das kulturelle Gedächtnis. Schrift, Erinnerung und politische Identität in frühen Hochkulturen.* Munich: C. H. Beck (Engl.: *Cultural memory and early civilization: Writing, remembrance, and political imagination.* Cambridge: University Press, 2011).

Bandura, A. (1962). *Social learning through imitation.* Lincoln, NE: University of Nebraska Press.

Barsalou, L. W., Niedenthal, P. M., Barbey, A. K., & Ruppert, J. A. (2003). Social embodiment. *Psychology of Learning and Motivation – Advances in Research and Theory, 43,* 43–92. https://doi.org/10.1016/S0079-7421(03)01011-9.

Barthes, R. (1967). *Système de la mode.* Paris Éditions du Seuil (Engl.: *The fashion system.* Berkeley, CA: University of California Press, 1967).

Bartlett, F. C. (1932). *Remembering. A study in experimental and social psychology.* Cambridge: Cambridge University Press.

Baudrillard, J. (1986). *Subjekt und Objekt: Fraktal.* Bern: Benteli.

Biddle, N. (2013). *CAEPR indigenous population project, 2011 census papers, paper 11: income.* Canberra: The Australian National University.

Blascovich, J., & Mendes, W. B. (2010). Social psychophysiology and embodiment. In S. T. Fiske, D. T. Gilbert, & G. Lindzey (Eds.), *Handbook of social psychology* (5th ed., pp. 194–227). New York: Wiley.

Blechschmidt, E. (2004). *The ontogenetic basis of human anatomy: A biodynamic approach to development from conception to birth.* Berkeley, CA: North Atlantic Books.

Bliege Bird, R., Bird, D. W., Codding, B. F., Parker, C. H., & Jones, J. H. (2008). The "fire stick farming" hypothesis: Australian Aboriginal foraging strategies, biodiversity, and anthropogenic fire mosaics. *Proceedings of the National Academy of Sciences of the United States of America, 105*(39), 14796–14801.

Boyd, R., & Richerson, P. J. (2000). Meme theory oversimplifies cultural change. *Scientific American, 283,* 54–55.

Brinke, J. (1977). *Im australischen Busch.* Leipzig: VEB F. A. Brockhaus.

Callaway, E. (2013). Fearful memories haunt mouse descendants. *Nature.* doi:https://doi.org/10.1038/nature.2013.14272. <http://www.nature.com/news/fearful–memories–haunt–mouse–descendants–1.14272>, accessed 6 May 2016.

Darwin, C. (1859). *On the origin of species.* London: John Murray.

Deela, C. (2013). *Sexual and gender based violence among the Batwa communities.* Kampala: Care Uganda.

Eco, U. (1968). *La struttura assente.* Milano: Bompiani.

Elias, N. (1969). *The civilizing process,* Vol. I: *The history of manners.* Oxford: Blackwell (Orig.: *Über den Prozeß der Zivilisation. Soziogenetische und psychogenetische Untersuchungen.* Vol. I: *Wandlungen des Verhaltens in den weltlichen Oberschichten des Abendlandes.* Basel: Verlag Haus zum Falken, 1939).

Elias, N. (1982). *The civilizing process,* Vol. II: *State formation and civilization.* Oxford: Blackwell (Orig.: *Über den Prozeß der Zivilisation. Soziogenetische und psychogenetische Untersuchungen.* Vol. II: *Wandlungen der Gesellschaft: Entwurf zu einer Theorie der Zivilisation.* Basel: Verlag Haus zum Falken, 1939).

Erdheim, M. (1988). *Die Psychoanalyse und das Unbewußte in der Kultur.* Frankfurt/M: Suhrkamp.

Erler, B. (1987). *Tödliche hilfe.* Freiburg i.B.: Dreisam-Verlag.

Fanon, F. (1986). *Das kolonisierte Ding wird Mensch. Ausgewählte Schriften.* Leipzig: Reclam.

Frazer, J. G. (1890). *The golden bough: A study in comparative religion*. Vols. 1 & 2. London: Macmillan (2nd ed., 3 vols., 1900, subtitle changed to *A study in magic and religion*; 3rd ed., 12 vols., 1906–1915; 1922 ed. as The Project Gutenberg EBook, 2003).

Frazer, J. G. (1910). *Totemism and exogamy. A treatise on early forms of superstition and society* (Vol. 4). London: Macmillan.

Freeman, D. (1983). *Margaret Mead and Samoa. The making and unmaking of an anthropological myth*. Cambridge, MA/London, England: Harvard University Press.

Freud, S. (1913). *Totem und Tabu. Einige Übereinstimmungen im Seelenleben der Wilden und der Neurotiker*. Wien: Hugo Heller. (Engl. translation by Strachey, J.: *Totem and Taboo. Some points of agreement between the mental lives of savages and neurotics*. Authorized translation by James Strachey. London: Routledge, 1950).

Frey, D. (1981). *Informationssuche und Informationsbewertung bei Entscheidungen*. Bern: Huber.

Frobenius, L. (1921). *Atlas Africanus*. Munich: Beck.

Frohmader, C. (2013). *Dehumanised: The forced sterilisation of women and girls with disabilities in Australia. WWDA submission to the senate inquiry into the involuntary or coerced sterilisation of people with disabilities in Australia*. Rosny Park: Women With Disabilities Australia (WWDA).

Gibbons, A. (1992). Rain forest diet: You are what you eat. *Science, 225*, 163.

Girtler, R. (2001). *Methoden der Feldforschung* (4th ed.). Vienna: Böhlau.

Gollwitzer, P. M., Sheeran, P., Michalski, V., & Seifert, A. E. (2009). When intentions go public: Does social reality widen the intention-behavior gap? *Psychological Science, 20*(5), 612–618. https://doi.org/10.1111/j.1467-9280.2009.02336.x.

Gomes Garcia, L., & Souza Nascimento, S. (2014). Family girls: A study about juvenile prostitution in the indigenous areas in Northeast of Brazil. *International Journal of Gender and Women's Studies, 2*(4), 1–25. https://doi.org/10.15640/ijgws.v2n4a1.

Groh, A. (1996). Psycholinguistische Aspekte der Transkription. *Semiotische Berichte, 20*(2–4), 353–381.

Groh, A. (2006). Globalisation and indigenous identity. *Psychopathologie Africaine, 33*(1), 33–47.

Groh, A. (Ed.). (2008). *Was ist Zeit? Beleuchtungen eines alltäglichen Phänomens*. Berlin: Weidler.

Haeckel, E. (1866). *Generelle Morphologie der Organismen. Allgemeine Grundzüge der organischen Formen–Wissenschaft, mechanisch begründet durch die von Charles Darwin reformirte Descendenztheorie. I: Allgemeine Anatomie der Organismen. II: Allgemeine Entwickelungsgeschichte der Organismen*. Berlin: G. Reimer.

Halbwachs, M. (1925). *Les cadres sociaux de la mémoire*. Paris: Librairie Félix Alcan, Collection Les Travaux de l'Année sociologique (Engl.: *On collective memory*, Chicago: The University of Chicago Press, 1992).

Halbwachs, M. (1939). *La mémoire collective*. Paris: Presses Universitaires de France, 1950 (Engl.: The collective memory, New York, Harper & Row Colophon Books, 1980).

Halfmann, D. (1998). *Die Tasmanischen Aborigines – Quellenkritische Bestandsaufnahme bisheriger Forschungsergebnisse*. Magister thesis. Freiburg: Albert–Ludwigs–Universität.

Harris, M., Carlson, B., & Poata-Smith, E. S. (2013). Indigenous identities and the politics of authenticity. In: M. Harris, M. Nakata, & B. Carlson (eds.), The politics of identity: Emerging indigeneity. Sydney: University of Technology Sydney E-Press, pp. 1–9. Available online at: <http://ro.uow.edu.au/lhapapers/845> (accessed 14 Aug 2017).

Heiber, H. (1958). Der Generalplan Ost. *Vierteljahrshefte für Zeitgeschichte, Dokumentation 6*, 3, 281–325. Available online at: <http://www.ifz-muenchen.de/heftarchiv/1958_3_5_heiber.pdf> (accessed 16 Aug 2017).

Herman, E. S., & Chomsky, N. (1988). *Manufacturing consent. The political economy of the mass media*. New York: Pantheon Books.

Herzog, R. (1988). *Staaten der Frühzeit. Ursprünge und Herrschaftsformen*. Munich: C.H. Beck.

Hobsbawm, E. J. (1978). Sexe, symboles, vetements et socialisme. *Actes de la Recherche en Sciences Sociales, 23*, 2–18.

Höhn, C. (1988). Von der Großfamilie zur Kernfamilie? Zum Wandel der Familienformen während des demographischen Übergangs. *Zeitschrift für Bevölkerungswissenschaft, 14*(3), 237–250.

Hossain, D. (2013). Socio-economic situation of the indigenous people in the Chittagong Hill Tracts (CHT) of Bangladesh. *Middle East Journal of Business, 8*(2), 22–30.

Johnstone, K. (2009). Indigenous birth rates—How reliable are they? *People and Place, 17*(4), 29–39.

Knorr-Cetina, K. (1981). *The manufacture of knowledge. An essay on the constructivist and contextual nature of science.* Oxford: Pergamon Press.

Kohler, T. A., & Matthews, M. H. (1988). Long–term Anasazi land use and forest reduction: A case study from Southwest Colorado. *American Antiquity, 53*(3), 537–564.

Kohr, L. (1977). *The overdeveloped nations: The diseconomies of scale.* New York: Schocken Books.

Kroeber, A. L. & Kluckhohn, C. (1952). *Culture. A critical review of concepts and definitions* (papers of the Peabody Museum of American Archaeology and Ethnoloy, Harvard University, vol. XLVII, no. 1). Cambridge, MA: Peabody Museum.

Lévi-Strauss, C. (1949). *Les Structures élémentaires de la parenté.* Paris: Presses Universitaires de France (Engl.: *The elementary structures of kinship.* Boston, MA: Beacon Press, 1969).

Lévi-Strauss, C. (1958). *Anthropologie structurale.* Paris: Librairie Plon (Engl.: *Structural anthropology.* Harmondsworth: Penguin Books, 1977).

Lévi-Strauss, C. (1962). *La pensée sauvage.* Paris: Librairie Plon (Engl.: *The savage mind.* Chicago: The University of Chicago Press, 1966).

Lévi-Strauss, C. (1973). *Anthropologie structurale deux.* Paris: Librairie Plon (Engl.: *Structural anthropology, Vol. II.* New York: Basic Books, 1976).

Lévi-Strauss, C. (1983). *Le Regard éloigné.* Paris: Librairie Plon (Engl.: *The view from afar.* New York: Basic Books, 1985).

Lewin, K. (1951). *Field theory in social science: Selected theoretical papers.* New York: Harper & Brothers.

Linton, R. (1945). *The cultural background of personality.* New York: D. Appleton-Century. This book, published in 1945, is based on a series of lectures that Linton gave already in 1943.

Luhmann, N. (1984). *Soziale Systeme. Grundriß einer allgemeinen Theorie.* Frankfurt/Main: Suhrkamp (Engl.: *Social systems.* Stanford: Stanford University Press, 1995).

Mayer, R. E. (1979). *Denken und Problemlösen. Eine Einführung in menschliches Denken und Lernen.* Berlin, Heidelberg: Springer (Orig.: Thinking and problem solving: An introduction to human cognition and learning. Glenview: Scott, Foresman and Company, 1977.)

Mead, G. H. (1934). *Mind, self, and society.* Ed.: C. W. Morris. Chicago: University of Chicago Press. Mead, M. (1928). *Coming of age in Samoa. A psychological study of primitive youth for western civilisation.* New York: William Morrow.

Mead, M. (1928). *Coming of age in Samoa.* New York: William Morrow & Company.

Mead, M. (1977). *Letters from the field, 1925–1975.* New York: Harper & Row.

Meier, B. P., Schnall, S., Schwarz, N., & Bargh, J. A. (2012). Embodiment in social psychology. *Topics in Cognitive Science, 4*, 705–716. https://doi.org/10.1111/j.1756-8765.2012.01212.x.

Miltenberger, R. G. (2012). *Behavior modification: Principles and procedures* (5th ed.). Wadsworth: Cengage.

Montenegro, R. A., & Stephens, C. (2006). Indigenous health in Latin America and the Caribbean. *Lancet, 367*, 1859–1869.

Moran, E. F. (1995). Rich and poor ecosystems of Amazonia: An approach to management. In: T. Nishizawa & J. I. Uitto (eds.), *The fragile tropics of Latin America: Sustainable management of changing environments.* Tokyo: United Nations University Press. Available online at: <http://archive.unu.edu/unupress/unupbooks/80877e/80877E00.htm>, accessed 26 July 2017.

Niedenthal, P. M., Barsalou, L. W., Winkielman, P., Krauth–Gruber, S., & Ric, F. (2005). Embodiment in attitudes, social perception, and emotion. *Personality and Social Psychology Review, 9*(3), 184–211.

Paasche, H. (1921). *Die Forschungsreise des Afrikaners Lukanga Mukara ins innerste Deutschland.* Hamburg: Goldmann Verlag.

Phillips, B., Daniels, J., Woodward, A., Blakely, T., Taylor, R., & Morrell, S. (2017). Mortality trends in Australian Aboriginal peoples and New Zealand Māori. Popular Health Metrics, 15(1), 25. doi: https://doi.org/10.1186/s12963-017-0140-6. Available online at: <https://pophealth-metrics.biomedcentral.com/track/pdf/10.1186/s12963-017-0140-6?site=pophealthmetrics.biomedcentral.com> (accessed 15 Aug 2017).

Purcell, T. (1998). Indigenous knowledge and applied anthropology: Questions of definition and direction. *Human Organization, 57*(3), 258–227.

Rigney, L. I. (1997). Internationalisation of an indigenous anti–colonial cultural critique of research methodologies: A guide to Indigenist research methodology and its principles. 632–639. Available on line at: <http://herdsa.org.au/wp–content/uploads/conference/1997/rigney01.pdf>, downloaded 14 Apr 2015.

Ritchie, J., & Lewis, J. (Eds.). (2003). *Qualitative research practice. A guide for social science students and researchers.* London, Thousand Oaks, New Delhi: Sage Publications.

Silburn, K., Reich, H., & Anderson, I. (Eds.). (2016). *A global snapshot of indigenous and tribal peoples' health. The Lancet-Lowitja Institute Collaboration.* Carlton South: The Lowitja Institute.

Skinner, B. F. (1948). Superstition in the pigeon. *Journal of Experimental Psychology, 38*, 168–172.

Smylie, J., Crengle, S., Freemantle, J., & Taualii, M. (2010). Indigenous birth outcomes in Australia, Canada, New Zealand and the United States – An overview. *The Open Women's Health Journal, 4*, 7–17.

Spengler, O. (1926). *The decline of the West.* Vol. I: *Form and actuality.* New York: Alfred A. Knopff (Orig.: *Der Untergang des Abendlandes. Umrisse einer Morphologie der Weltgeschichte.* Vol. I: *Gestalt und Wirklichkeit.* Wien: Braumüller, 1918. Revised ed. Munich: C. H. Beck, 1923).

Spengler, O. (1928). *The decline of the West.* Vol. II: *Perspectives of world–history.* New York: Alfred A. Knopff (Orig.: *Der Untergang des Abendlandes. Umrisse einer Morphologie der Weltgeschichte.* Vol. II: *Welthistorische Perspektiven.* Munich: C. H. Beck, 1922).

Tatz, C. (1999). *Genocide in Australia. An AIATSIS research discussion paper.* Canberra: The Australian Institute of Aboriginal and Torres Strait Islander Studies.

UN Millennium Project. (2005). *Investing in development: A practical plan to achieve the millennium development goals.* New York: United Nations Development Programme.

United Nations (1981–1983). *Study of the problem of discrimination against indigenous populations: Final report submitted by the Special Rapporteur, Mr. José Martínez Cobo.* E/CN.4/Sub.2/476 (1981); E/CN.4/Sub.2/1982/2 (1982); E/CN.4/Sub.2/1983/21 (1983). Geneva/New York: United Nations.

United Nations (1996). *Working paper by the Chairperson–Rapporteur, Mrs. Erica–Irene A. Daes. On the concept of "indigenous people".* E/CN.4/Sub.2/AC.4/1996/2. Geneva: UN.

United Nations Department of Economic and Social Affairs. (2009). *State of the world's indigenous peoples.* New York: United Nations.

United Nations General Assembly (2007). *Declaration on the rights of indigenous peoples.* Resolution adopted [without reference to a Main Committee (A/61/L.67 and Add.1)] 61/295.

United Nations Inter-Agency Support Group on Indigenous Peoples' Issues (2014). Elimination and responses to violence, exploitation and abuse of indigenous girls, adolescents and young women. Thematic paper towards the preparation of the 2014 World Conference on Indigenous Peoples. New York: United Nations. Available online at: <http://www.un.org/en/ga/president/68/pdf/wcip/IASG%20Thematic%20Paper_%20Violence%20against%20Girls%20and%20Women%20-%20rev1.pdf> (accessed 17 Aug 2017).

US Office on Colombia, ABColombia and Sisma Mujer. (2013). *Colombia: Women, conflict-related sexual violence, and the peace process.* London: ABColombia.

Watzlawick, P., Beavin, J. H., & Jackson, D. D. (1967). *Pragmatics of human communication. A study of Interctional patterns, pathologies, and paradoxes.* New York: Norton.

Weber, M. (1922). *Wirtschaft und Gesellschaft.* Tübingen: Mohr.

Weeber, K.-W. (1990). *Smog über Attika. Umweltverhalten im Altertum.* Zürich: Artemis & Winkler.

WHO. (2014). *Eliminating forced, coercive and otherwise involuntary sterilization: An interagency statement, OHCHR, UN women, UNAIDS, UNDP, UNFPA, UNICEF and WHO*. Geneva: World Health Organization.

Wicklund, R. A. (1990). *Zero-variable theories and the psychology of the explainer*. New York: Springer.

Wicklund, R. A., & Gollwitzer, P. M. (1982). *Symbolic self-completion*. Hillsdale, NJ: Lawrence Erlbaum.

Yehuda, R., Daskalakis, N. P., Bierer, L. M., Bader, H. N., Klengel, T., Holsboer, F., & Binder, E. B. (2015). Holocaust exposure induced intergenerational effects on FKBP5 methylation. *Biological Psychiatry*. https://doi.org/10.1016/j.biopsych.2015.08.005.

Zahavi, D. (2010). Empathy, embodiment and interpersonal understanding: From Lipps to Schutz. *Inquiry, 53*(3), 285–306. https://doi.org/10.1080/00201741003784663.

Zaumseil, M. (2006). Beiträge der Psychologie zum Verständnis des Zusammenhangs von Kultur und psychischer Gesundheit bzw. Krankheit. In E. Wohlfart & M. Zaumseil (Eds.), *Transkulturelle Psychiatrie – Interkulturelle Psychotherapie: Interdisziplinäre Theorie und Praxis* (pp. 3–50). Berlin: Springer.

Chapter 2
The Legal Framework of Research in Indigenous Contexts

Abstract The first historical account of a legal debate about the status of indigenous peoples dates back to the sixteenth century, when Bartolomé de Las Casas argued in favour of human rights to be granted to the indigenous peoples in the new Spanish colonies of the Americas. But it took very long until special consideration was given to indigenous peoples on the level of international law. From the 1950s, the International Labour Organization adopted specific conventions focussing on indigenous peoples' rights. And from 1982, another UN body was concerned with preparing what was then adopted by the General Assembly in 2007 as the Declaration on the Rights of Indigenous Peoples. Its observance is of major importance for anyone contacting indigenous peoples or working on any issue related to these cultural groups. Although the definition of indigeneity is a very difficult matter, researchers should ensure that they never violate any rights. In this chapter, we go into the details of the Declaration's articles that are particularly relevant for field research in indigenous contexts. Foremost, indigenous peoples are granted their right to self-determination. States are under obligation to protect indigenous peoples, their cultures and environments. Indigenous peoples have the right to revitalise their culture, they have cultural autonomy in education and lifestyle, and they have land rights. In media and education, indigenous culture has to be reflected correctly. Researchers have to make sure that they never obstruct the indigenous peoples' exercise of these rights but rather counterbalance existing impediments.

Keywords History of indigenous rights · United Nations Declaration on the Rights of Indigenous Peoples · Role of researchers · Culturally sustainable field research

There are many different good reasons as to why research in indigenous contexts has to be carried out cautiously, with respect towards the other culture and ensuring not to exert any destabilising influence on that particular social system. One reason is given by the ethical perspective, which makes clear that destabilising others, let alone their culture, is something to be avoided. A less altruistic and more selfish reason is given by the methodological perspective, according to which influences on the object of research – culture, in our case – would spoil the results. While we deal with these two reasons in other sections of this book, we shall look in this chapter at the legal aspects that determine the correct implementation of research in indigenous contexts.

These legal aspects are of major importance for anyone, who contacts traditionally living indigenous peoples. From the indigenous perspective, it does not matter much how the visitors define themselves. They might see themselves as tourists or as scientists or even as a mixture of both. Some would call themselves adventurers, globetrotters or backpackers; some come in groups, while others are alone. Some travel on their own accord; others have been sent by their bosses, as land surveyors, as prospectors or as researchers. If we try to take the indigenous peoples' perspective, then in all of these cases, someone intrudes into their daily routine, into their land and into their culture. Most, if not all, indigenous peoples have had quite negative experiences with intruders. During the past centuries, white people and others, who have become attached to the dominant culture, have taken indigenous peoples' land, have expelled them, have killed them and have done so many other nasty things to them that a book like this would not provide enough space to list them all. Very few investigations have looked into the psychological effects of these traumatising impacts on indigenous cultures.[1] Since there are indications that particular genetic properties can be found in the second generation of Holocaust survivors (Yehuda et al. 2015; also see Chap. 1 of this book, Sect. 1.1.1, on Transgenerational Traumata), there is a reason to consider the effects of traumatising impact on indigenous peoples, as it has been done by Bombay et al. (2009) or by Aguiar and Halseth (2015). These aspects are important for researchers in indigenous contexts, as we should be aware of the historical burden put upon those cultures. This burden is part of the indigenous context, in which we do our research. We are being perceived by the indigenous peoples under these premises. Furthermore, these aspects are important as we should refrain from stirring up collective traumata or even contribute to new destabilisations.

Bearing this in mind, the United Nations Declaration on the Rights of Indigenous Peoples can be welcomed as a guiding legal framework, which gives us some orientation and which helps to prevent any mistakes on our part. However, before we begin, the question might arise again as how to define indigeneity. That definition is a very difficult matter indeed. After we have addressed it from a socio-psychological perspective in Chap. 1 of this book, we shall take a closer look at it in Sect. 2.2, taking UN perspectives into account. But it can already be said here that, in order to ensure never to violate any rights, it makes sense not to focus on their narrowest possible definition but rather on the widest possible one. Therefore, we shall go into the details of the Declaration's articles that are particularly relevant for field research in indigenous contexts. Before we do so, let us start with looking at the historical processes that have led to the present legal positions. This is helpful not only for the reconstruction of their origin but also for clarifying their application, as well as for the extrapolation of the further path that these processes might take. We should be aware that we, as researchers in indigenous contexts, are part of these processes.

---

[1] Cf. Groh, A., Culture, Trauma and Psychotherapy (2009).

Therefore, we may not ignore the responsibility that we have. Our behaviour in the fields should never contribute to watering down the ongoing implementation of the indigenous rights. Rather, it is our ethical obligation to further sharpen, strengthen, specify and emphasise these rights in their concrete applications.

2.1 Historical Aspects

It took a long time, until indigenous peoples were legally recognised. However, this legal history did not occur all by itself. Rather, it was preceded by reflections on the part of the colonial rulers. From the beginning of the European expansion, these reflections were the reaction of some to the inhuman behaviour of many of the colonisers towards the indigenous peoples. Already in the early sixteenth century, the Dominican Order had sent some of their clerics to the New World, where they preached against the suppression and cruel treatment of the indigenous population. With the "Leyes de Burgos", the Laws of Burgos, of 1512, the Spanish Crown promoted the protection and humanitarian attitudes towards the indigenous peoples. The implementation of these laws, though, remained by far inadequate.

One person to be mentioned of the religious authorities in the Spanish colonies, who was motivated by the Dominican initiative to reflect and to rethink not only his own role but also the general position of the colonial power, was Bartolomé de Las Casas. From 1502, he had been involved with the submission of indigenous peoples in the Spanish colonies. He then became military chaplain and was confronted with the Dominicans' engagement for the indigenous cause. In 1511, the Dominicans had called together the legal scholars and the royal officials, including Diego Columbus, Christopher Columbus's son, to attend an Advent sermon at the Cathedral of Santa Domingo, which was held by the friar Antón Montesino. In this sermon, it was pointed out unmistakably that the cruel treatment of the indigenous population by the colonists was to be classified as mortal sin. But instead of repenting, the colonial officials were upset and urged the friar to revoke his statements the following Sunday. Yet, instead of revoking, Antón Montesino, with the backing of his confraternity, further substantiated the indictment and justified it theologically. As a reaction, Montesino was sent to Spain, but instead of being convicted, he succeeded in delivering his report on the atrocities to King Ferdinand personally and convincing him of the rightfulness of the criticism. This, then, led to the Laws of Burgos mentioned above. As the colonists remained unreasonably stubborn, the Dominicans resorted to the most drastic measures of refusing to hear their confessions and absolve them. When the field chaplain Bartolomé de Las Casas was affected by these measures, this triggered his process of rethinking, so that he then started to take stands for the indigenous population. In 1544, Las Casas became bishop of Chiapas.[2]

---

[2] Chiapas is now a federal state of Mexico.

Over decades, Bartolomé de Las Casas intervened several times with the Spanish Crown, advocating the indigenous cause. He accused the colonists and the colonial soldiers of committing atrocities against the indigenous population of the colonies. Between 1492 and 1536, he wrote detailed reports about the situation of the indigenous peoples. However, these writings where not accessible to the public and where later denounced as anti-Spanish propaganda. Due to this censorship, the first publications of Las Casas' books took place posthumously and outside the Spanish Dominion. The probably best known of his works is "Brevísima relación de la destrucción de las Indias occidentales" (A Short Account of the Destruction of the West Indies), written in 1542, which he had printed in 1552 in Seville and given to Prince Philip II of Spain.[3]

The efforts of Bartolomé de Las Casas had little but at least some effect, though. The Spanish Crown enforced the New Laws, "Leyes Nuevas", to protect the indigenous population. These laws prohibited the enslavement of indigenous persons, and it demanded that they should be paid when they worked for the colonists. But again, these laws were hardly translated into action. Rather, Las Casas was defamed and threatened with death. He then resigned from his office as Bishop but continued to campaign for indigenous issues and to take legal proceedings for it.

It then took some centuries until 1955 that the International Labour Organization (ILO) enacted a convention that focused on indigenous workers in particular, *Convention 104, concerning the Abolition of Penal Sanctions for Breaches of Contract of Employment by Indigenous Workers*, which entered into force in 1958. In 1957, the ILO approved *Convention 107, concerning the Protection and Integration of Indigenous and Other Tribal and Semi-Tribal Populations in Independent Countries* (entry into force: 1959).

Then, in 1989, the ILO passed *Convention 169* (entry into force: 1991), which grants tribal peoples equality, freedom, land rights, self-determination and own institutions, but only 22 countries ratified it.

In 1982, the Working Group on Indigenous Populations started its work at the United Nations High Commissariat of Human Rights, which at that time was a subsidiary body to the Economic and Social Council. It took 24 years until, more or less simultaneously, the Declaration on the Rights of Indigenous Peoples was completed, and a third council, the HRC/Human Rights Council, was constituted. I participated in the preparation of the Indigenous Rights Declaration in its final phase, from 1999 to 2006. The Declaration on the Rights of Indigenous Peoples was then adopted by the General Assembly in 2007 with the majority of the United Nations member states.

As the goal of compiling the Declaration was accomplished in 2006, the Working Group ceased to exist. We then had an extraordinary meeting in 2007 at the UN in Geneva to consider how we should proceed, and we recommended to the Human Rights Council that an Expert Mechanism on the Rights of Indigenous Peoples be created, complementary to the Permanent Forum on Indigenous Issues that takes

---

[3]After Bartolomé de Las Casas had returned to Spain in 1546, he lived at the court of Prince Philip II.

place once a year in New York. The recommendation was approved, and since 2008, we have annual meetings of the Expert Mechanism in Geneva, as a subsidiary body directly to the Human Rights Council.

It is often pointed out that the United Nations Declaration on the Rights of Indigenous Peoples was not a binding instrument of international law. But as most things in life, it is somewhat more complicated when we take a closer look. Not all scholars of law agree upon the distinction between binding and nonbinding rules, especially with regard to international law.[4] Even within the UN internal discourse, the engagement of the Declaration is discussed, with a claim for its high legal value to be accepted:

"The Declaration's wording, which has been endorsed by Members States, explicitly manifests a commitment to the rights and principles the Declaration embodies".[5]

Whereas declarations as such generally are not considered binding, the United Nations Declaration on the Rights of Indigenous Peoples is an extension, explication and clarification of the 1948 United Nations Universal Declaration of Human Rights. Therefore, the Indigenous Rights Declaration has the character of an amendment to the Human Rights Declaration. Consequently, as these declarations are inseparably linked with each other, in a way that the Indigenous Rights Declaration is built upon the Human Rights Declaration, the legal status of the extending declaration should be determined by the status of the underlying, primary declaration.

The United Nations Universal Declaration of Human Rights (United Nations General Assembly 1948), along with the International Covenant on Economic, Social and Cultural Rights[6] and the International Covenant on Civil and Political Rights[7], is part of the International Bill of Human Rights.[8] Since the covenants came into force in 1976, the whole Bill is on force as part of the international law.

In the discourse concerning the legal character of the United Nations Declaration on the Rights of Indigenous Peoples, it is stressed that this declaration has had an enormously complex history regarding the phase when it was generated, both in terms of the large number of persons being involved and the long time, which this process took, and that this declaration enjoys an unusually broad support within the UN mechanism, as well as on the international level; it is pointed out that therefore, the United Nations Declaration on the Rights of Indigenous Peoples is perceived "as an authoritative and legitimate document" (Barelli 2015, 56).

---

[4] Cf.: Indigenous Bar Association (2011).

[5] Cf.: UN Doc. A/65/264, General Assembly, Situation of human rights and fundamental freedoms of indigenous people: Note by the Secretary-General, Interim report of the Special Rapporteur on the situation of human rights and fundamental freedoms of indigenous people, section V. B.

[6] United Nations General Assembly (1976a).

[7] United Nations General Assembly (1976b).

[8] *International Bill of Human Rights* was the title of the 1948 UN General Assembly Resolution 217 (III) and is now a collective term comprising the Human Rights Declaration [i.e. Res. 217 (III), Part A] and the two Covenants mentioned.

2.2 Acknowledgement of Indigenous Identity

Whereas in the first chapter we have considered indigeneity in the sense of the question, what kind of culture can be called indigenous, the perspective taken here is rather characterised by the aspect of who is legally accepted as being indigenous. There is no final legal definition of indigeneity. However, there are some working concepts, which roughly outline the idea of which preconditions should be given in order to accept a person as being indigenous.

Within the discourse on indigeneity, it is often referred to the so-called Martínez Cobo Study, a "Study of the Problem of Discrimination Against Indigenous Populations", submitted by the Special Rapporteur to the Commission on Human Rights, the Ecuadorian José Ricardo Martínez Cobo (United Nations 1981–1983). In this report, Martínez Cobo compiled various official perspectives on indigenous issues, rather than formulating new ideas. One of the chapters deals with the "Definition of indigenous populations" (E/CN.4/Sub.2/1982/2/Add.6), and he arranged the various perspectives on this particular issue regarding the aspects of *ancestry*, *culture*, *language* and the *consciousness* of a group of being indigenous. Martínez Cobo pointed out that always more than one of the criteria were to be taken into account for acknowledging indigeneity to a social group and that actually *multiple criterion* consideration was necessary. As additional criteria, which had to be considered, he named the *acceptance by the indigenous community*, when a person claimed to be indigenous, and a community's *residence in certain parts of the country*, in order to accept that this is an indigenous community of that country concerned.

Another text that is often mentioned when it comes to the question, who is indigenous, is the working paper by Mrs. Erica-Irene A. Daes, *on the concept of* "indigenous people" (United Nations 1996). The Greek Erica Daes was the chairperson-rapporteur to the same UN body as Martínez Cobo, the Commission on Human Rights. In this working paper, she summarised the views of international organisations and legal experts regarding the constituents of the concept of indigeneity, namely:

(a) "Priority in time, with respect to the occupation and use of a specific territory;
(b) The voluntary perpetuation of cultural distinctiveness, which may include the aspects of language, social organization, religion and spiritual values, modes of production, laws and institutions;
(c) Self-identification, as well as recognition by other groups, or by State authorities, as a distinct collectivity; and.
(d) An experience of subjugation, marginalization, dispossession, exclusion or discrimination, whether or not these conditions persist".
(E/CN.4/Sub.2/AC.4/1996/2, para. 69, p. 22).

Like her predecessor Martínez Cobo, Erica Daes reaffirmed that the constituents mentioned were neither inclusive nor comprehensive. Rather than providing any definition, they were just factors that were present to a larger or lesser extent in different contexts and different regions of the world. Another focus of this paper was laid on correct wording, and during the years that followed its submission, the terminology was subsequently changed to "indigenous peoples" with the plural "s", and the working group that had been formally named "(…) on Indigenous Populations" was then renamed into the "United Nations Working Group on Indigenous Peoples", reflecting the self-conception of collective identity as claimed by indigenous representatives.

The next legal text, which is important with regard to the concept of indigeneity, on the timeline, is the above-mentioned ILO 169, the International Labour Organization's *Convention 169 concerning Indigenous and Tribal Peoples in Independent Countries* (International Labour Organization 1989). It is not a declaration but a treaty, and as such, it is the only international treaty that deals exclusively with the rights of indigenous peoples. It is open for ratification, and once ratified, it is binding for each state that has signed it. This binding character might be the reason for the states' reluctance to sign this convention. Until now, most countries of the world have not decided to ratify ILO 169.

ILO Convention 169 addresses tribal peoples, who are socially, culturally or economically distinct from other parts of a nation and who rely on their own traditions and customs. These peoples are understood as those who had been living in a country at the time of its conquest or colonisation or at the time when its present borders had been defined. In this convention, the criterion for assigning indigeneity is the self-definition that is found in a particular group. It is emphasised that the use of the term "peoples" does not imply any rights equivalent to the rights of nations within the framework of international law.

Emerged from the discourse of the past decades regarding the acknowledgement of indigenous identity is the consent that it would be less useful to define who is indigenous but rather to identify indigenous peoples with regard to a specific context and based on their self-definition. In the United Nations Declaration on the Rights of Indigenous Peoples, the aspect of self-identification is accentuated in Article 33: "Indigenous peoples have the right to determine their own identity or membership in accordance with their customs and traditions" (paragraph 1, sentence 1). Also as an emergence from the discourse, there is the understanding that indigenous peoples live in historic continuity of societies, which had lived in their areas already before any colonisation or before the arrival of dominant settlers. These areas do not have to be seen as being restricted to a particular dwelling place, as many indigenous peoples are hunting and gathering societies, or otherwise non-sedentary. Therefore, these areas are to be understood as the natural environments in which and from which the indigenous peoples live. Indigenous societies are characterised by notable feelings of attachment to these areas with their natural environments. They are also characterised by social and economic structures of their own and furthermore by their own language, a particular culture and their own worldview. Indigenous peoples are typically dominated by the non-indigenous society, and they see themselves as distinct from the non-indigenous society. Often, there is a notion of solidarity with other indigenous peoples. On the collective level, indigenous peoples designate themselves as indigenous, and on the individual level, the members of an indigenous society accept each other as being indigenous. They are typically determined to maintain their cultures with their particularities, which they want to pass on to the generations to come. Synoptically, we can extract the following central aspects, which reflect the general consent within the discourse on indigeneity:

Historical continuity Indigenous peoples are descendants of those who have lived in their traditional territories even before any colonisation, invasion or land acquisition took place. Today's indigenous peoples see themselves in ethnic and genealogical linkage with these ancestors.

Territoriality The claim of a people's linkage to a territory is to be accepted as justified if this particular people, in the historical process, has been living on that territory before any other people that is in relation to this land. This aspect is expressed, for example, in the self-describing term "First Nations" as used by North American indigenous peoples.

Cultural distinctness Indigenous peoples, by their own will, maintain certain cultural features and pass them on to the next generations. With regard to these cultural specificities, each indigenous people is different from other peoples, be it in comparison to neighbouring indigenous peoples or to a country's majority non-indigenous population.

Self-identification Indigenous persons identify themselves as being indigenous. However, in addition to this, it is necessary that their communities agree with that person's self-definition. Such a precaution shall help to prevent the abusive claim of indigeneity by non-indigenous persons (cf. examples in Sect. 1.1 of this book).

Collective experience of suppression Indigenous peoples have experienced various degrees of discrimination in the course of history, and this discrimination often still persists. It can take different forms such as forced displacement, genocide or dispossession.

We certainly cannot say that now, once and forever, it has been clarified who is indigenous and who is not. We still have to expect that there are some persons who claim to be indigenous while this status is being denied to them. Such denial can have various reasons. They can be politically motivated, because certain governments do not want to accept that indigenous peoples live in their countries. But it could also be the case that some persons have an individually constructed indigenous identity, which might be seen as being true by themselves, while, at the same time, that construction does not quite match with the criteria that others have set up with regard to indigeneity. Furthermore, we also have to expect that there are persons who do not want to be perceived as being indigenous, although there is a wide consent among others that they are to be awarded that status.

Such inconsistencies, contraries and heterogeneities can be found on either party involved, be it on the individual or on the collective level, among indigenous peoples, governments or non-officials. We will have to live with that. But we should always try to find the most appropriate way to deal with it. In any concrete case, we have to state reasons, justify and explain how we see things and why it is so.

Having said that about indigeneity, we shall now highlight some core aspects of the United Nations Declaration on the Rights of Indigenous Peoples, which are relevant for research in indigenous contexts.

2.3   Right to Self-Determination

Article 3

Indigenous peoples have the right to self-determination. By virtue of that right they freely determine their political status and freely pursue their economic, social and cultural development.

Article 3 of the United Nations Declaration on the Rights of Indigenous Peoples condenses many of the aspects covered by the Declaration. One very important implication is the right of indigenous peoples to say no. This even pertains to Article 3 itself or to certain aspects that are addressed within this article. For example, some indigenous peoples might say that they do not want to become involved with economy at all. Also, the concept of "development" could be seen very critically. It is often taken as granted from the globalised society's point of view that everyone needed and wanted "development". But we have to admit that even the term itself is problematic. Only those things can be developed, which had been enveloped before. A human being can develop from the fertilised egg through embryonic and foetal statuses, childhood and youth to the fully developed adult. Likewise, when you put a grain of seed into the soil, it will develop a plant under the appropriate conditions. This is determined by the genetic programme encoded in the DNA and can only be modified to a certain degree by external factors. In other languages, the term contains the same etymological meaning, be it the German *Entwicklung* or the Spanish *desarollo*.

Using such a term, which reflects determination, with regard to social issues, suggests that there is also a determination regarding historical processes of social and cultural systems. By such a usage, the term becomes a political instrument, claiming that those who are *not yet* like us are somewhat slow in their *development*, and because they are *backward*, they needed some aid to become like us. And implicitly, we claim that the historical processes that have led to the state in which we are now all went perfectly fine or that at least the state in which we are is the optimum, towards which all others have to orientate themselves. We are perfect, whereas the others still are imperfect. They can ameliorate the situation by adapting to us, modifying their behaviour, changing their lifestyles, giving up their traditions and converting to globalisation.

Some advocates of globalisation might deny that they demand full conversion from indigenous peoples. They might claim that they only want to give them punctual improvements. However, by claiming that, they ignore the systemic character of culture. As if it was possible to only build a road, without affecting the community that is reached by this road. As if it was possible to only install a school, without changing the people's way of thinking. Of course, there are cases where humanitarian intervention is necessary. But any intervention needs to be carefully planned, in order to avoid collateral damages. When people have to stay in refugee camps, living in tents neatly arranged in rows and accustomed to canned food, the passing on of cultural information is interrupted, be it the information on how to hunt and gather, how to fish, how to build the hut or any other of the techniques, which characterise and distinctively constitute indigenous culture. After some years in such camps, indigenous culture is deteriorated. Unfortunately, such situations are not so rare. So surprisingly, Article 3 even provides assistance for critical circumstances. It should not be rendered inoperative by focusing on the mere survival of peoples in emergency. Consulting them and involving them in planning and realisation of any intervention would, on the one hand, facilitate the daily routine, for example, in refugee camps, it would be cost-efficient, and, on the other hand, it would benefit the survival of their culture instead of approving its cease.

Article 3 exemplifies that the whole Declaration is the result of a tenacious struggle between the representatives of indigenous peoples on the one side and those acting in the interest of states on the other side. Looking at this article, we can see that the first, short sentence rather reflects indigenous interests, while the second, longer sentence seems to be formulated under strong influence exerted by governments. However, former decrees in countries like Thailand and Kenya, which have prohibited indigenous peoples due to decency conventions to appear in public in their traditional, unclothed way, have de facto been rendered inoperative by the adoption of the United Nations Declaration on the Rights of Indigenous Peoples.

Article 3 also shows that indigenous peoples' self-determination is not seen as something self-evident. If it was a matter of course, then it would be needless to mention it. There are systemic effects on both sides: The industrial culture, being heir to the colonial powers, habitually takes a dominant position, while indigenous peoples often see themselves and behave in a subordinate position. Consequently, there are not too many practical examples of indigenous peoples exercising their rights as defined in Article 3 of the United Nations Declaration on the Rights of Indigenous Peoples. For instance, the chiefs of some Pacific islands in the Western Carolines have banned globalised clothes from their territories. So even the few backpackers arriving to these places may wear no more than the traditional grass skirt. This not only has a strengthening effect on the indigenous peoples' cultural self-confidence, but it also is a much more authentic experience for the visitors, who are integrated on the decisive level of visual semiotics. With this regulation, reciprocity and mutuality are installed, like indigenous peoples also integrate themselves when they happen to visit industrial countries. By the chiefs' decision, destabilising influence is prevented. This self-determination of their own cultural context parallels the self-determination exercised by the globalised people within globalised contexts.

The circumstance that indigenous peoples, due to the imbalance of dominance, have been victims of intrusion and various destructive forms of interference exerted by non-indigenous people is taken account of by granting self-determination to indigenous peoples while leaving it up to their free choice if they want to participate in the political or otherwise non-indigenous activities of the state. This perspective becomes quite clear in Article 5:

Article 5

Indigenous peoples have the right to maintain and strengthen their distinct political, legal, economic, social and cultural institutions, while retaining their right to participate fully, if they so choose, in the political, economic, social and cultural life of the State.

The formulation, "if they so choose", implies, in a balanced way, that indigenous peoples can decide pro or contra such participation. Furthermore, such choice is necessarily done as an act of freedom, since the freedom of choice is a conditio sine qua non that is stressed throughout this and similar UN documents.

In theory, any act of biasing a choice, which is supposed to be made in freedom, would be a violation of fundamental human rights principles. In practice, however, indigenous peoples are heavily influenced when they are in touch with globalised culture and thus exposed to cultural dominance. Yet, the dominant are responsible for whatever effect results from their contact with indigenous culture. Therefore, the members of the globalised culture are under obligation to ensure that indigenous peoples can, in fact, determine their concerns freely. As theory, in this case, does not match with practice but rather is far away from reality, at least researchers should not contribute to this imbalance. We should do our best to understand the mechanisms behind it, in order to provide the best possible counterbalance.

Here, it is necessary to shine a light on the aspect of dominance. The mere dichotomy of indigenous peoples versus the state is an oversimplification, which does not live up to the much more complex reality. Due to various degrees of contact with the non-indigenous superdominant culture, indigenous peoples have gone through different extent of synthesis and accordingly enact various degrees of dominance upon each other. With the help of the concept of the spectrum of cultures, we can visualise these relations between the different indigenous groups as different locations of these groups within the cultural spectrum, which we have already referred to in the first chapter of this book, in connection with the modelling of cultural synthesis. Those indigenous groups, who have been influenced by the non-indigenous superdominant culture to a large extent, are more heated up, to speak in terms of this concept, while the other indigenous groups, who have had less contact with the non-indigenous superdominant culture, are less heated up. In the metaphorical visualisation, the least heated up are located furthest to the blue end of the spectrum. What we have to take into account is the fact that these indigenous peoples are in contact with each other, forming a hierarchical line or chain, in which those who are the most influenced ones on this chain exert their dominance on those below their position, who are somewhat less influenced. Then, these latter ones exert their dominance on those below their position, etc.

Furthermore, we have to take into consideration that these are dynamic processes, with the present state only reflecting the situation of an indigenous group, which has lived a more traditional lifestyle before and which is most probably about to move towards a more and more globalised lifestyle. For example,[9] the hierarchy between the different indigenous groups in the region of the Uaupés River in Brazil is expressed in the fact that some of them have maintained gardens along the smaller feeding streams. They consider the other indigenous groups, who still follow a traditional hunter-gatherer lifestyle, as being inferior to themselves. On the other hand, they maintain trading relations to the globalised settlements along the main river. What is happening right now is that those garden owners spend more and more time in town and eventually settle down there, and they order the inferior groups to take care of their gardens, who are now becoming established there, being more and more kept away from the forest and thus from their traditional hunting and gathering way of life.

It would rather be a convenient excuse to say that all these actors within the connected social systems are making their free choices and are fully determining their lives themselves. The truth is that social pressure is passed down in this hierarchy. The globalised non-indigenous superdominant culture puts pressure on the indigenous peoples who come to town, who put pressure on those who have to take care of their gardens and who are inferior to the town-goers while acting superior to the more traditional indigenous peoples in the forest.

Unfortunately, one of the shortcomings of the United Nations Declaration on the Rights of Indigenous Peoples is that oversimplification of reducing the constellations and mechanisms of dominance to the imbalance between the state on the one side and indigenous peoples on the other side. By this, the processes of cultural change, which are taking place *because of* the dominance constellations, are not sufficiently taken into account. The aspect of time should be given more attention. As the cultural change is taking place due to pressure being exerted from one cultural group to the next, it cannot be accepted as being good in an evaluative sense and not even as a neutral. Free choice is restricted, in the relation between the globalised culture and indigenous peoples in immediate contact to it, as well as between indigenous peoples, in their interethnic and hierarchical relations. Those indigenous peoples who have partially adopted globalisation and who treat the more traditionally living indigenous peoples as being inferior to them should feel addressed by many of the articles of the United Nations Declaration on the Rights of Indigenous Peoples, which all call for acceptance and respect, the granting of self-determination, as well as full, free, prior and informed consent and which forbid any destabilisation of their cultures. Here, again, the cultural spectrum comes to bear: Those peoples, who have partially converted to globalisation, are accordingly acting in globalised ways. Therefore, the call for protecting indigenous cultures (Article 8) and the imperative to ensure the unbiased choice that indigenous peoples can revitalise their culture, if they wish so (Article 11), are directed to the non-indigenous global

---

[9] Renato Athias gave an excellent presentation on this example in 2015 at the "Eleventh Conference on Hunting and Gathering Societies" held in Vienna, titled "The Hupdah and their mobility in the Region of the Uaupé Basin" in the section "Amazonia from East to West: synthesizing perspectives on foraging societies in lowland South America".

culture, as well as to indigenous peoples, who behave dominantly towards other indigenous peoples, who they consider to be inferior to them. From the Human Rights point of view, the summoning to give up the perspective of others being inferior to oneself pertains to everyone, non-indigenous and indigenous humans alike.

2.4 Protection of Culture

Article 8

1. *Indigenous peoples and individuals have the right not to be subjected to forced assimilation or destruction of their culture.*

2. *States shall provide effective mechanisms for prevention of, and redress for:*

   (a) *Any action which has the aim or effect of depriving them of their integrity as distinct peoples, or of their cultural values or ethnic identities* [.]

Paragraph 2 of this article carries on with further subparagraphs, which condemn land theft, population transfer with the aim or effect of violating indigenous peoples' rights, forced assimilation or integration and discriminatory propaganda against indigenous peoples.

"The question of culture enjoys a prominent position" (Barelli 2015, p. 47) not only in these two articles but also throughout the United Nations Declaration on the Rights of Indigenous Peoples. As an aspect central to the whole document, it is not only acknowledged that indigenous peoples have cultures of their own, but that these cultures have to be protected. The duties of ensuring that these rights are respected by any party involved are delegated to the states.

Subparagraph 2. (a) of Article 8 is of particular relevance for researchers. It pertains to cultural destabilisation that is to be averted from indigenous peoples, especially detriments brought about by "depriving them of their integrity as distinct peoples, or of their cultural values or ethnic identities". And it is clearly said as to what is forbidden: "Any action which has the aim or effect". As the words of the Declaration have been pondered cautiously, this formulation ensures that no one can use excuses like, "I didn't want to", "I didn't mean it" or "It was not intended". Not only the aim of bringing about such cultural destabilisation would be a trespass but also the effect.

As researchers, we should be eager to avoid any such effect. Subparagraph 2. (a) ends with the reference to *identities*. Social identities are always mediated by means of self-presentation: For the peer group, it does not matter what a person thinks about himself or herself, as long as this is not communicated. But the way persons show themselves, the way they are seen by the others, matters most. This defines their social identity, whatever they say about themselves or even if they would be mute. At the same time, we know that there are dominance effects between persons from different parts of the cultural spectrum. These effects are especially strong, when these persons are representatives of the different ends of the spectrum, that is, from an indigenous culture on the one side and from the global culture on the other side. A central effect of cultural dominance is the asymmetry of mutual perception and influence. Because the dominant persons are perceived as role models, their cultural elements are likely to be picked up by persons from indigenous cultures, where the dominant elements replace and delete the traditional ones.

These two aspects taken together – identity relevance of visual self-presentation and indigenous cultural elements being ousted by the dominant globalised elements – have severe implications for any globalised person contacting an indigenous culture. Whatever cultural elements the globalised person carries into the indigenous context involves the risk of destabilising the indigenous culture. But this is what we want to avoid. So what to do? Should we completely stay out of indigenous cultures, because we cannot behave and because any behaviour of ours could potentially transfer an element of our culture?

Well, first of all we can take a closer look at cultural elements and their relevance to identity. They differ quite much in this respect. Whereas clothing defines a person very much, technical gadgets do so to a lesser extent. Moreover, indigenous persons usually cannot afford or would hardly be able to buy costly technical devices, but they might receive pieces of clothing from someone, which would then have an effect if they would present themselves with this clothing that represents the dominant culture. And as we know from research on social embodiment (e.g. Niedenthal et al. 2005; Gallagher 2005), it would also change those persons' way of thinking. What it comes down to is that the closer cultural elements are to the body of a person, and the more permanently they are perceived by others, the more they determine the cultural identity of that person.

Because we cannot hide the fact that we are representatives of the globalised culture, and because there is a dominance effect, which causes that we are perceived as role models, we should avoid to import any body-related standards, and we should not make use of any bodily self-presentation other than predefined by the indigenous tradition. Article 8 forbids anything that could possibly have any destabilising effect on indigenous culture and in particular on identity.

By identifying the level of body semiotics as identity relevant, we can differentiate between intrusive and nonintrusive acts of communication. At the same time, this enables the formulation of policies that do not exclude people from each other. Isolating indigenous peoples would collide with human rights in general. But if we acknowledge the relation of indigenous cultures with the respective territories, then mutual respect can be practised. Indigenous peoples have the right to leave their places and go into globalised areas. But it is expected then that they comply with the globalised behavioural rules. Mutuality, in observance of the United Nations Declaration on the Rights of Indigenous Peoples, requires that, likewise, globalised persons respect the culture-specific rules within indigenous areas. However, this applies to the visual level and not to the exchange of thoughts. The United Nations Conference on Freedom of Information (1948) has particular relevance to this. Free exchange of thoughts implies that the sides involved do not exert any pressure upon each other. As a practical example, this also pertains to missionary activities, as we may not forbid the conveyance of certain information. Thus, we may not prevent that any knowledge or perspective is passed on to indigenous peoples, in order to ensure the freedom of information. But at the same time, the freedom of choice has to be granted. With regard to religion, forcing anyone into a certain faith would hardly have any theological value, as assumably, there would be no personal conviction. Due to these specified perspectives of international law, visual and material culture on the one side has to be separated from information and intellectual exchange on the other side. But an exchange of thoughts, free of dominance, can only work when visitors respect the indigenous culture by integrating into it for the time of the visit. Otherwise, there would be the danger of cultural destabilisation. So again, we see that the level of visual semiotics is of major importance with regard to communicating respect and acceptance. Once this is ensured, then information can be exchanged freely in a way that ensures the freedom of choice.

The next important communication channel to be taken account of is the auditory one. It is, in fact, the most important channel with regard to intellectual exchange. The visual channel, though, is more prominent for different reasons.[10] One of the reasons is that visual communication takes place permanently, and another reason is that people can communicate with each other visually without using language. In any culture, people see each other much more than they talk with each other. Even if you speak an indigenous people's language and you tell them verbally that you accept and respect their culture but your visual appearance does not communicate the same, then there would be a contradiction, and you would have lost your credibility. In the following section, we shall see how the United Nations Declaration on the Rights of Indigenous Peoples seeks to protect indigenous languages as core elements of the indigenous cultures.

2.4.1 The Role of Language Within Indigenous Peoples' Cultural Rights

Article 13

1. *Indigenous peoples have the right to revitalize, use, develop and transmit to future generations their histories, languages, oral traditions, philosophies, writing systems and literatures, and to designate and retain their own names for communities, places and persons.*

2. *States shall take effective measures to ensure that this right is protected and also to ensure that indigenous peoples can understand and be understood in political, legal and administrative proceedings, where necessary through the provision of interpretation or by other appropriate means.*

---

[10] In our industrial culture, the notion of the visual channel's priority is due in no small part to the omnipresence of script. However, script is a converted form of auditory communication. It is actually verbal communication, which has been shifted into the visual channel.

All aspects addressed in this article have to do with language, either with spoken or written language or with the conveying of cultural elements – immaterial, in particular – or with issues of communication that are of distinctly linguistic nature.

Language constitutes, to a large extent, cultural identity for the members of any particular group that speak their common idiom. This is not only so because they have something in common, which could be anything. Language enables humans to convey complex, and even abstract, ideas. Through language, possibilities and options can be debated, past events can be evaluated, the future with its hopes and envisaged chances can be discussed, questions can be asked, fairy tales with imagined mythical beasts can be told, jokes can be made, and laughter and tears can be elicited. Language enables us to communicate in the most intimate way; it is the interface at which our thoughts interact. And this always happens in a culturally specific way.

Therefore, language is also a central paradigm for categorising culture. Concretely, this means that we can determine the number of cultures by the number of languages spoken. So if you want to know how many cultures are presently counted in the world, you can simply look up at the start page of *ethnologue.com*, where the present figure is displayed. This number varies all the time, as new indigenous languages are recognised, while others die out. During the past years, the number has been ranging around 7000. Taking into consideration the past 500 years with the European expansion, colonisation and extermination of many cultures, the number might have been much higher during previous phases of human history. The important role of language within culture, as well as its significance for a person's identity, has led to special attention being paid to linguistic aspects in the United Nations Declaration on the Rights of Indigenous Peoples. It is clear that, when the protection of culture is demanded, one should also be mindful of the protection of language. The latter is part of culture, as one of its core elements. Depending on the kind of communication, language can be, at times, the only representation of a particular culture.

Being mindful of the prominence of language for human cultures, it is not surprising that linguistic aspects are also addressed in further articles of the United Nations Declaration on the Rights of Indigenous Peoples. Article 14, which deals with the indigenous peoples' right to have their own educational systems and at which we are going to have a closer look later on, underlines that the culturally specific education be carried out in the indigenous language and that states, when they provide access to education for indigenous peoples, should take care that this is an education "in their own culture and provided in their own language" (Art. 14, para. 1). Furthermore, Article 16 grants indigenous peoples the right to "their own media in their own languages" (Art. 16, para. 1).

The issue of traditional knowledge, which is to be addressed in the following section, is already taken up in Article 13, which, inter alia, protects indigenous peoples' rights "to designate and retain their own names for communities, places and persons" (Art. 13, para. 1). In many cases, names of places are the only reminders that are retained regarding the former existence of an indigenous culture, which has been extinct by the dominant culture. However, due to the large variety of indigenous cultures, these rights, like many other rights, will have to be adapted to particular situations and circumstances. The Yanomami, for instance, do not directly address persons by their name. Rather, when speaking to them, they would say something like "Hey, you there". Yet when these persons are absent, they would use the given name when speaking about them.

2.4.2   Indigenous Culture and Intellectual Property

Article 31

1. *Indigenous peoples have the right to maintain, control, protect and develop their cultural heritage, traditional knowledge and traditional cultural expressions, as well as the manifestations of their sciences, technologies and cultures, including human and genetic resources, seeds, medicines, knowledge of the properties of fauna and flora, oral traditions, literatures, designs, sports and traditional games and visual and performing arts. They also have the right to maintain, control, protect and develop their intellectual property over such cultural heritage, traditional knowledge, and traditional cultural expressions.*
2. *In conjunction with indigenous peoples, States shall take effective measures to recognize and protect the exercise of these rights.*

Though it is not explicitly said, Article 31 of the United Nations Declaration on the Rights of Indigenous Peoples has a strong information-theoretical perspective. At the same time, it links cultural information, such as *traditional knowledge*, to non-cultural information, such as *seeds*, which is a specification of the immediately preceding naming of genetic resources. It is clear that this linkage is justified by culture-specific preoccupation with particular noncultural carriers of information, exemplified by the mentioning of *knowledge of the properties of fauna and flora*. Whenever research in indigenous contexts is targeted at things like *medicines* or *oral traditions*, then it touches the issue of the respective indigenous peoples' intellectual property.

Although paragraph 2 of Article 31 says that states shall ensure the observance of these rights together with the indigenous peoples, we, as researchers, should observe these rights anyway. Neither should we look for loopholes nor should we prey upon situations, in which national laws to protect indigenous intellectual property have not yet been enforced. The concept of Article 31 is clearly explained in paragraph 1. Therefore, if there is no national legislation, we should nevertheless seek permission from the respective indigenous people. Actually, regardless of if there are national laws or not, the indigenous peoples' right to control their intellectual property even overrides national legislation.

The question of how to handle intellectual property issues should be considered well before we go into the field; it should be part of the planning procedure already. As part of this, we should also look ahead – who will own the data once we have collected them? Who will own the outcome of the comparison of our collected data with secondary data? Who will own the overall results of the research? Well, the answers depend upon the specific type of investigation, as well as on the type of data.

Intellectual property, and in particular indigenous intellectual property, is a topic that enjoys intensive discussion. The basic problem lies within the cultural differences of jurisdictional systems. Many, if not all, indigenous peoples have their proper conceptions about ownership, entailing complex ideas concerning such things as depictions, music, dance or even the culture as a whole. Sometimes, rights of ownership are even coupled to each other, for example, the right to produce and own a particular piece of art and the right to possess a certain piece of land. Concepts of ownership vary extremely between cultures, so that they often are incompatible and cannot be synchronised. Even within the industrial nations, there is lack of clarity, when it comes to law cases, in which persons from different countries are involved. British, German, Spanish or US American laws are all different from each other. Some have their historical roots in the law of the ancient Roman Empire; others have quite different approaches of determining legal ruling. So how could we expect that an indigenous peoples' point of view regarding intellectual ownership would be in harmony with the idea that we have about it? Even the idea of intellectual property itself might be typical for our globalised culture. Moreover, this idea only came up quite recently. A starting point of this discourse might have been an article by Brush (1993) on indigenous knowledge.[11]

On the international level, previous organisations, which covered partial aspects of intellectual property, have been merged to the World Intellectual Property Organization (WIPO) in 1967, and the member nations of the World Trade Organization have made an Agreement on Trade-Related Aspects of Intellectual Property Rights (TRIPS) in 1994, but as the name of the latter says, this agreement is relevant to trade. For research, it might be relevant, for example, when a publication, in which indigenous medical knowledge is reported, is used by the pharmaceutical industry to produce and sell new drugs. Such a relation to trade would not be given under different circumstances like research regarding social structures. Somewhere in between are those cases, in which indigenous peoples demand the return of certain objects, such as feather crowns, which had been collected by ethnologists in former decades or centuries and which are now on display in museums. Some of these cases might rather be an issue for legal philosophy, especially those where it can be assumed that these objects would not exist anymore if they had not been preserved in museums under special conditions and protection. Furthermore, such cases tend to be instrumentalised for political or other dogmatic reasons. Somewhat related are again other cases of archaeological objects from cultures, which do not exist anymore, and the return of which is demanded by modern governments.

Generally, when anything is transported across borders, which could potentially be considered under the aspect of trade, it should be ensured that the minimum standards of the country of origin are observed, even if these standards are higher than the standards of one's own country, to which the particular item is being transported.

---

[11] Cf. the excellent overview by Mazzola (2016).

Let us look at some particular types of data collected in indigenous contexts.

- Language related data are usually not considered intellectual property. When linguists compile a dictionary of an indigenous language or a grammar book, or when psychologists ask indigenous peoples how they designate colours, then this is the research of these scientists; they are free to write about it and to publish the results.
- With regard to the export of objects, the regulations of the respective countries have to be observed. This also applies to the acquisition of the objects. When they belong to a person or to a group, they may only be acquired by consent. That means, they may be accepted as a gift, they may be purchased, and they may be bartered or otherwise legally obtained (e.g. they might come into one's inheritance). Any unlawful acquisition would have to be considered as theft.
- When it comes to the export of recorded sounds, it is necessary to differentiate between commercial and non-commercial use. When the sounds are used for non-commercial research purposes, then the trade agreements do not apply. In the case that researchers do not use the sounds, which they have recorded and exported, in a commercial way themselves, but these sounds are copied by artists, or adopted and modified, and then used in a commercial way by these artists, without the knowledge, approval or involvement of the particular researcher, then this commercial use did not occur under the responsibility of that researcher, who would therefore be indemnified against any liability.
- Regarding film and photography, the indigenous people should be informed what is going to happen with these pictures. It is necessary to obtain the full, free, prior and informed consent before taking the pictures. Ideally, this consent should be given in written form. But this is often not possible, as the persons concerned are illiterate. Then, that consent should be sought in the presence of witnesses. In those cases, when money is demanded for taking pictures, then the acquisition of rights for further use is covered by this payment. Here, too, the presence of witnesses would ensure legal certainty.
- As for the export and import of plants or seeds, the Plant Variety Protection laws of the countries concerned need to be observed, which are, if they exist, regulations on national levels.
- Although the Convention on International Trade in Endangered Species of Wild Fauna and Flora (CITES) explicitly addresses trade, it generally targets import and export, with a special focus on animals. Applicable are the lists compiled by the countries concerned.

The both last points mentioned, which are targeted at species, are of relevance to the issue of indigenous intellectual property, insofar as there is extensive indigenous knowledge pertaining to plants and animals. This knowledge touches the very objective of the Convention on Biological Diversity (CBD) that was enacted at the 1992 Rio Earth Summit and which has been signed by 168 states and the European Union (status as of March 2017). Traditional knowledge on plants and animals arises from the relationship of the indigenous culture with the natural environment. Any destruction of the natural environment makes that knowledge obsolete and, at the same time, destroys some central aspects of the indigenous culture concerned. But the culture-land relationship can also be destroyed when the indigenous people is expelled from their territory, as it often happens when national parks or nature reserves are installed. In these cases, the separation of the indigenous peoples from their ancestral land is particularly absurd, as they are the ones who have the knowledge pertaining to the species that live in the respective area. Those who set up the national park or nature reserve are external forces, represented by dominant officials, who cannot have recourse to such knowledge of the local fauna and flora like the indigenous persons, who have grown up not only in that ecosystem but also in a culture, which had been interconnected with that environment for long periods of time, in a homoeostatic, systemic way. Therefore, destroying the natural environment of indigenous peoples or expelling them from their land is a much more radical interference with indigenous traditional knowledge, as it not only harms single elements of it but also entails the deletion of traditional knowledge. It can be topped, however, by forms of sociocide, which delete the culture altogether – as it permanently happens in the course of globalisation – or by ethnocide, which regrettably has not only happened during dark chapters of the past but which still is a constant companion even in the present age.

Indigenous peoples' knowledge of the natural environment and especially their knowledge of the pharmaceutical use of natural resources are also particularly addressed in Article 24 of the United Nations Declaration on the Rights of Indigenous Peoples, which acknowledges the right of indigenous peoples "to their traditional medicines and to maintain their health practices, including the conservation of their vital medicinal plants, animals and minerals".

Similar to the aspect of sounds or pictures being collected with non-commercial purpose but then used commercially by artists, one could also think of plant or other biological material being collected or data pertaining to species or biological material, which is collected by researchers without any commercial purpose but then used by the pharmaceutical industry in a commercial way. Such data could even exist of the mere information mentioned in a journal article, about the prevalence of a particular plant with specific characteristics and certain active agents, and information about the region, where this plant can be found. But again, as long as it was not the intention of the researchers that any commercial use takes place, and as long as the researchers are not involved in these commercial activities, then they cannot be held responsible for such commercial use.

Yet, these perspectives, taken from legal positions of the dominant culture, are only one side of the coin. On the other side of that coin, there are those many indigenous perspectives, which literally count by the thousands, as each and every of the several thousand indigenous societies has their own legal perspectives. It is therefore impossible to take a comprehensive view of "the" indigenous position. The advice that can be given here is that, in observance of Article 31 of the United Nations Declaration on the Rights of Indigenous Peoples, researchers in a particular indigenous context should seek all relevant information regarding the respective people's ruling on what is understood as intellectual property and then obtain their consent and approval with regard to any further action.

Within the present situation of the globalising world with its imbalance of dominance, indigenous peoples are, to a large extent, forced to accept the industrial culture's regulations. The problems arising from the differences between the globalised and the many indigenous concepts of intellectual property are a matter of intense discussion (e.g. Rimmer 2015; Gervais 2015). The general tenor that prevails in this discourse is that we are at a loss when we try to synchronise the globalised with the indigenous concepts. Even, when we look at a single indigenous group's handling of their traditional knowledge, there are hardly any overlaps of their ideas on their traditional knowledge with the globalised idea of intellectual property. Rather, the conceptualisations diverge extensively. Not even the attempt to tackle the complicated situation by applying cognitive or social psychology approaches, as Simon (2005) has tried it, seems to bring about any real solution.

Indigenous perspectives are often unique in ways that globalised lawyers have never dreamt of. A good example for this is the law cases about depictions of Aboriginal drawings on Australian bank notes (Mazzola 2016). From the Aboriginal point of view, the right to print these drawings could not be transferred to anyone, because they could neither belong to a single person, like an Aboriginal artist, nor could it be allowed that they existed anywhere outside their ancestral context. These drawings did not only belong to the community, but due to their embeddedness into the very complex system of the Aboriginal metaphysical world view, such artwork is also connected to land ownership. Likewise, it is an infringement of Aboriginal legislation when certain drawings are reproduced on carpets or T-shirts.

We tend to forget that in the cultures antecedent to the global society, law and metaphysics were not only intertwined; rather, metaphysics is the very source of the law. Mazzola (2017) presents an example of an indigenous word, the meaning of which designates the sacred as well as the law. And not without reason, indigenous traditional knowledge and beliefs, as well as indigenous relations to nature, are addressed in the United Nations Declaration on the Rights of Indigenous Peoples in the same articles. Like the legal perspectives, the profound relationship to the natural environment is also entrenched in indigenous metaphysics. In the globalised society, such spiritual connectedness to nature is only left over in a rudimentary way in the form of positive feelings related to natural landscapes (cf. Smuda 1986). After all, the indispensable value of nature not only for individual well-being but also for the culture at large is indeed approved in the non-indigenous discourse (Tisucká 2014).

Here is another example of a perspective unknown to the globalised way of thinking: Even when consent and approval have been obtained from an Aboriginal community to take pictures of community members, these pictures might have an expiration date. Among some Aborigines, it is customary to destroy pictures of community members, once these persons have died. If these pictures or films had been stored electronically, then the relevant parts are deleted by the living members of the community. To comply with this indigenous regulation, it would be necessary for visitors to keep themselves updated after the visit, regarding the well-being of the persons of whom they had taken pictures, in order to react immediately in the case of any of these persons' passing away. Such an observance would be problematic, though, when these pictures have already been reproduced and printed in publications. Also, when they had been put online, it might be easy to take them from the server, but one would not know who had already downloaded them.

These examples might give but little idea of how complicated the question is, as who owns the data, which researchers collect in indigenous contexts. This question concerns the primary, raw data, as well as the secondary data, which result from value added by any sort of data processing based on previous studies and also the results of the research, after these data have been interpreted, discussed and led to new insight. On the one hand, there is the governing non-indigenous law that has to be respected. On the other hand, there is the ethical aspect to respect indigenous intellectual property even beyond the boundaries of the dominant legal systems. Article 31 of the United Nations Declaration on the Rights of Indigenous Peoples, in a way, tries to bridge these two aspects.

Barelli (2015) discusses the "soft" character of the United Nations Declaration on the Rights of Indigenous Peoples in comparison to "hard" legislation and with special focus on intellectual property. He argues that although this UN declaration was not binding per se, one would have to differentiate between various degrees of softness, and that the United Nations Declaration on the Rights of Indigenous Peoples, by virtue of its particular normative content, was enhanced in its legal status. Nevertheless, he also points out that the disparity of the "system of intellectual property law and Indigenous (…) concepts of cultural and intellectual property" (p. 63) is problematic.

One of the UN papers on the path to the position taken in Article 31 of the Declaration on the Rights of Indigenous Peoples was a report of 2000, which not only addressed "principles and guidelines for the protection of the heritage of indigenous people [sic]" (United Nations 2000, E/CN.4/Sub.2/2000/26) but which also referred implicitly to researchers. Let us take a synoptical look at the very ambitious guidelines formulated in that paper (Chapter V, Annex I, para. 26 to 34): *That section*, addressing "Researchers and scholarly institutions", *says that indigenous peoples' heritage may not be exploited; rather, scientist should fully inform indigenous peoples in the case that they (the scientists) have any indigenous cultural property in their (the scientists') custody. Such property should either be returned upon demand, or formal agreement should be obtained regarding the use and interpretation of the indigenous property. Donations or sale of any parts of indigenous heritage should only take place after consultation with the traditional owners. Any biological material in the possession of* "traditional owners" *(para. 30) may only be studied with these owners' consent, the obtaining of which needs to be documented. When indigenous peoples have assisted researchers by giving them information, or helping them in their studies, about any parts of nature, then it is necessary to obtain the indigenous peoples' consent and to identify the traditional owners in the case of any citation of publication related to these parts of nature; in the case of any commercial benefit, the indigenous people must receive compensation. Human genome research and applications need to be subordinate to the respect for indigenous persons or peoples. All possible efforts should be made* "to increase indigenous peoples' access to all forms of medical, scientific and technical education" *(para. 33), as well as their participation in any research that could possibly affect indigenous peoples or from which they might benefit. Academics should cooperate with indigenous peoples to promote these guidelines, to sponsor seminars and to take disciplinary measures in the case of contravention.*

These guidelines were suggestions, which were made several years before the United Nations Declaration on the Rights of Indigenous Peoples was completed. Now that the declaration exists, some of the positions taken in that paper (United Nations 2000) could not be upheld. Though certainly made in good intention, all recommendations that imply the involvement of indigenous peoples with the global culture would need some overhauling. Especially the passage from paragraph 33 quoted above sounds as if it pledges for pushing indigenous peoples into globalised education. However, that would collide with the very central concern of the United Nations Declaration on the Rights of Indigenous Peoples of protecting their culture and of preventing any destabilisation thereof. The particularities of indigenous culture, together with the indigenous peoples' determination to preserve their culture, have led to the focus being directed on culture in the UN Declaration on the Rights of Indigenous Peoples (Barelli 2015). Therefore, the idea of undertaking utmost efforts to involve indigenous peoples in education and to conduct seminars together with them could be critical with regard to Article 14, which grants indigenous peoples to have their own educational systems. Any cooperation without ensuring the protection of indigenous culture (e.g. Art. 8) would also not be compatible with the securing of indigenous peoples' right to revitalise their culture (Art. 11). Observance implies that there is no bias regarding any external input that indigenous peoples receive. If, for example, researchers would act in a way that communicates a position like "well, theoretically, you have the freedom of returning to your old-fashioned traditions, but we suggest that you appreciate the globalised lifestyle", then this certainly could not be counted as observance of the United Nations Declaration on the Rights of Indigenous Peoples, its general principles and main ideas.

So, what are we left with, considering intellectual property related to indigenous peoples and their cultures? The United Nations 2000 paper (E/CN.4/Sub.2/2000/26) highlights various aspects pertaining to this question in detail. However, these are recommendations from the time before the United Nations Declaration on the Rights of Indigenous Peoples was adopted. We can, on the one hand, receive impulses from this United Nations 2000 paper that help us reflect on details of the issue; however, on the other hand, we have to carefully check these positions against the rights granted in the Declaration. The United Nations 2000 paper was, in a way, still immature, and in 2007, the United Nations Declaration on the Rights of Indigenous Peoples was ripened.

Bearing in mind the discourse regarding the nonbinding character of the United Nations Declaration on the Rights of Indigenous Peoples and yet its influence as an authoritative legal instrument, as shown above in Sect. 2.1, we should use our reasonable endeavour to always find ways to respect the parties concerned – the indigenous peoples, as well as the legal governmental authorities. For the latter, paragraph 2 of Article 31 of the United Nations Declaration on the Rights of Indigenous Peoples offers large opportunities to cement and establish more firmly the rights granted in paragraph 1. By securing the maintenance of indigenous peoples' relationship to the land, a lot can be achieved. As it has been explained in this section, indigenous peoples' traditional knowledge and their worldview are both strongly related to the natural environment. This also becomes evident, as "knowledge of the properties of fauna and flora" is explicitly mentioned in paragraph 1 of Article 31. While traditional knowledge, as well as any worldview, consists of cognitive elements, thus being intangible heritage, land is, by all means, very material and concrete. Therefore, ensuring that the natural environment is protected and the indigenous peoples living therein are not expelled from it would be an essential starting point for the implementation of Article 31 of the United Nations Declaration on the Rights of Indigenous Peoples.

2.5   Revitalisation of Culture

Article 11

1. *Indigenous peoples have the right to practise and revitalize their cultural traditions and customs. This includes the right to maintain, protect and develop the past, present and future manifestations of their cultures, such as archaeological and historical sites, artefacts, designs, ceremonies, technologies and visual and performing arts and literature.*

The first sentence says it explicitly, and the second sentence points out certain things that shall be included in "the right to practise and revitalize their cultural traditions and customs". The principle that is underlined here is the right of indigenous people to live in their culture-specific way.

The special thing about this article is the right to "revitalise" their culture as granted to indigenous peoples. Accepting the ways they *are* is a not-so-new demand. Quite often, the present state, the way they *are* is already characterised by cultural destabilisation or even loss of culture. This has been taken as an excuse by believers in globalisation to push them further, modernise them, globalise them and "develop" them. Criticism has been quashed with catchphrases like "You cannot turn back the clock".

Yes, they can. Indigenous peoples have the right now to "revitalise" their culture. Even, if their culture has been heavily influenced, if they wear shorts, bras and T-shirts, live in houses and eat canned food, they have the right to decide to turn back the clock. And when this is their decision, we have to respect that.

But do they have the chance to make a free decision? In order to analyse the freedom of decision in such a situation, we should ask ourselves: What is our role with regard to the observance of the right granted to indigenous peoples in Article 11 of the UN Declaration? If we take a closer look, then it becomes evident that this article defines not only a right relevant to indigenous peoples. It is relevant to anyone contacting an indigenous people as well. Once such a contact happens, then there is systemic interaction taking place. The persons, who are present in such a contact situation, communicate at least via the visual channel, perhaps also via the auditory and further channels. As this is an encounter of persons from different parts of the cultural spectrum, dominance effects come to bear, as explained above.

There is an imbalance of mutual perception and an imbalance of mutual influence, and the dominant persons are perceived as role models by the indigenous persons. Since we *cannot not* communicate (Watzlawick et al. 1967), it matters very much *what* and *how* we communicate. As cultural identity is constituted by means of bodily self-presentation, our own appearance has a significant impact, *because* we are perceived as role models by the indigenous persons. If our self-presentation is based on globalised standards, then that is the input we give. Since perceivable behaviour patterns are acts of communication, then, due to our function as role models, we would implicitly convey those standards to the indigenous culture. Once arrived there, they would unfold their culture-destabilising effects. But if we orientate our self-presentation towards the traditional standards, uninfluenced by the dominant culture, then we communicate acceptance and respect towards the indigenous culture. We shall go into more details about this in Chaps. 3 and 4.

In reality, the influence exerted on indigenous cultures is very much biased. They are almost exclusively being pushed towards globalisation. As researchers with ethical values, we have the obligation to counterbalance this influence. If we would not do that, then we would be complicit in depriving indigenous peoples of their right to maintain and all the more of their right to revitalise their culture. Only if we counterbalance the dominant input, we at least contribute to the indigenous peoples' freedom of choice with regard to maintenance or revitalisation of their culture.

There are some interesting examples of cultural revitalisation in southern Africa. Both the Swazi and the Zulu are cultures that have a king. Whereas the kings have been educated in Europe, the peoples of both kingdoms have revitalised old traditions, which particularly become evident in the reed festivals, when tens of thousands gather before their kings. Thus, unlike in the example given in 2.3 of the chiefs maintaining culture by decree, the driving force regarding the practising of tradition in this case are the people. The Swazi and the Zulu were acting by consent, when they revitalised their cultures. It was a bottom-up rather than a top-down process. Remarkably, the revitalisations of the Swazi and Zulu cultures happened after the end of Apartheid. I remember that when I was in Zululand in the early 1980s, one could have the impression that the culture was about to die, as so much of tradition had been gone in Southern Africa already. In many parts of the world, the end of colonial rule brought about the phenomenon that the peoples concerned turned away from their traditional culture in favour of a more globalised lifestyle. Instead of saying "Now that we have become rid of the oppressors, we can follow our own style", they said, "Now we want to be like them". One could have expected that the course of events would be similar after the end of Apartheid. But the contrary happened. A probable socio-cognitive explanation would be that the Zulu, like other peoples of that region, had witnessed that Apartheid was abolished due to external pressure and that they now wanted to contrast themselves from the Whites living in South Africa.

Although in both cases, the decrees of the Pacific islands chiefs and the indigenous peoples' consent in southern Africa, self-healing capacities have manifested themselves, we cannot rely on such a course of events. Most indigenous peoples have been intimidated and therefore do not dare to stand up for their rights, not to mention that in most cases, they do not even know that they have any rights at all.

For the sake of completeness, it should also be mentioned that Article 13 of the United Nations Declaration on the Rights of Indigenous Peoples takes up again the aspect of revitalisation by saying that indigenous peoples have the right "to revitalize (…) and transmit to future generations their histories, languages, oral traditions, philosophies (…)" (Art. 13,1), thus highlighting the role of language for processes of revitalising culture. This touches the question, if language is an indispensable prerequisite for cultural revitalisation. However, if that would be the case, then this could be taken as an argument to prevent indigenous peoples, who have already been deprived of their traditional language due to colonial or otherwise dominant influences, from even starting with the revitalisation of their culture as granted in the United Nations Declaration on the Rights of Indigenous Peoples. There is, by the way, a prominent case of language revitalisation. Hebrew had survived in the sacred realm until it was revitalised as a spoken language by Eliezer Ben-Yehuda, although not even his own family had believed in the cause he pursued. This shows us that it is possible to bring language back to life, which is quite a significant aspect for cultural revitalisation, as language is very momentous with regard to cultural identity. Therefore, even those indigenous peoples who have already been deprived of their native tongue should not give up the hope that they can also bring their old language back to life, when they want to exercise their right to revitalisation as granted in the United Nations Declaration on the Rights of Indigenous Peoples. In such cases, it might be helpful when the old languages had been preserved by researchers prior to the extinction in linguistic studies with their grammar and vocabulary.

The indigenous peoples' right to cultural revitalisation entails for us, the researchers, the very important aspect that we must make sure that this right can be practised. We may neither obstruct that nor should we be part of the social pressure, which globalisation exerts on indigenous peoples. Rather, it is our ethical obligation to provide counterbalance to this pressure in the most appropriate and most effective way. In the case that an indigenous people has decided to revitalise its culture, researchers can make valuable contributions to this, if knowledge about the culture is stored in archives, museums or in detailed descriptions of former research. This knowledge can then be used to reconstruct what has been lost. For example, Senft (2016) thoroughly describes a particular type of boat, which is about to vanish from the Trobriand Islands. It could well be that in a few years or decades, the Trobriand Islanders decide to revitalise their culture, and they could then resort to such descriptions. This aspect of preserving knowledge can also be interesting for the elders of an indigenous community, when we explain our intended research and seek their permission for it.

2.6 Cultural Autonomy in Education and Lifestyle

Article 14

1. *Indigenous peoples have the right to establish and control their educational systems and institutions providing education in their own languages, in a manner appropriate to their cultural methods of teaching and learning.*

In every culture, knowledge and skills are passed on to the next generation. Those knowledge and skills cover the aspects necessary for living in the culture's particular context. As long as the context does not change, this is fine, and this system can prove itself successful over long periods of time. When the context changes slightly and slowly, then the culture usually can adapt to the new requirements. But when the context changes rapidly and when there are large-scale changes, then it becomes more difficult to find solutions, because the people have no strategies at hand as how to cope with the new challenges. They have not been taught the necessary strategies, and they cannot teach the next generations what would be necessary.

If rapid environmental changes are caused by natural forces, like volcano eruptions, then the only chance for the culture to survive might be to migrate to another region. Obviously, they can only take the knowledge with themselves, which they have. But the new territory might require other skills hitherto unknown, and it might already be inhabited by another people. These other people possess knowledge appropriate to their well-known specific context. Principally, the immigrants could then adopt the knowledge of the long-established residents.

If such an adoption of knowledge takes place, if so, to which degree and how fast depend on various factors. Paradigmatically, Herzog (1988) has reconstructed such a situation for Mesopotamia in early history. As already mentioned in Chap. 1 of this book, according to the reconstruction reported by Herzog (1988), a foreign people once came into that marshy landscape. But these immigrants did not fully integrate into the culture of the dwellers, who already lived there. Apparently, the newcomers were not used to marshlands. Archaeologists found that they erected artificial hills. After a certain time, there was a mixed culture, which was characterised by a language that contained elements of the two very different origins. This blended culture was then to become a great and significant civilisation.

In this example, knowledge was contributed by both parties. The emerging culture, a synthesis of the two predecessor cultures, then possessed knowledge that was of relevance even beyond its own context, so that long-distance political relations and trade could be established. The joining of knowledge in the course of cultural synthesis generally leads to higher efficiency – and thus power – due to the recombination of cultural elements. Yet, by all means, this can and should be seen critically. Certainly, at least some, if not many, of such a resulting culture's people enjoy the power and efficiency. But as history has shown, this has always also been used in a destructive way. Even in ancient times, the natural environment has been destroyed massively by human activity (Weeber 1990). Moreover, the efficiency is also used to wage wars and to suppress other people. If we virtually step back and look at the devastation caused by humans on this planet, then, in the end, the synthesis of knowledge, passed on over generations and escalated to high efficiencies, has brought about unsolvable problems. The break with linearity of passing on knowledge brought advantages to those who profited from it. But when the systemic functions of the global culture with the global context collapse, we'll ask ourselves if it was worth it. The alternatives are or were long-term stability versus power and efficiency for a limited timeframe.

These reflections on the passing on of knowledge seem necessary to convey an idea of indigenous perspectives. Outsiders often see indigenous persons as uneducated. But the truth is that we, coming from the industrial culture, are educated in our ways, and indigenous peoples are educated in their ways. So they could just as well claim that we are uneducated, which would be true with regard to their traditional knowledge. Once there is mutual insight into the other side's culture, there can be culture comparative reflections. Often, the mutuality is quite unbalanced. The dominant is much less interested in the culture of the dominated than vice versa. Frequently, the dominated is even forced to become familiar with the globalised thinking in order to be able to claim their rights or even to argue in favour of their bare existence. There are indigenous elders, who have pondered about the pros and cons of the different ways of living and about the different degrees to which these lifestyles are sustainable. When they decide to pass on their traditional culture to their children, then we have to accept that.

Article 14 by no means represents an isolated aspect. As part of the UN Declaration on the Rights of Indigenous Peoples, it has to be seen in conjunction with the other articles. Especially, when we take Articles 8, 11 and 31 into consideration, it becomes clear that the right to say no should be particularly respected. If indigenous peoples decide against externally induced education, we have to acknowledge it. Some globalised persons might criticise that. But should the global industrial culture collapse one day, then humankind might have a chance to survive due to those indigenous cultures living in voluntary isolation or at least pursuing a lifestyle based on a truly sustainable concept of culture-nature relation. If this is what they want to teach their children, then it would probably not be very wise of us to prevent them to do so.

There are other indigenous peoples who accept globalised education, for reasons that we shall discuss in Chap. 3 with regard to the relativity of the freedom of choice and to the effects of external social pressure. And there are again other indigenous peoples, who, on the one hand, accept governmental schooling but who make sure that they otherwise maintain their cultural identity by refusing globalised clothing, let alone school uniforms. The maintenance of cultural identity is reflected in their bodily self-presentation, which is consistently practised across situations. For example, there are indigenous people in the Pacific region, who not even at school, with teachers and pupils alike, but also at church keep up their traditional appearance, in the same way as they do throughout their everyday life.

Unfortunately, there are negative examples as well. Some agencies that proclaim to help indigenous peoples actually commit infringements against various of the UN Declaration's articles, when they misuse the schooling of indigenous peoples to impose globalised standards on them. When representatives of the FUNAI (Fundação

Nacional do Índio, the Brazilian National Indian Foundation) encounter traditionally living indigenous people, they regularly urge them to cover their bodies, although these peoples have walked on their land free and totally unveiled since ages. In Ethiopia, we met a teacher in the Hamer people's region of the South Omo Valley. She was an urbanised African, paid by a Norwegian initiative, teaching the Hamer children in a donated building roofed with corrugated metal, and she was wearing a turtleneck pullover, although this was not only a breach with local customs but also incompatible with the tropical climate. Clothing, in general, and school uniforms, in particular, lead to the deletion of the indigenous children's cultural identity. In Venezuela, where the Yanomami people try to maintain their culture, this is purposefully undermined, especially by outmanoeuvring the indigenous women. As the Yanomami reject clothing, textile necklaces are given to the women as gifts. By and by, bigger and bigger necklaces are given, so that they are worn like sashes across both shoulders, with the aim of making them accustomed to feeling textiles on their bodies, so that eventually, they can be persuaded to put on clothing. External teachers[12] play a central role in deleting traditional culture and replacing it with unified global standards. Targeted disintegration of indigenous culture is taking place worldwide. It is commonplace now to hire teachers of the same country, but with urbanised background, and send them to indigenous villages, without in the least sensitising these teachers for indigenous issues or informing them about indigenous rights.

What happens cognitively on the part of the globalised, culturally non-adapted teachers can be explained in terms of dissonance reduction (Festinger 1957). To maintain their own cognitive consonance and to justify their own modernity, teachers have to look down at the indigenous peoples' traditions and pledge for so-called "development". Appreciating the traditional indigenous lifestyle would be dissonant to their own modernised lifestyle. But by persuading the indigenous to abandon their traditions and to also appreciate modernity, the teachers reduce their own cognitive dissonance.

The cognitive processes on the part of the indigenous peoples can also be explained within other socio-cognitive approaches. According to the theory of symbolic self-completion (Wicklund and Gollwitzer 1982), persons compensate presumed, identity relevant deficiencies by using symbols, in order to make others believe that they already have the striven-for identity. Therefore, if other persons, like teachers, give indigenous peoples the feeling to be incompetent, less worthy, backward or primitive (which happens on a regular basis), then the indigenous persons concerned will try to escape this status by becoming like the dominant persons. And the easiest way to do so is to look like them. Self-presentation on the visual level is the most effective definition of one's identity.

These mechanisms are taking place within the processes of globalisation. They make it very difficult for indigenous peoples to exert their right to cultural autonomy in education and lifestyle. Basically, it is possible for both of the participating sides to escape these mechanisms. By reflecting about them, as well as about one's own

---

[12] E.g.: <http://previews.agefotostock.com/previewimage/bajaage/7cf0439c7ff6597dcc871a115c3 52e01/h44-10830509.jpg> (accessed 31 Aug. 2017).

role, a person cognitively deals with these problems on a metalevel, which gives access to alternative decisions, positions and behaviour. Metalevel reflections are important for consciously governing one's own behaviour, changing things and avoiding mistakes.

In the case of teachers, who destabilise indigenous cultures, these are single persons, who each time destabilise whole communities and destroy their culture, because of their personal incompetency regarding respectful integration into the indigenous traditions. As a result, not only Article 14 (indigenous peoples' right to establish and control their educational systems) is infringed but also Articles 3 (right to self-determination), 8 (indigenous peoples' right not to be subjected to forced assimilation or destruction of their culture) and 31 (right to traditional knowledge and traditional cultural expressions). In effect, the invasive intrusions result in the deletion of indigenous culture.

Whereas, principally, it would be possible to make it compulsory for teachers to receive a training targeted at imparting the necessary intercultural competence for integrating themselves into traditional indigenous contexts (see also Chap. 4 of this book, Sect. 4.4 on Education and Training), boarding schools are a different problem. Children are deprived of their social contacts, which are necessary for them to be socialised within their culture and to internalise the specific indigenous knowledge and skills. Moreover, these boarding schools are often, if not usually, emotionally void. In many places of the world, indigenous children have been or still are taken away from their people. The aim is to civilise them, to change their identity and to make them speak and think in another language. In India, we visited such a place in Biligiri Rangana Hills, Karnataka. The Education Centre is located inside the territory of the Soliga people. It is a protected area, but with the support of an aid organisation, more than five hundred children are being educated there in line with governmental preferences. They are raised in a Hindu worldview; they have to sing nationalistic songs and to wear school uniform. Those who are responsible for that are probably convinced that they do a good work.

The involvement of indigenous representatives in the planning of curricula for indigenous children is often a fig leaf. When indigenous authorities are invited to participate in the planning of education, then this might be very selective, with those being chosen who agree with governmental ambitions. Thus, in spite of the United Nations Declaration on the Rights of Indigenous Peoples, the integration of indigenous perspectives into the mainstream education implies that indigenous perspectives only play a subordinate role with regard to the education of indigenous children and youth. If indigenous peoples are to be adjudicated autonomy of raising and educating their younger generations, then the task is to integrate mainstream education into the culturally specific indigenous education and not vice versa. A curriculum for indigenous pupils should not be predominantly defined by state authorities, to which the fields of indigenous knowledge, like the use of specific plants, are unknown.

Whatever schooling measures are planned, they should be thoroughly scrutinised to make sure that they support the respective indigenous people's existence as a community, a culture and a social system. If such planned measures contain any factors that could possibly lead to destabilisation or even disintegration, then they may not be applied due to Article 8, 2 (a). Rather, forms of education should be intended that strengthen the indigenous identity of the children and youth. Just leaving some room for folklore is not enough. Culture needs to be fully lived; otherwise the identity of the young generation will be stunted. It is outmost important that the education takes place in the traditional visual appearance, because this is the basis for the constitution of the identity. Any compromise in this respect would inevitably compromise the development of an indigenous identity. Especially, it should be absolutely avoided to educate indigenous pupils in boarding schools, because they are tools to almost certainly eradicate their indigenous self-confidence, due to the psychological mechanisms of cultural dominance.

2.7 Reflection of Culture in Media

Article 15
1. *Indigenous peoples have the right to the dignity and diversity of their cultures, traditions, histories and aspirations which shall be appropriately reflected in education and public information.*

Article 16
1. *Indigenous peoples have the right to establish their own media in their own languages and to have access to all forms of non-indigenous media without discrimination.*
2. *States shall take effective measures to ensure that State-owned media duly reflect indigenous cultural diversity. States, without prejudice to ensuring full freedom of expression, should encourage privately owned media to adequately reflect indigenous cultural diversity.*

The responsibilities of states are addressed in several ways with regard to the correct reflection of indigenous culture in media. The existence of indigenous peoples and their ways of living shall not be concealed in state-owned media, and indigenous culture shall be properly reflected in education and public information as well. Likewise, states should encourage the private media *to adequately reflect indigenous cultural diversity.* If these obligations are pointed out, then there must be reasons for that. Why should states try to hide indigenous people? Why should they refrain from telling their young citizens about them? Why should indigenous issues be kept out of public information? Why do private media need encouragement to adequately reflect indigenous culture? For what reasons should indigenous culture be incorrectly reflected? Many questions.

From the perspective of some governments, indigenous peoples are embarrassing. At least, when it comes to their authentic traditional culture. Uninfluenced by globalisation. The way it was before any external, modernising, European, colonial or otherwise dominant influence. For tropical areas around the world, this means: naked. That is embarrassing for civilised persons. Too much human skin is embarrassing. Uncovered breasts are embarrassing. Private parts are embarrassing.

From such a perspective, indigenous peoples should not be shown in media or public information, and they should not be thematised in education.

Apart from nudity, the mere fact that indigenous peoples are also, from that point of view, uneducated, primitive and backward is also embarrassing. It is a shame to have such folks in the country, a shame for the glorious nation. This is another reason for concealing the existence of indigenous peoples.

Furthermore, some states might consider it strategically appropriate not to mention their indigenous population in order to avoid that any land right issues might be stirred up. The more commonly known is that there are indigenous peoples in certain regions, the more likely it is that some human rights activists would try to make sure that the indigenous peoples are in charge of those territories.

But generally, the existence of indigenous peoples cannot be kept as a secret. So those responsible for media, education and public information find ways to modify the image to an extent that is deemed acceptable. As there is constant impact on indigenous peoples to push them towards globalisation, it is relatively easy to find some, who wear clothes. If that is not the case, then preparatory measures are taken, like in the following example:

In Brazil, Orlando Villas Bôas, together with his brothers Cláudio, Leonardo and Álvaro, fought for the establishment of the Xingú National Park, one of the few hotspots on earth, where there is still a high density of indigenous cultures. As long as he was alive, he kept an eye on the policies regarding indigenous peoples in Brazil and took stands for their protection. Soon after his death in 2002, the FUNAI pursued a policy to promote tourism to indigenous areas. One of our research institution's[13] representatives reported from the 2005 World Tourism Organization conference in Rio de Janeiro about a promotion film for tourism to the Pataxo people, who live in a natural reserve near Porto Seguro, Bahia. Apparently, the FUNAI had brought a box with bras and distributed them to the women and girls before the shooting of the film, so that even 11-year-olds were wearing bikini tops. Authentic pictures would have embarrassed potential tourists from certain globalised countries. But since the FUNAI wanted to win international customers, they adapted the indigenous people to civilised standards. Such a way of treating indigenous peoples like toys was a violation of ethical principles even at that time.

Since the commencement of the United Nations Declaration on the Rights of Indigenous Peoples in 2007, such procedure would be an offence against international law. But still, governmental organisations, as well as tour operators, seem to expect that indigenous peoples adjust themselves to the standards of tourism and not the other way around. From the indigenous rights perspective, adaptation should actually take place in the other direction, in terms that the tourists should adapt to the indigenous cultures, when they visit them. Yet, in that Pataxo case, it was obvious that those responsible were less interested in the protection of the indigenous peoples than in their questionable commercial exploitation and that financial aspects were given priority before cultural sustainability.

---

[13] Structural Analysis of Cultural Systems (S.A.C.S.), <https://s-a-c-s.net>.

Well-renowned magazines operate according to the same principles as portrayed in this example. They claim to report seriously about cultures worldwide, but with regard to the authenticity of indigenous culture, this claim is questionable, too. Unwanted body parts are not shown on the pictures, or they are far in the background, very small and blurred. While men's chests are shown, women are either shown from the back or with objects "incidentally" in front of them or not at all. Anyway, *indigenous cultural diversity* is not correctly reflected as demanded by Articles 15 and 16 of the United Nations Declaration on the Rights of Indigenous Peoples.

A popular ploy is to either pick those indigenous persons to be shown on pictures, who already are covered according to the dominant modesty standards, or to give them clothing as presents first, before taking the photos. Systemically, this has a backlash on the indigenous culture. Some of the indigenous persons concerned might go to town occasionally, where they see themselves depicted in the particular magazine or in the TV documentary. Or a tourist brings along the report and shows it to the indigenous people. Both through such a media-based self-perception and through the confrontation with the media people when the pictures are taken, standards are being mediated to the indigenous peoples regarding their appearance that is appreciated by the dominant culture. When they become acquainted to literally see themselves looking the approved way, then they internalise this standard. This is a media-based way of modifying indigenous identity and another breach with Article 8, 2. (a).

2.8   Land Rights

Article 8
[…] 2. States shall provide effective mechanisms for prevention of, and redress for:
   […] (b) Any action which has the aim or effect of dispossessing them of their lands, territories or resources [.]

Article 10
Indigenous peoples shall not be forcibly removed from their lands or territories. No relocation shall take place without the free, prior and informed consent of the indigenous peoples concerned and after agreement on just and fair compensation and, where possible, with the option of return.

Article 25
Indigenous peoples have the right to maintain and strengthen their distinctive spiritual relationship with their traditionally owned or otherwise occupied and used lands, territories, waters and coastal seas and other resources and to uphold their responsibilities to future generations in this regard.

Article 26

1. *Indigenous peoples have the right to the lands, territories and resources which they have traditionally owned, occupied or otherwise used or acquired.*
2. *Indigenous peoples have the right to own, use, develop and control the lands, territories and resources that they possess by reason of traditional ownership or other traditional occupation or use, as well as those which they have otherwise acquired.*
3. *States shall give legal recognition and protection to these lands, territories and resources. Such recognition shall be conducted with due respect to the customs, traditions and land tenure systems of the indigenous peoples concerned.*

It goes without saying that land rights are a major issue for states with regard to indigenous peoples. In many, if not most, cases, land issues are the main obstacle for acknowledging indigenous peoples' autonomy or indigenous peoples' rights altogether. On the part of the governments, a psychological factor of the reluctance to make concessions towards indigenous peoples is the philosophy of keeping sovereignty over the entire national territory. But usually, there are financial interests involved. Extractive industries are after natural resources that are situated on and below the surface. Rainforests are being cut down for agricultural purposes, although agriculture often turns out to be not feasible and leads to irreversible land degradation and erosion. Large areas of lower-quality woods are destroyed in order to access the relatively few trees of valuable timber that have grown scattered and dispersed in the natural forest. And underneath, precious metals and minerals, coal, oil and gas are in the focus of mining companies.

Even if there are no known mineral deposits, governments want to keep the option open of being in charge of potential future exploitation. Researchers are often involved in the assessment of possible mineral resources and the profitability of deposits. Such research is often carried out in indigenous contexts, although the researchers in charge are no social scientists. They might find it difficult to resist the temptation of turning a blind eye on the indigenous issues. However, although they have no explicit mandate of taking care of the indigenous peoples, they will implicitly be responsible for the consequences of the activities, which are going to take place, and in the preparation of which they are participating.

2.8.1 Protection of Territories

Article 27

States shall establish and implement, in conjunction with indigenous peoples concerned, a fair, independent, impartial, open and transparent process, giving due recognition to indigenous peoples' laws, traditions, customs and land tenure systems, to recognize and adjudicate the rights of indigenous peoples pertaining to their lands, territories and resources, including those which were traditionally owned or otherwise occupied or used. Indigenous peoples shall have the right to participate in this process.

Article 29

1. *Indigenous peoples have the right to the conservation and protection of the environment and the productive capacity of their lands or territories and resources. States shall establish and implement assistance programmes for indigenous peoples for such conservation and protection, without discrimination.*

Whereas formulations of Article 27 seem to be somewhat reserved, ending with the assertion that indigenous people may participate in the process pertaining to the land rights, Article 29 formulates in a much clearer way that indigenous peoples have the right to the protection of their lands. It even goes beyond that, as conservation of indigenous lands means that they may not be exposed to, or involved in, measures of so-called "development". Furthermore, the article addresses resources, and they do not necessarily have to be located on a particular land or within a particular territory. If, for example, a river is a natural resource, from which an indigenous people live, then this river needs to be protected. The river might have its source very far away from that indigenous land. However, without this river, the region would be dry, there would be no forest and the indigenous people would have no water and no fish.

This is the reason why hydroelectric dams can pose a threat to indigenous peoples, and this is not only so because their communities have to move when the reservoir is filled after the building of the dam is finished. In the popular case of Belo Monte in Brazil, a dam has been built, although there is no river. It is planned now to divert the river towards the dam, in order to fill the reservoir and to keep it filled. But this river waters the Xingú area, one of the world's hotspots of indigenous cultures. It is the traditional territory of 11 indigenous peoples. Additionally, three other indigenous peoples were rescued from other places, where their further existence had been threatened and brought to the Xingú area by the Bôas brothers, who were anthropologists and who had successfully advocated for that area to become a national park. Apart from other threats as mentioned above (2.7), the indigenous peoples therein are now threatened in their mere existence, as an ecological catastrophe is imminent. Indigenous peoples, when neighbouring each other, usually have selective dietary customs (Gibbons 1992; also see Chap. 1 of this book Sect. 1.1). If one of the indigenous groups lives on fishing, while all of the others are each hunting their preferred animal species, none of them encroaches on the other. But what is going to happen when the river runs dry? In order to survive, the fisher folk will have to abandon the traditional diet, so that conflicts with the other cultural groups will be inevitable. However, when the forest will dry out, all will lose their bases of existence. The Brazilian government, though, has made provisions for that: the hydroelectric dam will produce lots of electricity, so that it is already planned to build factories there. As for now, they do not have the workers for these factories yet. But this will change soon, when, as expected, indigenous peoples will have to abandon their traditional land.

2.8.2   Land Use

Article 32

1. *Indigenous peoples have the right to determine and develop priorities and strategies for the development or use of their lands or territories and other resources.*
2. *States shall consult and cooperate in good faith with the indigenous peoples concerned through their own representative institutions in order to obtain their free and informed consent prior to the approval of any project affecting their lands or territories and other resources, particularly in connection with the development, utilization or exploitation of mineral, water or other resources.*

Another of the world's few hotspots of indigenous cultures is the South Omo Valley of Ethiopia, where 19 indigenous peoples have their traditional lands. Up to now, they have lived a self-sufficient lifestyle, and although neighbouring each other, they have maintained their own cultural characteristics. These cultures are about to be eradicated now, because the Ethiopian government has leased their land to investors from India and South Korea, who are growing energy plants such as maize and sugarcane, which are not meant for consumption as food but as biomass to produce renewable energy. The modern road for fast connection of the South Omo Valley with central Ethiopia has already been built, and it is planned to build a railway line parallel to this road.

There is no question that the indigenous peoples are denied to *determine* the *use of their lands*. Likewise, appropriate consultations of, or corporation with, the indigenous peoples *in good faith* are lacking. The indigenous peoples of the South Omo Valley do not know what is happening to them. It seems actually impossible to explain to them the high-tech agriculture, which is worlds apart from their way of life, for which sustainability can certainly be reclaimed, rather than the attempts of the technological solution with energy plants. For me, it felt quite bitter to look into the eyes of these cultures that are doomed to be extinct, just for the sake of profit. They have no idea what is about to happen to them. I saw men carrying old muzzle-loading guns, probably still from the First World War. They seemed to feel strong with these weapons. But they will be useless to keep away the tsunami of globalisation.

It has to be mentioned, though, that there are indigenous peoples, who have decided to make use of the land by having casinos build there, so that they can make money from the gambling visitors. It is their decision, and when they have made it in full, free, prior and informed consent, then it apparently has to be accepted. Certainly, they don't always make the best deal with the external contractors, who run the facilities. But even more certain is the fact that conversion of formally natural indigenous land to a gambling resort opens doors to globalising influences that wound indigenous culture to the core.

2.8.3   Mitigation of Adverse Impact

Article 32

3. *States shall provide effective mechanisms for just and fair redress for any such activities, and appropriate measures shall be taken to mitigate adverse environmental, economic, social, cultural or spiritual impact.*

The wording "any such activities" refers to projects affecting indigenous peoples' "lands or territories and other resources, particularly in connection with (…) mineral, water or other resources" as mentioned in the previous subparagraph. In many cases however, the term "mitigation" would be a euphemism. The term suggests that an impact could be absorbed or cushioned, or that intervention could take place with the result that an impact could be made mild in its intensity. But many indigenous territories are damaged to an extent that the situation could not be reversed anywhere near the situation that was there before.

With regard to mining, it doesn't make too much difference for indigenous communities, which kind of mining takes place in the territories. Even when companies are only drilling for oil, collateral damages are immense, because an enormous infrastructure is involved. The forest is cut down to build roads to the site. A few indigenous persons might become involved with cheap labour, but a large number of specialised workers are brought to the place. They are given some on-site housing, and usually, indigenous women will find themselves in prostitution shortly after the strangers have found their way to their place. Opencast mining has probably the worst impact, as the land as such ceases to exist to a depth of many, often tens of, metres. Endemic flora and fauna are not only damaged or reduced but fully eradicated. After the end of the project, indigenous peoples cannot find their way back to the village, because the surface of the earth, as they knew it, is not there anymore. The Dongria Kondh indigenous people in the eastern Indian state of Odisha were lucky in 2014, when they won the trial against the British company Vedanta Resources, and thus stopped the plans for opencast mining in their territories. But there are numerous other indigenous peoples, who have lost their land completely to such projects and who have no hope for any mitigation, let alone redress.

2.8.4   Right to Redress and Compensation

Article 28

1. *Indigenous peoples have the right to redress, by means that can include restitution or, when this is not possible, just, fair and equitable compensation, for the lands, territories and resources which they have traditionally owned or otherwise occupied or used, and which have been confiscated, taken, occupied, used or damaged without their free, prior and informed consent.*

2. *Unless otherwise freely agreed upon by the peoples concerned, compensation shall take the form of lands, territories and resources equal in quality, size and legal status or of monetary compensation or other appropriate redress.*

These two subparagraphs cover aspects that are very similar to those, which are covered by Article 32, 3. They concern situations, when damage has already happened. One can easily assume that states are not too happy with these passages. For one thing, redress and compensation are quite costly, and for another thing, it is not feasible to fully compensate the loss of land.

Each land or territory is unique in various respects. Since, especially in tropical areas, there is a high density of species, which goes along with endemism, the governments won't be able to retrieve them, once they are exterminated. Furthermore, indigenous peoples often link their land to their spiritual concepts. It is not seen as just a material value, as it is the case from the legal perspective of the industrial culture. Rather, the manifold features of the land, such as rocks, rivers or hills, are seen as entities, with each of them having a meaning to the indigenous people.

Even, when indigenous peoples, after having been evicted, are allowed to return to their ancestral lands, permanent damage has already taken place. If the natural environment has not been destroyed, as it might be the case with national parks, then the indigenous people concerned has suffered not only from the eviction itself, but the traumatisation has continued during the exile from their land, being exposed to the arbitrariness of the dominant culture. In Chap. 1 of this book, we have briefly highlighted the fate of the Batwa people (1.4). Even the ethnic continuity of the Batwa is threatened, due to cannibalism committed by Bantu, as well as permanent rape of Batwa women by Bantu men. Since the 1990s, the next generations result in a large proportion from these rapes. These young people are neither accepted by the Bantu as belonging to them nor can they really internalise the Batwa hunter-gatherer culture and thus obtain that indigenous identity. One also has to keep in mind that these children grow up with parents, who are heavily hit by humiliation, sexual abuse and other violence, malnutrition and illnesses that were previously unknown to their people and threats to their lives. These traumatisations often entail further problems, such as substance abuse. These are collective traumata, and the young generations do not have psychologically or socially stable family backgrounds.

Yes, it is imperative to let these evicted indigenous peoples go back to their territories. As long as their lands still exist, like nature reserves or national parks, there is no alternative to letting the indigenous peoples return immediately. This should be out of any question. However, the damage that has done to them is immeasurable.

Researchers might be involved in these problems in different respects. This might even be the case in preceding preparations to these problems, when a national park or nature reserve is planned, and they are called in as experts. They might be asked to investigate the area and the natural environment, while the indigenous people, who are to be evicted, are still living there. Then, human rights and ethical aspects should prevail over financial interests. Besides, it is possible to accept such a job, do the investigation in a culturally sustainable way and then come to the conclusion in the expertise that any resettlement of the indigenous people, as well as any interference with their natural resources, must be ruled out, because these would be violations of particular laws, regulations, declarations and agreements, which should then be addressed in detail. When researchers are called in when it is already too late, in situations characterised by the damage that had taken place before, then they should do their best that remedial actions take place immediately, and they should press for all measures to be taken in the best possible way, according to a strict interpretation of the United Nations Declaration on the Rights of Indigenous Peoples and according to ethical principles.

2.8.5   Indigenous Cultures and Borders

Article 36

1. *Indigenous peoples, in particular those divided by international borders, have the right to maintain and develop contacts, relations and cooperation, including activities for spiritual, cultural, political, economic and social purposes, with their own members as well as other peoples across borders.*
2. *States, in consultation and cooperation with indigenous peoples, shall take effective measures to facilitate the exercise and ensure the implementation of this right.*

The collective identity of indigenous peoples became particularly evident in the discussion about the "s" at the end of the word "peoples". This discussion was ignited around the last turn of the millennium during the Working Group's efforts to prepare the Indigenous Rights Declaration at the United Nations. Originally, the title of the Working Group, which had commenced its work in 1982, was "Working Group on Indigenous Populations". It was then argued that "populations" did not sufficiently reflect the aspect that indigenous cultures had a strong group identity, which means that they saw themselves as collectives rather than individuals. One could have worked around it by changing to terms like "cultures", "issues" or "nations", but due to the familiarity with the abbreviation "WGIP", a term with "P" was preferred. Participants in this discussion, which was a matter of a couple of years, were very mindful that not the term "people" was used, but "peoples". "People" would have meant something like "folks" in the sense of "many individuals". But "peoples" is the plural of an equivalent to "nation", meaning a collective that shares a common culture.

Dividing such an indigenous people by borders means literally cutting such a collective in two, along with its culture. For each side of that people concerned, such an encroachment feels like an amputation, if there is a strong collective identity. Even from a more distant point of view, it is clear that dividing a cultural group implies that family relations are cut and likewise other social interconnections. This has negative effects on the functioning of a culture, as communication using the indigenous language is affected and also the exchange of all other cultural elements is impaired, be it of architectural, alimentary, self-representational or other relevance. A benchmark for the survival of a language is a group size of 1000 speakers, who are interconnected in a way that all regular verbal communication takes place as linguistic exchange within that group. Indigenous peoples often have a small group size anyway, and they usually are characterised by a language of their own. When they are cut in two, chances are high that the group size on either side will be below 1000. Such a small group below the benchmark for language survival is then exposed to the official language of the country on the respective side of the border. In most cases, such a group is also exposed to the languages and cultures of other ethnic groups that have not been affected by the drawing up of the border and that are outnumbering the split-off group. It is likely that dominance effects will then arise, leading to the destabilisation of the affected community and eventually to its cultural deterioration. Language is only one, though important, domain contributing to cultural identity. An example of the effect of cutting an indigenous people in two, on the cultural identity of those affected, is reflected by the fact that such a divided people, now living in Benin and Togo, even has two different names for themselves – those living in Benin are called Somba, while those in Togo are called Tamberma.

Yet, dividing indigenous peoples has been commonplace, when colonies were established, and this still has significant effects until today. The Berlin Conference of 1884–1885 was a major event, where borders were drawn with a ruler across the map of Africa, dividing it between the colonial powers. But even much earlier, during the European Expansion, as well as in the decades following the conference, land was claimed in connection with the idea of establishing a territory with borders, recognised by countries with European culture. Double standards become evident, if we imagine an indigenous people coming to the shores of Europe now and claiming land for themselves. Even if they would correctly hoist a flag in a land-taking ceremony, it would not be taken seriously.

An example of a border that impairs indigenous communication is that between Morocco and Algeria. There are Berber groups on both sides of that border, who can hardly maintain their relations. Berber organisations point out that Berber culture has been present in north and north-west Africa long before the arrival of Arabs, and it is generally expressed by these organisations that they feel dominated by the Arab-Muslim culture. Indeed, during the Arab invasion into that region, there was strong resistance by the Berbers, which was eventually put down. In consequence, Arab language and culture were introduced. During the resistance, some Berber groups had even converted to Judaism, which is now recalled as part of modern resistance. Berber organisations that refer to the ancient Queen Kahina or show a Berber flag have to sense governmental repressions. With regard to this situation, the border dividing the ancient Berber land can be seen as convenient by both sides' governments, as it prevents cooperation between Berber organisations and a flaring of the conflict, especially as there have been ongoing tensions since a number of years between Morocco and Algeria. Anyhow, that border is a result of colonial policy, as are most borders outside of Europe.

For researchers, of course, this also has practical consequences. It is not possible to do research across the Moroccan-Algerian border, for example. In the case of the Somba-Tamberma, there is a special regulation in, at least partial, accordance with Article 36 of the United Nations Declaration on the Rights of Indigenous Peoples, as on Wednesdays, the border is opened at Boukombé, in order to allow a common market for those living on both sides. Although this one crossing point, being open for only 1 day per week, is by far not enough to allow the maintenance of contacts for the whole Somba-Tamberma people, it is better than nothing. But, again with regard to practical research, there is no border control. This is problematic, because if we want to use the opportunity for some cross-border research and go to from Boukombé to the market itself, which is on the territory of Togo, we find ourselves acting illegally without entry stamps in our passports. The weekly opening of the checkpoint is supposed to be used by the locals only, who are expected to return home by the end of the day. This goes along without official procedures, and those who cross the border for the market are not asked for a passport. So always try to be on the safe side and enquire for the present circumstances and correct procedures, in order to avoid any trouble.

References

Aguiar, W., & Halseth, R. (2015). *Aboriginal peoples and historic trauma: The processes of intergenerational transmission*. Prince George, BC: National Collaborating Centre for Aboriginal Health.

Barelli, M. (2015). The United Nations declaration on the rights of indigenous peoples: A human rights framework for intellectual property rights. In M. Rimmer (Ed.), *Indigenous intellectual property: A handbook of contemporary research* (pp. 47–63). Cheltenham/Northampton: Edward Elgar Publishing.

Bombay, A., Matheson, K., & Anisman, H. (2009). Intergenerational trauma: Convergence of multiple processes among first nations peoples in Canada. *Journal de la santé autochtone/Journal of Aboriginal Health, 5*, 6–47.

Brush, S. B. (1993). Indigenous knowledge of biological resources and intellectual property rights: The role of anthropology. *American Anthropologist, 95*(3), 653–671.

Festinger, L. (1957). *A theory of cognitive dissonance*. Stanford, CA: Stanford University Press.

Gallagher, S. (2005). *How the body shapes the mind*. Oxford: Oxford University Press.

Gervais, D. J. (Ed.). (2015). *International intellectual property: A handbook of contemporary research*. Cheltenham/Northampton: Edward Elgar Publishing.

Gibbons, A. (1992). Rain forest diet: You are what you eat. *Science, 225*, 163.

Groh, A. (2009). Culture, trauma and psychotherapy. In S. Madu (Ed.), *Trauma and psychotherapy in Africa. Proceedings of the 5th African conference on psychotherapy* (pp. 32–42). Limpopo: University Press.

Herzog, R. (1988). *Staaten der Frühzeit. Ursprünge und Herrschaftsformen*. Munich: C.H. Beck.

Indigenous Bar Association. (2011). *Understanding and implementing the UN declaration on the rights of indigenous peoples. An introductory handbook*. Winnipeg: University of Manitoba, Faculty of Law.

International Labour Organization. (1955). *Convention 104, concerning the abolition of penal sanctions for breaches of contract of employment by indigenous workers* (Entry into force: 7 June 1958). Geneva: ILO.

International Labour Organization. (1957). *Convention 107, concerning the protection and integration of indigenous and other tribal and semi-tribal populations in independent countries* (Entry into force: 2 June 1959). Geneva: ILO.

International Labour Organization. (1989). *Convention 169 – Indigenous and tribal peoples in independent countries* (Entry into force: 5 Sept 1991). Geneva: ILO.

Mazzola, R. (2016). *Copyright and Tjuringa: Can aboriginal dreaming be owned?* Draft paper of the presentation held at the Seventh Multidisciplinary Meeting on Indigenous Peoples (EMPI VII), Milan, 12–13 May 2016.

Mazzola, R. (2017). *Alienating the Inalienable: Copyright and Madayin.* Paper presented at the international seminar Coloquio internacional de estudiantes de doctorado Italia–Mexico, UNAM (Mexico City), 19 June 2017.

Niedenthal, P. M., Barsalou, L. W., Winkielman, P., Krauth–Gruber, S., & Ric, F. (2005). Embodiment in attitudes, social perception, and emotion. *Personality and Social Psychology Review, 9*(3), 184–211.

Rimmer, M. (Ed.). (2015). *Indigenous intellectual property: A handbook of contemporary research.* Cheltenham/Northampton: Edward Elgar Publishing.

Senft, G. (2016). *"Masawa–begeokwa si tuta!":* Cultural and cognitive implications of the Trobriand Islanders' gradual loss of their knowledge of how to make a *Masawa* Canoe. In P. Meusburger, T. Freytag, & L. Suarsana (Eds.), *Ethnic and cultural dimensions of knowledge* (pp. 229–256). Cham/Heidelberg/New York/Dodrecht/London: Springer.

Simon, B. S. (2005). Intellectual property and traditional knowledge: A psychological approach to conflicting claims of creativity in international law. *Berkeley Technology Law Journal, 20,* 4(Art. 5), 1613–1684. Available at: <http://scholarship.law.berkeley.edu/btlj/vol20/iss4/5> (accessed 26 July 2017). https://doi.org/10.15779/Z38F69H.

Smuda, M. (Ed.). (1986). *Landschaft.* Suhrkamp: Frankfurt/M.

Tisucká, B. (2014). The intertwinedness of forest and cultural landscapes in the context of cultural ecology. *Envigogika: Charles University E-journal for Environmental Education, 9,* 1. Published 30. 5. 2014. Available at: <https://envigogika.cuni.cz/index.php/Envigogika/article/view/428/566> (accessed 28 July 2017). https://doi.org/10.14712/18023061.428.

United Nations. (1981–1983). *Study of the problem of discrimination against indigenous populations: Final report submitted by the Special Rapporteur, Mr. José Martínez Cobo.* E/CN.4/Sub.2/476 (1981); E/CN.4/Sub.2/1982/2 (1982); E/CN.4/Sub.2/1983/21 (1983). Geneva/New York: United Nations.

United Nations. (1996). *Working paper by the Chairperson–Rapporteur, Mrs. Erica–Irene A. Daes. On the concept of "indigenous people".* E/CN.4/Sub.2/AC.4/1996/2. Geneva: UN.

United Nations. (2000). *Human rights of indigenous peoples. Report of the seminar on the draft principles and guidelines for the protection of the heritage of indigenous people.* E/CN.4/Sub.2/2000/26. Geneva: UN.

United Nations Conference on Freedom of Information. (1948). Held at Geneva 23 March – 21 April 1948. *Final act.* Lake Success, New York: UN.

United Nations General Assembly. (1948). *Resolution 217 (III): International Bill of Human Rights/Charte internationale des droits de l'homme. Part A: Universal Declaration of Human Rights/Déclaration universelle des droits de l'homme; Part B: Right of Petition/Droit de pétition; Part C: Fate of Minorities/Sort des minorités; Part D: Publicity to be Given to the Universal Declaration of Human Rights/Publicité a donner à la déclaration universelle des droits de l'homme; Part E: Preparation of a Draft Covenant on Human Rights and Draft Measures of Implementation/Preparation d'un projet de pacte relatif aux droits de l'homme et des mesures de mise en œvre.* Paris: Nations Unies.

United Nations General Assembly. (1976a). *International covenant on economic, social and cultural rights.* New York: United Nations.

United Nations General Assembly. (1976b). *International covenant on civil and political rights.* New York: United Nations.

United Nations General Assembly. (2007). *Declaration on the rights of indigenous peoples.* Resolution adopted [without reference to a Main Committee (A/61/L.67 and Add.1)] 61/295. New York: United Nations.

Watzlawick, P., Beavin, J. H., & Jackson, D. D. (1967). *Pragmatics of human communication. A study of interctional patterns, pathologies, and paradoxes.* New York: Norton.

Weeber, K.–. W. (1990). *Smog über Attika. Umweltverhalten im Altertum.* Zürich: Artemis & Winkler.

Wicklund, R. A., & Gollwitzer, P. M. (1982). *Symbolic self-completion.* Hillsdale, NJ: Lawrence Erlbaum.

Yehuda, R., Daskalakis, N. P., Bierer, L. M., Bader, H. N., Klengel, T., Holsboer, F., & Binder, E. B. (2015). Holocaust exposure induced intergenerational effects on FKBP5 methylation. *Biological Psychiatry.* https://doi.org/10.1016/j.biopsych.2015.08.005.

Chapter 3
Methodology: How to Optimally Collect Data in the Fields

Abstract The methodological aspects of this chapter cover a wide range, starting with research questions to consider even before the beginning of any field research preparations; then looking at the designing of the field research itself, the techniques to apply in the field, the data analysis and evaluation methods; and also addressing issues to be mindful of regarding the presentation of the results after the return from the research. Ethical aspects play a major role throughout these aspects, as transcultural dominance effects would not only debilitate the data but could also have detrimental impacts on the indigenous people concerned. Therefore, it is necessary to apply minimally invasive techniques, which should not only go along with the researchers' total immersion into the indigenous context but also, in most of these field situations, due to previous destruction of the indigenous culture, with rescue work. Some of the legal aspects, which have been extensively looked at in the previous chapter, such as the issue of full, free, prior and informed consent, are taken up, where necessary, along with particular articles of the UN Indigenous Rights Declaration. This chapter also reviews the common methodological concepts of validity, reliability and objectivity and their purport for our topic, looking at field encounter as quasi-experimentation, as well as at the application of qualitative and quantitative methods. With regard to the actual field research situation, socio-cognitive mechanisms pertaining to the persons involved are analysed with special attention to the constellations of influence, and the role of translators is investigated. Furthermore, researchers exemplary for the history of transcultural field encounters are referred to.

Keywords Epistemology · Data collection · Philosophy of science · Research ethics · Vulnerability and resilience · Transcultural copying · Social cognition

Even before you start to plan how to collect data in an indigenous context, please thoroughly think about the question if it is necessary at all to go there. Does the research issue make sense? And if so, are these data that you want to collect really needed to answer the research question? Couldn't it just as well be answered by relying on secondary data, which already exist and which you could evaluate for

© Springer International Publishing AG 2018   93
A. Groh, *Research Methods in Indigenous Contexts*,
https://doi.org/10.1007/978-3-319-72776-9_3

your particular purpose? Even if this is not the case, it is very likely that you will consult existing sources during the planning phase, just as you will correlate primary and secondary data after the collection phase. The primary data result from the actual research, which you carry out, whereas the secondary data result from previous studies, which usually have already been published and which have been analysed again. This is often done to produce alternative views, systematic reviews or meta-analyses. When you use the same dataset again with regard to statistical testing of the data for significances, then you will have to apply the Bonferroni correction. Although you do not have to go into such details, informing the indigenous people about the general purpose of what you are doing, obtaining their consent regarding the practical procedures and what you are planning to do is not only an ethical principle and sign of respect, but it is also possible that the discussion of the research topic with the elders or other indigenous persons will yield new ideas and insight that you would not come upon on your own. As a matter of course, the research should never be to the detriment of the indigenous peoples, but rather to their benefit and in support of the indigenous cause.

Most research designs of field research in indigenous contexts are criteria based or the so-called purposive sampling. The researchers have a reason for selecting a particular indigenous people, or at least a particular region, before they start with more detailed preparations of the excursion. However, things don't always work out. It could happen that you are in search of a certain nomadic group, but that you are not successful with your search, because these people are in search, too, yet they are searching for particular fruits in the forest, which are just in season. Or other unforeseeable events could stop the excursion halfway. Anyway, when you want to do research with a certain indigenous group, then you have your reasons due to the particular research issues that you pursue. As the term says, the sample of people is chosen with the purpose of doing specific research with them according to preset criteria. If you want to go more into detail, Ritchie et al. (2003) differentiate various approaches to purposive sampling, such as extreme case, intensity, typical case or critical case sampling.

Depending on your research question, please consider if you could just as well draw on national or international surveys, censuses or administrative records, to conduct some essential meta-research, which might already be sufficient to answer your questions, or which would at least partially do so, so that you can minimise the time of your stay in an indigenous community. The less time you spend with indigenous people, the smaller is the risk of causing any destabilisation. Nevertheless, bearing this risk in mind, it always makes sense to not only try to minimise this risk as far as possible but also to design field research from the outset in a stabilising or restabilising manner. The issue of rescue work shall be approached in Sect. 3.5.2.

Although this is a book on research methods in indigenous contexts, it can briefly be mentioned that data analysis and evaluation do not only pertain to quantitative research, which yields data that are then evaluated with conventional statistical procedures, but that qualitative research also yields data, which can be processed with more complex methods and not only narratively be reported. Some of these analysis methods are in the tradition of linguistic or sociological research; others have been elaborated in the context of psychotherapy. Ryan and Bernard (1994) give an overview on systematic approaches of categorising, analysing and evaluating qualitative data. When you're working with text-based data, in particular with narrations or recordings of spoken language, then there are different standardised qualitative evaluation procedures, the most prominent of which might be the Grounded Theory of Glaser and Strauss (1967) and the Qualitative Content Analysis by Mayring (2000). The latter is generally done with the ATLAS.ti software.[1]

Ethical Clearance

The question, whether researchers have to seek ethical clearance before starting a project, depends on national regulations in their country of origin and in the country, where the research is carried out, as well as on international regulations and on general consent in the academic world. The legal regulations partially overlap with other regulations, such as those concerning intellectual property, which we have looked at in the previous chapter.

Generally, data collection that takes place in the form of everyday communication does not need any ethical permission. If you ask indigenous peoples how they designate or how they like something, then that is a way of communicating, which any non-researcher could do just as well. However, when you present something to indigenous peoples, which you want them to evaluate, comment or designate, then you must take care that this is not done in an obtrusive way. Keeping Article 8 of the United Nations Declaration in the Rights of Indigenous Peoples in mind, all contacts with indigenous peoples should be carried out in a minimally invasive way, and no action should take place that could possibly have the effect of destabilising their culture or individual persons.

Ethical aspects are addressed in many passages of this book, as indigenous peoples are concerned by, and exposed to, many unethical decisions, policies and practices. It does not seem unreasonable to assume that scientists in general, and field researchers in particular, have a pronounced obligation to support the observance of ethical principles and to guide their own behaviour in orientation towards these principles. Regarding ethical aspects, we shall go in more detail in Sect. 3.4.5.

Full, Free, Prior and Informed Consent

Like ethical aspects, the concept of full, free, prior and informed consent is mentioned in many of this book's passages. It is of comparable central importance and actually an essential part of the ethical foundation upon which research can take place in indigenous contexts. Due to its central importance, it is addressed in several articles of the United Nations Declaration on the Rights of Indigenous Peoples, for example, with regard to land rights. Principally, it is of major significance in connection with many issues pertaining to the topic of intellectual property that we have dealt with in Sect. 2.4.2.

When the concept of full, free, prior and informed consent is treated, the "full" is sometimes omitted, and even shorter, it can be referred to as "FPIC" only. Nevertheless, one should strive for informing the participants as full, that is as

---

[1] Cf. <http://atlasti.com> (accessed 29 Aug. 2017).

comprehensive, as possible. If that goal can always be fully, that is, totally, reached is certainly a practical, as well as a philosophical, question. This even pertains to research in our own culture. Are we able to explain all scientific aspects to the participants of a study? Even if they are no specialists and if they are from outside the subject area? Often, they are not really interested in details, though they might enjoy to participate in the research. When we carry out research in another culture, the language barrier is an additional hindrance. Yet, we should do our best to give a *full* explanation of what we are doing.

There is a well-known methodological problem that in certain cases, the full explanation given *prior* to an experiment might or would spoil the results, because the knowledge of what we want to find out about would already bias the participants' answers or behaviour. A famous example is the two-factor theory of emotion, which we owe to the brilliant research design of Schachter and Singer (1962), who told some of their subjects that they had received a vitamin product, but, in fact, these participants had been administered epinephrine. Otherwise, the experiment wouldn't have worked, and these researchers would not have found out that emotion is based on the two factors of adrenalin-based bodily arousal plus the cognitive labelling of that arousal. But there is consent, though, among social scientists that even if subjects need to be naive about the epistemological interest, nothing harmful may be done to them and nothing that could possibly be expected to be against their will and that, after the experiment, they have to be fully informed about the actual goal of the study. In indigenous contexts, the requirements are stricter, which makes sense, in the face of the abuse indigenous peoples have been subject to in the past. Therefore, we should give a clear and full explanation what the study is about that we want to carry out.

Indigenous persons should be *free* to give the consent, and likewise, they should have the freedom to refuse their participation. In any case, we have to accept their decision. But what does the freedom of decision mean? If we look at this question from the perspective of field theory,[2] then human behaviour including thinking, motivation and decision-making is a result of the "sum of the forces bearing on the individual" (Wicklund 1990, p. 123). In a more metaphorical way, we can imagine a cotton ball on a table and people standing around the table blowing at it. If the cotton ball moves at all, and if so, in which direction it moves, in what line it goes on, how fast it goes and how far – all that is a result of the forces bearing on it. In this example, these forces are the winds caused by the people blowing at the cotton ball. Human behaviour usually results from different forces – social forces, our genes, beliefs and environmental forces, to sketch a few. We have been socialised, and during that process, we have internalised principles, standards, rules, ways of looking at things and other behaviour patterns. Much of this is specific to the culture, in which we have grown up. However, this should not render the impression that we are just puppets on the strings of our fate. Although there have been some scientists who have denied that humans had a free will, they were just a few, and

---

[2] Lewin (1951).

their idea had been refuted by later experiments.[3] The majority shares the consent that what makes humans so special is their ability to not only change perspectives but also to look at things from a metalevel. We can see ourselves in relation to others, and we can reflect about this constellation. We can even consider the meta-metalevel, that is, the way we look at the reflections, and the meta-meta-metalevel and so on.[4]

However, there are various forces, which are, for example, present in economical, ecological and relational aspects, which bear on our thinking. These aspects do not fully determine our thinking, as we can reflect about our automatic responses to them and intervene to counteract the automatism. At least to a certain degree, we should add. Some huge topics that we don't want to go into now are things like subliminal perception and depth psychology. Leaving that aside, we still have to consider that there are interindividual differences as to what extent persons actually do reflect things from meta-perspectives. This extent might be a matter of habituality, or it might be specific to particular situations. Perhaps it could be explained by cultural factors. But that does not really matter. The fact as such – that there are these interindividual differences – is enough. This means that we have to take into consideration the aspect that total freedom of thinking, of decision and of consent cannot be guaranteed. But we have to make the best of it.

Practically, that means that we have to minimise anything that could restrict the freedom of the indigenous peoples, and as we focus on research, we have to prevent that the freedom of the indigenous peoples' decision regarding their *consent* be impaired in any way, once they have been *informed* about our research intention. We can of course only minimise those factors that are under our control. One major factor that has an impact on indigenous peoples' freedom is the dominance of the industrial culture. When we think back to the cultural theories outlined in Chap. 1, then we could point out now that a culture is not a being like a plant or an animal.[5] Dominance is an attribute of behaviour. So, how can a culture be dominant? Well, cultures are made up of people. Culture is the essence of collective behaviour. And we, as researchers, are representatives of the industrial culture, if we like it or not. We are associated with our culture's dominance. At least, as long as the indigenous people know of our culture. Most, if not all, do. Does that mean that we cannot escape that role and that our mere presence would be exerting dominance upon the indigenous people we are visiting? Yes and no. Yes, we generally cannot escape the role of being representatives of our culture. And no, we do not have to exert dominance on the indigenous people in any repressive way. We can actually use the fact that our culture is seen as influential – in whichever way – to ameliorate the situation. If we orientate ourselves towards the specific standards of the indigenous culture, then this communicates acceptance and respect. As we are talking about

---

[3] Those, who claimed that consciousness was just an illusion, referred to an experiment by Libet et al. (1979) on readiness potentials. But Schultze-Kraft et al. (2016) could show that our free will can veto against automatic reactions of the brain.

[4] Cf. Watzlawick et al. (1967).

[5] In an early twentieth-century conceptualisation, Spengler (1926, 1928) understood cultures as beings that even featured youth, maturity and senility.

traditionally living indigenous peoples, the standards by which we should orientate ourselves are the precolonial ones, which means those dating from the time before any external impact from the dominant culture. We shall go into more detail on this issue in Chap. 4.

The Role of the Translators

One issue that needs to be addressed is the fact that in most cases, we have to rely on translators, when we carry our research in indigenous contexts. There are about 7000 languages, which are presently still spoken in the world, and the majority of these are indigenous languages.[6] It is not possible for a non-indigenous researcher to perfectly learn an indigenous language. Once we have passed the phase of language acquisition,[7] we cannot learn a new language intuitively any more. Past puberty, when we are researchers, it is too late. Especially, when we do comparative research in different indigenous cultures, there is no chance that we can become a sovereign user of the respective languages where we carry out our studies.

Many indigenous persons have knowledge of a colonial language, to different extents – some are perfect in it, others barely manage with it. Independent of their competence in the colonial language, some indigenous persons dislike to use it because of their ideological attitudes towards it. The colonial language is often associated with genocide, land theft, forced displacement and other atrocities committed against indigenous peoples. As researchers, we need to be careful and sensitive, in order not to hurt the indigenous peoples' feelings.

So, there are several reasons why it might be necessary to involve translators – our own lack of competence in the indigenous language, indigenous peoples' critical view of colonial languages and perhaps the indigenous persons' limited skills of the colonial language. Unless we are linguists ourselves and equipped with the necessary knowledge, we might be lucky and enjoy the company of a colleague from a university of the country where we are just carrying out the research, who might be able to translate for us. But usually, the translators available are persons, who normally earn their living as tour guides. Yet, we have to be sceptical with regard to the quality of the translations, as long as the translator does not originate from exactly the same social group for which he[8] is translating. Indigenous languages and their dialects are endemic to the particular territory, which means that the linguistic changes show enormous territorial variances. In India, for example, 417 indigenous languages are spoken and in Cameroon 225.[9] Languages usually have dialects as subcategories. The differentiation of dialects from languages is not easy and often arbitrary. Depending on the linguists' consent, what is spoken in two neighbouring villages can either be considered as two dialects of the same language or as two

---

[6] The present figure is regularly updated at <ethnologue.com>.

[7] Cf. Chomsky (1972).

[8] In this case, I use only the male personal pronoun, as I have never encountered a female tour guide or translator in these contexts ever since the 1980s, when I started my research with indigenous peoples.

[9] Figures vary over time; <ethnologue.com> presents regular updates.

different languages. These distinctions determine whether the figure given for the number of languages within a country is higher or lower. In the field, it might happen that the languages spoken in villages only a few kilometres apart are linguistically related, but they are as different as English and Spanish, which both belong to the family of Indo-European languages.

We have to consider the social-cognitive situation of the translator. He usually is paid for his job, which he does not want to lose. He is expected to translate, so even if he is uncertain about an expression, he will deliver a translation. Another serious problem is the influence exerted by the translator, which is often uncontrollable. He might phrase questions in a leading way instead of striving for neutrality, and we usually cannot understand what he is talking with the indigenous people. It is helpful, therefore, to install security measures within the research design. Otherwise, validity would perish.

If possible, the answers given in the original indigenous language should be recorded and then blind checked. This means that we try to find another person of the same mother tongue, who also speaks a language that we know well, in a different place, for example, in the nearest town. We should then read the indigenous words, which we have noted down, to this person, and ask what they meant. But we should be careful not to give any suggestions by telling about our research interest before that person translates the words, because then, we would have to expect that this translation might be biased. In fact, just presenting the words is a good choice. When we have an audio or video recording taken with the indigenous people's consent, then this contains much context. Nevertheless, it would be interesting for colleagues of that region who know at least some of that language and who want to contribute to the evaluation of the research.

When we take notes of the answers given in the indigenous language, along with writing down the translations given, we should also be sure how to pronounce the words. There are languages without the correspondence between the written and the spoken words as we know it. This is especially the case with regard to certain tonal languages. For example, in the Ditamari language spoken by the Somba-Tamberma people of Benin and Togo, the phonemes do not matter as much as the tone given to them. So, when you ask a native speaker from that group to repeat a word, vowels and even consonants might be exchanged. In such a case, a solution would be to present the answered words singled out from the audio recording, for blindcheck, if we find another native speaker – which does not always work out. Sometimes, we have to accept that data are left unprocessed.

For projects, in which the government of the respective country is involved, official translators might be provided. However, these translators might be rejected by the indigenous people concerned for at least two reasons. Firstly, there might be distrust towards the government and related officials. Secondly, due to the endemic characteristics of indigenous languages, the translators, who have received some academic training, are unlikely to speak exactly the dialect of the village concerned. Probably the second aspect will be taken as an argument for not accepting the official translator. If then, for a government-related project, a local translator will be accepted by both sides, this translator will be in a conflict of loyalty. With every bit that he (in most cases, also these translators are men) translates, he might make clear with his formulations that he does not share the government's position, thereby making sure that he has only been forced into the role of the translator. In other projects, a local translator might feel himself to be in a very different position. When the topic to be translated concerns indigenous peoples' rights, then he might agree very much with it.

It should also be mentioned that indigenous peoples are often fluid in quite a number of languages, besides their own also those of neighbouring peoples plus at least one colonial language. In these cases, translators would even be redundant.

In the following sections of this chapter, we shall first take a look at the history of transcultural field encounters. Ever since indigenous cultures were studied, or certain aspects, like their languages, were investigated, there have been some researchers at least, who tried to minimise their own invasiveness when visiting these peoples. Researchers of this kind generally had much better access to such cultures, and were more successful in obtaining useful data than other researchers, who were not so considerate. Unfortunately, even in present times, transcultural encounters are taking place in the fields without due regard being given to the indigenous peoples. However, since 2007, this might even be a violation of indigenous rights.

Keeping this in mind, we shall further focus in this chapter on the reasons why, and especially how, we should strive for validity, reliability and objectivity in indigenous contexts. It is necessary to understand the theoretical framework of research design, in order to be able to draw causal conclusions on the basis of empirical findings. Some theorists have particularly examined the researcher's role and his or her influence on the findings. These considerations point to the stringent necessity to apply techniques in the fields that minimise any destabilising influence.

3.1   History of Transcultural Field Encounters

Minimally invasive field encounter, total immersion and integrative and participatory research are not so new. They have been practised by many, mostly individual, persons in contact with other cultures. For example, the Portuguese colonial army had problems, because many of their soldiers were going indigenous. They deserted and took shelter in indigenous communities, where they remained, married and had a family. Apparently, they found that much more enjoyable than serving in the army.

With the emergence of modern science, there were also researchers who realised that immersion was the way to understand another culture much better than looking at it from the distance or as bystanders. To name but a few, Frank Hamilton Cushing (1857–1900), an American ethnologist, was the pioneer of the so-called intensive studies by systematically applying as one of the first, if not the first, participatory research during his fieldwork with North American First Nations. The approach of participatory research has often been attributed to the Polish social anthropologist Bronisław Malinowski (1884–1942). Yet, this is not quite correct, for two reasons. Firstly, Malinowski carried out his famous research in the Trobriand Islands during the time of the First World War, which was about three decades after Cushing did his fieldwork. Secondly, after the publication of Malinowski's diaries, it became clear that he did not fulfil the goals set by himself regarding the application of participatory techniques in field research. Curt Unckel Nimuendajú (1883–1945) was a German anthropologist, born in Jena. Shortly after the turn of the century, then only by the name of Curt Unckel, he went to Brazil, where he lived with indigenous peoples. His fully immersive research led to some ground-breaking publications. The Guaraní gave him the surname Nimuendajú, meaning "the one, who has settled down". Paul Wirz (1892–1955), a Swiss ethnologist, did research predominantly in New Guinea. Due to his integrative fieldwork, he gained much more insight into the culture visited than others, who avoided too much contact with indigenous peoples. The Bôas brothers, who have already been mentioned in the previous chapter of this book, promoted the establishing of the Xingú National Park in Brazil, where they were very much integrated into the indigenous cultures during their work as anthropologists, especially Orlando Villas Bôas (1914–2002), who, upon his death, was bemoaned by the indigenous people like a major chief. The Austrian ethnologists Gerhard Kubik, born 1934, stayed with indigenous peoples in Malawi, where he even underwent initiation including circumcision during his integrative field research. Bruno Manser, born 1954, another Swiss ethnologist, went to Borneo to do fieldwork with the Penan people in full immersion into their culture. During the time of his activities, we were also in the field on Borneo, not too far away, with the closely related Punan people. Bruno disappeared in 2000 and was officially declared missing by the Swiss authorities in 2005. It is supposed that he was killed because he organised the indigenous people to stand up against the logging of their forest. In 1998, we happened to speak to a tour guide in Tarakan, who, as one of the few external persons, had met Bruno in the jungle by chance. According to the guide's account, Bruno was already fearing for his life at that time.

In each of these cases, deep familiarity with the indigenous peoples and insight into the cultures was accomplished by immersion and integration, which was practised and manifested on the visual level by adapting to the bodily appearance of indigenous people. Without this, immersion, integration or participation would remain but empty catchphrases. What counts is how the indigenous peoples see you. If you keep your clothes on, you are just an alien object. Therefore, if you genuinely want to be in contact with indigenous cultures, you need to be accepted by them. But is only possible if you communicate acceptance and respect towards their standards yourself. If you take methodology, ethic values and indigenous rights seriously, which you should, then you have to minimise your invasiveness. The researchers, who have practised minimally invasive field encounters, have given us impressive examples.

You might have noticed that all of the researchers, who are known to do immersive fieldwork, are men. In the literature, and when you go through archives very carefully, you can only find hints about female researchers. Especially with regard to the nineteenth and twentieth century, one reason for this is that almost all researchers were indeed men, although there were some exceptions, and only a few male researchers took their wives with them. Another reason, in particular for the present time, is that women are already stigmatised when they dare to uncover their chests. We regularly have female members in our research teams, and of course they are scared that any depiction of their immersive field encounter with indigenous peoples could be abusively posted on the Internet, causing a so-called shit storm in the social media. It is easy to understand that nobody wants to be treated negatively. But it is not these women who are to be blamed. They are good examples, as they behave correctly, when they associate themselves with the indigenous women. They support the indigenous women's self-confidence and thus help to stabilise or even restabilise indigenous culture. Those, who are to blame, are the irrational globalised persons, who with ridicule and sexualisation subvert female self-confidence even in the global culture and directly or indirectly promote deterioration of indigenous culture.

Taking a synoptic view on the history of transcultural field encounters, it seems that each time had its chances, each time had its shortcomings and each time had persons, who tried to make the best out of it. What impeded integrative behaviour of the researchers in the late nineteenth until well into the twentieth century was the implicit conviction of the white men's supremacy. Cushing (similar to people like Las Casas, by the way) was ahead of his time with his belief that all peoples have a culture. While this is commonplace today, there are other absurdities, which are impeding field research. As described by social embodiment and other socio-cognitive approaches, modifications that are targeted at people's bodily appearance lead to modifications of these people's state of mind. Although in each era the prevailing zeitgeist has a formative influence on those living in it to an extent that they are taking these attitudes as a matter of course, there are always some who manage to escape from this and to understand that truth must be something unaffected by fashions. This search for truth is the originary impetus of science, and it certainly also was and is the impetus for those field researchers, who do not only say that they respect indigenous cultures but also act in this way.

3.2 Field Encounter as Quasi-Experimentation

Scientists, who have theoretically dealt with field research, have most probably come across Cook and Campbell's (1979) reflections on *Quasi-Experimentation*, perhaps also the successor book by Shadish et al. (2002).

Cook and Campbell (1979) paved the way towards intensive considerations and justifications of the comparability of the significances of field research versus laboratory research. In both cases, subjects can be observed, who are under different conditions, and the actions or reactions under these different conditions can be compared. Therefore, both in the laboratory and in the field, there are independent variables, which have a bearing on the subjects, and there are dependent variables, which are the outcomes of these different situations. Consequently, Cook and

Campbell (1979) use the term quasi-experimentation for field research situations, in reference to experimentations, which are carried out in laboratories. One major difference between quasi-experimentation and experimentation can be found with regard to the randomising of subjects, which does not take place in field research. In the field setting, one usually has to be content with the persons, who are present in the particular setting, as one neither makes the selection by kicking anyone out, nor does one bring other persons along, as persons to be studied. In the laboratory, in contrast, the denotation of randomising can be somewhat confusing, as one actually wants to exert control about the participants in the experiment. The laboratory researcher wants to make sure about such characteristics as the age groups that are participating, their sex ratio, education and socio-economic background. Since such a control does not take place in field research, where natural groups are investigated and perhaps compared, possible influencing factors can be confounded, which are features or traits of the subjects or influences caused by the investigation itself, so that the internal validity (see Sect. 3.4.2) could be impaired, in the sense that one cannot be quite sure about the causal relations of independent variables and dependent variables and one has to take over- or underestimations of this relation into account.

However, there are often no alternatives to field research. Methodological hardliners might suggest that only highly controllable laboratory research should take place. But this is not an option, if it would leave indigenous peoples exposed to threats, which are diminished when those in charge of the threats know that researchers, and thus witnesses, are around. Laboratory studies certainly have their point, and I have done some laboratory research myself, but sticking merely to laboratory research would be an expression of a very narrowed worldview, perhaps caused by some fear of the not-so-comfortable world out there. By the way, even in laboratory research, as long as humans are involved, one should be cautious to ever assume complete internal validity, as it is defined by constructs, which always have to be interpreted. When we do laboratory research, then we use the opportunity of restricted complexity, to control the situation as far as possible. In comparison, quasi-experimental designs substantiate their significance on concepts of causality and put increased weight on external validity and construct validity, thus compensating possible uncertainties regarding the internal validity.

Quasi-experimentation designs can investigate, for example, the differences between two or more groups. This is what you do when you go to different indigenous peoples and present them the same stimuli, like certain colours, or ask them the same questions, as we presently do in a study regarding the orientation towards cardinal directions. But depending on the research question, doubts pertaining to confounding variables can become more imminent, so that it is indicated to try to reduce them. This could be done by measures such as keeping these confounding variables constant or resorting to matched samples (Bortz and Döring 2003).

3.3   Researchers' Influence and Philosophy of Science

The aspect of influence is often treated in a much-too-sweeping way with regard to the researcher's behaviour in field settings. While it is true that the object of research should not be influenced, because otherwise, the results would not be valid, it is at the same time also clear that any interaction implies some form of mutual influence. Therefore, one has to differentiate with regard to where influence has to be avoided and where influence is part of the interactions and thus even necessary.

Which are the areas, in which influence needs to be avoided? First of all, in any setting, in which culture plays a role, this is the main sphere, which we have to reflect thoroughly about. Indigenous cultures are located in a constellation of tensions caused by systemic hierarchies of dominance. The present state of the culture is usually the result of previous human rights violations, social pressure and other forms of dominance, which have been exerted on them. This means that they have not moved voluntarily to the cultural position, in which they actually are, but rather, force or strain has been, or still is, in effect. A good way to model the respective situation is provided by the field theory of Lewin (1951) or, rather simplified, by the cotton ball example given above. With regard to the researchers, we have to bear two important aspects in mind. One of them pertains to the ethical perspective; we may not ignore any unjust or even merely unfair treatment of people. The other one pertains to the fact that we cannot not behave; once we are aware of wrongful actions against an indigenous people, and we are involved with their situation and probably could take a stand against the wrongful acts by virtue of our position, then we would be complicit in these wrongful acts if we decided to ignore them and be bystanders only. Therefore, we should always be vigilant by looking at our own behaviour and analysing it from a meta-perspective, which, among other advantages, also helps to prevent others from practising any diffusion of responsibility, which is a phenomenon that is well-known in social psychology.

Consequently, researchers have to make sure that they do not complicit in putting pressure on anyone, and specifically, researchers in indigenous context have to exclude that they exert any cultural dominance on indigenous persons or that they contribute to pushing them away from tradition and towards globalisation. Such pushing would be a form of social pressure and thus unacceptable. The directive resulting from this with regard to field research in indigenous contexts is that any influence has to be ruled out, which would have the aim or effect of moving the indigenous culture or people thereof towards the "warmer" part of the cultural spectrum.[10]

Other areas, in which influence has to be avoided, are of course those that directly pertain to research questions. A negative example can be found in instructions, which were given to indigenous persons during field research on colour concepts, where researchers had restricted beforehand what the indigenous subjects were

---

[10] Please see Chapter 1 of this book for the concept of the cultural spectrum.

allowed to answer, when they were shown the colour samples.[11] If we want to find out about indigenous peoples' colour concepts, that kind of manipulation makes no sense at all. To avoid such mistakes, we always have to step back and look at the design and the procedure and ask ourselves, What do we want to find out, and is this the optimal way towards finding the answers?

When we talk about influence, we should also be aware that researchers themselves are under influence not only from their cultural background in general but also from their specific academic context. Thomas Kuhn (1962) revealed that there are periodic fashions in science, like in other areas of social life. There is a hype of certain theories for a while until they have completed their service and are considered to be worn out. When people have become tired of them, they look for new heroes and will then be hyped along with their theories. Karin Knorr-Cetina (1981) went into more details by analysing concrete research situations. Many minor decisions and concessions are made due to the particular research circumstances, the availability of resources, the preferences of superiors or colleagues, personnel policies and unforeseen events. In principle, the situation of researchers is not that much different in comparison to journalists or other persons, who are obliged to their social and occupational subsystem. So, what should be the consequence? Should science be condemned altogether (cf. Feyerabend 1975)? Of course not. But we have to keep an eye on the influence, which we are exposed to, as well as on the influence, which we might exert on others.

Seen from the perspective of epistemology, influence is part of the condition, under which a study is carried out. There are forms of influence, which cannot be avoided, as each communication already influences the one who receives it. But as they cannot be avoided, we need to control them at least. Interaction is an intrinsic part of field encounter, and therefore, certain forms of interaction are even necessary. Controlling the necessary parts of influence first and foremost means that we have to reduce any invasiveness in terms of possible destabilising aspects of our own contributions within the interaction that is taking place. With regard to verbal communication, even leading questions can make sense in field research (Girtler 2001), as long as they are applied in a controlled way, targeted at identifying reasons and making out meaning, details and truth. In any case, we need to be fully aware of the influence exerted, which, by the way, could also take place directed to us. Being conscious of not only the existence of influence but also of its particular functions and taking these into account in our evaluations are the preconditions for the correct procedures in the field, as well as for the avoidance of misleading interpretations of the outcomes.

---

[11] Overview: Groh (2016a).

3.3.1 *Vulnerability and Resilience*

The concept of vulnerability has been applied to various aspects, such as the vulnerability of ecosystems or people's vulnerability to health hazards. Of particular pertinence to field research in indigenous contexts is the perspective of cultural vulnerability, as it is used in connection with ethnography, which also implies the focus on those individuals, who are subject to increased vulnerability due to particularities of their culture and its relation to other, especially dominant, cultures.

The vulnerability of individuals can be understood as decreased resilience towards stress in their relation to their environment, be it social or otherwise environmental, as compared to other individuals in similar situations. The decreased resilience, in turn, can be understood as relevant thresholds being lowered in the sense that the majority of the other individuals do not react in the way as the vulnerable individuals do.

Resilience, as a concept, is defined complementary to vulnerability. Persons, who can be described as being resilient, do not react with psychological or otherwise health-related impairment to stressful conditions of their environment (Rutter 2006). They are adaptable to changing situations, to which they react flexible and adequately. In developmental psychology, the concept of resilience is applied to the dealing with adversity and risk, which children or adolescents might be exposed to (overview: Daniel 2010; Olsson et al. 2003). Generally, individual dispositional factors, a cohesive and warm family and external social support factors are seen as being positively related to the person's resilience. A perspective, which is of particular relevance to field research in indigenous contexts, is that of community resilience (Vos and Sullivan 2014; Eshel and Kimhi 2016). It is applied predominantly to a community's dealing with disasters and war. A factor, which positively contributes to both individual and community resilience, has been found in the role of churches with regard to coping with personal hardship, as well as communal dealing with catastrophes (Shean 2015; Aldrich and Meyer 2014). On the individual cognitive level, correlations have been found of resilience with attributional styles, in terms of more optimistic (Kelly 2013) and with more complex (Narayanan 2009) causal attributions.

The predecessor of the current resilience concept was Aaron Antonovsky's concept of salutogenesis (overview: Lindström and Eriksson 2005). The term is a neologism derived from Latin, with the meaning *origin of health*. Antonovsky had found that some Holocaust survivors had particular abilities to cope with the horrors they had gone through, and he became interested in the factors, which contributed to this, what later would be called resilience. Antonovsky came to the conclusion that a *sense of coherence* was responsible for the well-being of people and that this sense was based on the aspects of *comprehensibility* regarding life events, the conviction of the *manageability* of one's life and the belief in the *meaningfulness* of life.

Up to now, research pertaining to indigenous peoples' vulnerability and resilience[12] has primarily focused on the coping with disasters, either with regard to communal coping strategies or to the question, if indigenous knowledge can be generally useful for disaster management. In this connection, a particular focus has been put on the effects of climate change. Although there is wide consent that indigenous peoples are more vulnerable than non-indigenous persons or communities, targeted research on vulnerability and resilience on the individual level of indigenous persons seems not to be taken adequately into consideration, and the same can be said for the connection between their individual and communal resilience.

3.4   Epistemology

Research is always carried out in order to gain knowledge. Research in indigenous contexts is no exception to that rule. To know and to better understand, from a meta-level, what we are doing, we should look at the methodological peculiarities that are applicable to research in these particular, indigenous, contexts. Although these contexts are very specific, all general epistemological aspects are relevant, since we claim to do scientific research. The term epistemology designates the branch of science that is preoccupied with studying the generation of knowledge.

If we want to explain certain phenomena within the scientific discourse, it would not be enough to just give a personal opinion.[13] Scientific explanations have to avoid inconsistencies and gaps, and they also have to justify their argumentations. The practical side of this is the methodology that we apply in our research. The theoretical side is the epistemology constituting the reasons for our actions. Both have to comply with the particular conditions. We should pay special attention to three aspects of meeting these conditions: Researchers, of course, have to (1) adhere to the *law*, like anyone else; they should (2) comply with *ethical* principles; and they should (3) gather their data according to scientific *methodological* rules.

When we try to comprehend the differences between indigenous and globalised contexts, then it might be helpful to see those settings as social fields in the sense of the approach of Pierre Bourdieu (cf. Champagne 2013). In such fields, cultures or subcultures are structured by social practices. These practices, in turn, remain largely implicit. The reason for this implicitness lies in the historical genesis of these structures and practices, which have always occurred in culturally (or sub culturally) specific ways.

As researchers, we perceive phenomena, and as long as they are not static, they are processes. And especially as researchers, who focus on culture or culture-related issues, the phenomena that we perceive are notably complex. For whatever we see, hear or otherwise perceive, there must be a reason. This pertains to processes as well as to static phenomena, for which we can assume a process that has preceded and

---

[12] See also United Nations General Assembly (2014).

[13] Schülein and Reitze (2010) give an excellent overview on epistemology and theory of science.

led to the present state. With regard to the physical world, there is a set of natural laws, on which we can draw for explanations. But culture consists of humans, and these humans are equipped with cognitive aptitudes, which enable them to violate, in a certain way, the natural laws. Even picking up a pen is such a violation, as the pen would not have gone into its new position by itself. If there would be no life in our bodies, we could not perform such an action, although every single atom would be available just like in a living body. A dead grain of seed, an unfertilised egg would simply decay according to natural laws. Life is a break with these laws. However, processes of living organisms are subject to different, more complex, laws. And human behaviour occurs according to psychological laws. Cognitions are part of the psychological mechanisms, along with many unconscious processes, which also are determinants of behaviour. In every culture, the phenomena that we can perceive result from interactions of the individuals within that culture. Even, when persons perform a self-given task individually, they have received input during their hitherto socialisation from their contextual culture and thus from other persons of that culture. It is of secondary importance, when this input has been generated. Be it a parent giving advice, or be it a book written more than a century ago, it is culturally specific input for a person. In the special case that a person receives input across cultural boundaries, that is, from persons belonging to a different culture, then this input is perceived, processed and interpreted in a culturally specific way, according to the previous socialisation.

We, the researchers with globalised backgrounds in indigenous contexts, are such persons. We perceive something in a different culture, but we are equipped with means to handle this input in a manner that we have been taught in our culture of origin. It might be a certain advantage that our culture has been synthesised out of many preceding cultures, so that, to a certain degree, we might have recourse to understanding things form a meta-perspective. But by all means, we should not rely on that. There have been appalling misunderstandings in the past by scientists. Most prominent examples are the misconceptions of interpreting indigenous nudity in a sexual way. When we do research in different cultures, we have to scrutinise even our premises. Correlations that we take for granted might not be applicable to the other context.

Science tries to optimise the accuracy of attributions and explications. Over the past centuries, science as a system of thought has been elaborated and established by people, who systematically have been searching for answers. A reasonable scientist knows that there is a world outside science and that scientific procedures are mere conventions upon which academics have agreed that these are suitable customs to find out about causal relations. This basic agreement about causalities underlies any formulation of a theory, as it implies the existence of reality and truth to which a logic is inherent that, in principle, can be understood.[14]

---

[14]Attempts to call reality into question, such as radical constructivism (e.g. Watzlawick 1977), have not been long-living and did not find broad acceptance. The consent that there is a reality, regardless of individual accuracy to reflect it, is the basis for any legal system, as well as for scientific discourse (without that, the discourse itself would be redundant).

However, there are different epistemological traditions of approaching insight, recognition and understanding (overview regarding qualitative research: Guba and Lincoln 1994). These different traditions do not only exist between cultures but also between different academic disciplines, and within the disciplines, between the different schools. With regard to research in, on or related to indigenous contexts, these traditions differ especially in their perspectives of the specific versus the general. One, even central, objective of cross-cultural research is the search for culturally specific versus universal phenomena. Only when we can tell what can be found in all cultures, and what can be found only in some cultures, we can justify claims for the former to be typical for the human being and for the latter to be specific for particular cultures, but not across cultures. There are various words for expressing this distinction, like unique versus general, emic versus etic or indigenous versus universal. Eckensberger (2015) uses the different perspectives on culture, as we can find them in cross-cultural psychology, cultural psychology and indigenous psychologies, as criteria to assign psychologists to one of these schools. However, sticking to such categorisation might do wrong to all those who do not take dogmatic positions, but first look at circumstances and then decide how to proceed, be it with regard to taking theoretical approaches or research-wise. Therefore, such categorisations should be understood as distinctions between procedures, but not between scientists.

There have been descriptions of the different psychological perspectives on culture, for example, by Greenfield (2000), but these descriptions are neither precise, nor are they comprehensive. This would not be possible, anyway, as there have never been agreements upon boundaries between these schools or any allotting of methods to be accepted for one of these schools, but not for the others. The different psychological perspectives on culture are "fuzzy concepts with partially overlapping sets of exemplars" (Greenfield 2000, p. 223). There are some cultural psychologists and even associations of cultural psychology, who leave the inter- or trans-ethnical perspective out of focus, but deal with interpretations of paintings or linguistic phenomena of their own culture of origin. So, we could only use the distinctions between the schools in the sense of accumulations of typical methodological procedures and ways of interpreting phenomena.

Now, what is typical for which school? – Cross-cultural psychology uses instruments of a particular culture to measure phenomena in other cultures. Obviously, the typical cross-cultural researcher has a globalised background, so that these instruments have usually been constructed within the industrial society. Therefore, they reflect the way of seeing things and reasoning of the dominant culture's science. But it is only natural that an instrument is characterised by its constructor's background. If indigenous peoples carry out examinations of other cultures, their instruments can be expected to be each characterised by the respective culture, in which they have been constructed. But there is another thing that is somewhat problematic, though in rather philosophical respect. From a cross-cultural psychology perspective, it is quite common to understand culture as an independent variable (Eckensberger 2015). It is seen as a force outside the persons, although the persons themselves make up their culture. However, it certainly depends on the particular question, if this perspective has any debilitating effect on the data, on conclusions and further considerations. As long as we bear in mind that we only use the conception of culture as a source of influence in a simplified, abstract model for the purpose of having a feasible research design, there should not be any problem with it. It is all right if it elicits some philosophical debates; they might be quite fruitful.

More problematic is the individualistic versus collectivistic distinction, which has reached cult status in certain cross-cultural circles. This is in fact used like a password by which people signal each other their preferences. That would be fine outside science. But it is problematic when the individualistic versus collectivistic distinction is taken as a basis, unquestioned. And there is a lot to question. That distinction, in the cross-cultural discourse, usually refers to Hofstede (1980, 2001), who had carried out a study based on data collected among employees in IBM branches of 40 countries. Again, this is fine, as long as we keep in mind what kind of data we talk about.

Data collected among a certain sample of persons allow us to make points about that particular sample, and they allow us to make inferences about further persons only insofar, as the sample group can be claimed to be representative for those further people. For example, responses given by a randomised and sufficiently large sample taken from the population of a country would allow us to assume that the population of this country in general would show the same or a quite similar distribution of answers, as the persons of our sample do. But if that sample is preselected, then we cannot make such assumptions any more. If we only ask students, or only women, or only persons above a certain income, then we can expect the answers to have a bias, because attitudes often correlate with the social status, age group, education and so forth. And of course, the content of such a survey's questions matters. If we ask people about their political opinion, then we cannot make any conclusions regarding their preferences to be expected when they have to choose between pears and apples or bananas and oranges.

Hofstede (1980, 2001) presented several dimensions of culture, among which the individualistic-collectivistic dimension is the most popular one. In the underlying study, the IBM employees had been surveyed with items regarding their values, attitudes and behaviour patterns. But can IBM employees of, for example, a sub-Saharan African country be claimed to be representative for that country's culture? Of course not. Such countries are usually the results of colonialism, with straight borders that, on the one hand, cut indigenous societies in pieces and which, on the other hand, coerce indigenous peoples into unities which they often do not want and in which the weaker ones are exposed to the dominant ones. Therefore, even the question regarding such a country's culture is flawed. It is very common that in such countries, there are many, sometimes hundreds, of cultures, each with its own lifestyle – its own language, its own worldview, its own way of housing and its own dietary rules. And it is no secret that the upper classes are very much segregated from the more traditional cultural groups and often reject any relation in terms of cultural identity with the latter, although these traditional cultures embody the cultural background of the *nomenklatura*. The upper social stratum is very thin but powerful. Moreover, political key positions are generally filled with people from the same ethnic group, which therefore abandons traditional life even faster, widening the gap between them and the other ethnic groups.[15] Therefore, by no means can persons with a high-tech job in such countries be taken as being representative of these countries' cultures. The nonrepresentativity of the persons investigated is a major point of critique regarding Hofstede's concept. Any follow-up studies should be carefully scrutinised in this respect.

Having said that much about cross-cultural psychology, the delineations of the other schools can be kept relatively short. Cultural psychology has a strong focus on qualitative approaches. Some cultural psychologists even reject quantitative studies. Of course, they have their points, and this qualitative focus can be understood within a philosophical framework. Yet, when it is practised to an extent that the discourse is impeded, then it becomes somewhat questionable. After all, we do want to understand what culture is, how it works, what happens within and between cultures and how the processes of cultural change can be explained. As long as we are interested in what the others do for the sake of realising and of gaining knowledge, then we would not close our mind to other approaches, as long as they comply with academic standards. Striving after insight, we should rather consider to apply any approach when it makes sense and when it is helpful. Like the other schools, cultural psychology also has researchers in it, who are not too dogmatic. If they see themselves as representatives of that school, they might do so because they are very apt to work with their specific approaches, which are considered typical for cultural psychology. Because of their experience, they can find answers on ways that others do not even know how to pursue while at the same time being open for the most reasonable methodology in a given situation. Whereas cross-cultural psychology bears the comparative aspect already in its label, it is also customary that cultural psychology is applied focussing on single cultures. One has to admit, though, that even then a cross-cultural aspect comes to bear, as the academic researcher carries out his or her work as a representative of the dominant industrial culture. Yet, whereas so-labelled cross-cultural psychology relies on classical types of studies and only applies them in a culture-comparative way, it is not uncommon that cultural psychology designs an investigation especially for a particular culture. As cultural psychologists try to understand the systemic complexity of human behaviour in a given culture, they often do so, perhaps often without being aware of it, in ways that are typical for semiotics. And not only they do so, but likewise anthropologists, ethnologists, sociologists and others preoccupied with studying culture. Analysing social structures, like Lévi-Strauss (1949, 1958, 1973) did, or categorising weaving patterns and colours used in handicraft of a certain culture, as Greenfield (2004) did, actually means studying sign systems and sign processes. Therefore, these approaches can justifiably be called semiotic.

Indigenous psychologies are labelled so in plural, because there is more than one indigenous psychology. Meanwhile, there are a number of persons with indigenous backgrounds, who have become psychologists. Psychology as a discipline exists

---

[15] It should be noted that in some indigenous languages, the word for human being is reserved for persons of that particular cultural group sharing this mother tongue.

within the globalised context, historically rooted in European culture. Although these psychologists with indigenous backgrounds are fully integrated into this context and part of the global culture's researchers, at least some of them still know about worldviews, conceptualisations and specific approaches to analyse or categorise things that are typical of the culture they come from. These ways of handling things might overlap in some points with the ways of industrial culture's science (e.g. Kim et al. 2006). But they also add new aspects, which might entail unique ways of seeing things and thus lead to perspectives, which would not have been reached with the conventional academic strategies alone. However, all these indigenous aspects added to customary psychology come from different directions, so to speak, as each indigenous culture has its own worldview and approaches. However, indigenous psychologies are not just connections of different strategies to investigate collective human behaviour. Rather, they are amalgamates of globally customary science with a respective indigenous approach. In such an amalgamation, psychologists with indigenous backgrounds formalise their culture's particular approach according to the rules of the dominant culture's science or, more precisely, psychology. This then enables them to carry out empirical studies with a methodology that is accepted by the global culture's scientific journals. Otherwise, indigenous perspectives would hardly have a chance to enter into the academic discourse. Yet, caution is recommended regarding the labelling of indigenous psychologies. This pertains especially to the indigeneity of such an approach. If, for example, someone talked of Indian psychology, labelling it as an indigenous psychology (e.g. Chakkarath 2013), then we could swiftly point to the number of cultures in India, making clear that there is not *the* Indian culture. Aside from the fact that India is largely globalised, there are more than 400 cultures in this country, if we take language as the criterion. So, the mislabelling of psychological approaches as indigenous features certain similarities to the confounding of nation and culture in the IBM study mentioned above.

Whereas the labelling of a school or the type of approach refers to persons, who produce insight, other preconditions for reflecting upon research are clarifications of concepts such as causality and method. Theories generally imply a logical connection of cause and effect. In science, the investigation of such connections has become institutionalised and bound to defined procedures. Methods are procedures, by which researchers aim at working out the characteristics of an object of investigation. To a certain degree, it is determined by the object of investigation, which methods are appropriate and can be applied. Therefore, one's research should not be motivated by the wish to apply a particular method, which is fashionable at the moment. Rather, one should look at the object of investigation and at the research question and then ponder, which methods are suited best to yield answers to that question. Methods are filters between the object of investigation and the researcher (Clauß and Ebner 1979). As filters, they do not pass all characteristics of the object on to the researcher but only those that are of interest to the research question. However, we have to be aware that some characteristics of the object, which are represented by applying a particular method, might be exaggerated, while others might be weakened, and even other characteristics might only be pretended due to the particular method used, while in fact, they do not exist. We should, of course, always strive after applying methods that are as distortion-free as possible, which means that the relevant characteristics are represented in an unambiguous way.

Not all issues are eligible for empirical research. Especially such issues, which are based on unclear conceptions, are hardly or not seisable with scientific methods. When the issue itself is ill-defined, or when there are various opinions with no consent regarding the definition of the issue, then its investigation does not make much sense. It is necessary that there is a clear research plan, that the research question is formulated precisely, that the findings are documented systematically and that the collected data are of a nature, which enables their interpretation, which then allow for meaningful inferences and conclusions.

That does not mean that every investigation has to follow the customary scheme of formulating a hypothesis and an alternative hypothesis, then collect the data, evaluate them and finally decide between the hypotheses on the ground of the results. When linguists go to indigenous peoples to find out about the structures of their languages, their grammar and their vocabulary, they do not need to formulate hypotheses. But still, they have to observe other principles, especially regarding their own behaviour in the indigenous context. The same is true for botanists, who want to learn from indigenous peoples about plants and their use, for anthropologists or sociologists, who are interested in kinship and family structures, and so forth.

3.4.1 Qualitative and Quantitative Methods

There is a basic distinction between qualitative and quantitative data. Qualitative data are nonnumerical and rather descriptive, whereas quantitative data are those that are expressed by numbers. If carried out systematically, both kinds of data collection can be called empirical, as they are based on experience.[16] When we go into the field, we always have some experience there, and therefore, the qualitative aspect is always of importance. The collection of quantitative data would be something additional, if we decide for it.

If we want to answer the question, how to design a quantitative study that respects the rights and values of indigenous peoples, it is helpful to take orientation from the United Nations Declaration on the Rights of Indigenous Peoples, as it gives legal certainty by also addressing ethical aspects. The key concept here is that of full, free, prior and informed consent. This means concretely that an indigenous people, where data for a quantitative study is collected, needs to be consulted before, and the procedure, as well as the aim of the study, has to be explained. When doing so, the researchers must make sure that the explanations are understood. The study can be carried out when the consent of the indigenous people has been obtained.

---

[16] Greek εμπειρία, experience.

The data collection itself may not be carried out in a way, which could possibly have any destabilising effect on the indigenous culture (UN Indigenous Rights Declaration, Article 8, 2a). This also pertains to nonquantitative studies. For example, researchers should carefully ponder if they want to use technical devices and, if so, which could be acceptable. In many cases, the presence of technical equipment does not entail the threat of destabilising a traditional indigenous culture, because it cannot be expected that the indigenous persons will ever obtain our own such a device. But whereas, for instance, a camera as such does not pose a threat, certain pictures, that are shown, potentially could. As we try not to import any cultural elements, which could modify the indigenous person's self-presentation on the level of visual semiotics, and therefore refrain from clothing and even watches and sunglasses, it would not make sense to show them pictures with persons wearing those things. When we carried out our gesture study (Groh 2002), for example, we had to present the gestures by performing them, although they all existed as video clips, though performed by globalised actors. This necessarily requires that the gestures have been well trained beforehand, so that they can be performed in a standardised way.

When quantitative data is collected in indigenous communities, this can never be done without a qualitative research framework. You always have to be present in the indigenous context, and your presence has an impact on the people. Since these facts are unalterable, the question can and must always be for researchers or other visitors, *how* to be present. You are being perceived, primarily on the visual level, and therefore, you predominantly have to take all precautions that this does not have any detrimental effect. It is not possible to exclude the qualitative aspect by focusing on the data collection only. If you cannot ensure that you minimise your invasiveness, an alternative for collecting data from indigenous persons could be events in the globalised context, like conferences, in which indigenous persons participate. But then, you will still have to obtain full, free, prior and informed consent from the indigenous persons concerned, and you will probably also have to organise the data collection in cooperation with the host of the conference.

The rest of this book takes much consideration of qualitative approaches and procedures, anyway. But there are cases in which quantitative studies are of high explanatory power, not least because the globalised culture and its subcultures have their rituals, too, just like indigenous cultures. This is what humans have in common. In more traditional societies, persons have to pass particular initiations to obtain a certain social status, and in principle this is not really different from the rituals one has to pass in the global society, for example, to obtain a PhD. So, when some of our subcultures are only willing to accept a discourse that is based on quantitative data, let them have the quantitative studies. As research scientists, we would not be too beneficial if we would become dogmatic in the support of either the quantitative or the qualitative side. Rather, we would disclose ourselves from some of the academic discourse and furthermore prove a lack of flexibility.

However, if you have decided to carry out a quantitative study in an indigenous context, you have to put sufficient weight on all the qualitative aspects that are extensively treated in the chapters of this book. It is very advisable not to consider these qualitative aspects merely as a framework. You would make the most of it if you consider them as at least as important as the quantitative data, which you want to collect. This can be said for several reasons: For one thing, the methodological aspects of validity, reliability and objectivity are all very much supported by an increased understanding of the indigenous context with the particular setting and social system. The more you are integrated in the culture, though only temporarily, the more you can gain insight into it. And for another thing, as many indigenous peoples live in rather precarious conditions, in which they often have to suffer from being subject to general human rights violations or particular indigenous rights violations, the deeper understanding of the situation could also enable you to be helpful by taking a stand for the indigenous people and engaging yourself beyond academic profiling.

3.4.2   Validity

Validity pertains to the question, do we really investigate what we claim to investigate? For example, if we want to measure the temperature in a lecture hall, but before doing so, put up a fan heater, which usually is not there, then we would correctly be blamed of falsifying the result. Now, we could claim that the presence of persons has an influence on the measurement, anyway, as each human body maintains a core temperature of 37 °C. Each additional person would increase that temperature. That is correct, but if we claim to measure the air temperature under normal conditions, then we should specify that and say how many persons were in that hall during the measurement. But heating up the air first, without mentioning the heater, and then announcing the alleged temperature would not be correct. Likewise, if the thermometer or whatever more sophisticated apparatus for measuring the temperature is heated up itself due to some malfunction, then the result would not be valid.

Indeed, every measurement has an influence on the results. Even, when we move the apparatus for the measurement to its place, then we stir up air molecules and thus increase the temperature. However, that increase would be negligibly small, but it would be there. Now, someone might come up with an example like, if astronomers measure the spectrum of a distant star, they would by no means influence that spectrum, especially, as it might be some light years old already and therefore had been emitted long before that measurement took place. Although this is correct, astronomers still influence the data, because these results depend on the instruments used.

What does this mean for us now? – If we carry out any study in an indigenous context, then we are there, physically, bodily. All the psychological mechanisms are at work that have an influence on perception, interpretation and resulting behaviour. Due to the imbalance of dominance, researchers with globalised background are generally perceived as role models by indigenous persons. The researchers exert an influence on the indigenous culture by their mere presence. There is no reason to ask *if* we exert any influence. But we should ask *how* and to which extent we influence the indigenous culture.

Like in the example with the temperature and the heater, it does not make sense to exert any cultural influence when we investigate cultures, cultural issues or other things that are somehow related to culture. Since we are physically present, we can only strive for minimising our influence as far as possible. There is a wide range of possible influences. People can import words or even languages into other cultures, as well as particular food, architecture, technical devices or behaviour patterns. It has been shown in the previous chapters of this book that cultural elements can have very different effects when they are imported into another culture. If the other culture is very much characterised by hegemony, then imported cultural elements won't have too much effect on it. The people from the hegemonic culture will pick up those elements that they expect to bring them further advantages, and it is unlikely that those elements will then have a weakening effect on that culture. However, the relation between the researchers' background culture and indigenous cultures usually is quite different. If not reflected upon, aspects of hegemony might even be most prevalent in the researchers' cognitions. Indigenous persons, in turn, often feel subordinate, as they cannot compete with globalised effectiveness. Globalised persons can talk with the family back home, with colleagues or friends in different parts of the world with their mobile phone. Indigenous persons witness that the globalised persons are capable of communicating in such an enormously effective way with the help of such a little gadget. Even, when indigenous persons use mobile phone themselves,[17] they do not attribute it to their own culture, but by making use of this technical devices, they implicitly acknowledge the effective technology of the industrial culture. Indigenous peoples all over the world see aeroplanes flying, and most of them, who are in contact with the dominant culture, have reflected about the effectiveness of this means of transport. They also know, or even have made the experience themselves, that a little white tablet from the industrial culture can quickly bring down fever.

We have already addressed indigenous peoples' feeling of inferiority in the first chapter of this book. Unless you have measured it, or the persons have told you, or you have otherwise reliably found out, you do not know to which extend the indigenous people, where you are carrying out the field research, are affected by the feeling of inferiority. But you cannot rule it out; rather, it is to be assumed that this feeling of inferiority is substantially existing. This probability, in interaction with your own behaviour, is of relevance to the validity of your research, because, if you do not minimise all aspects of dominance in your own behaviour, or, in other words, if you behave dominantly, then you would contribute to the indigenous people's feeling of inferiority by reactivating those parts of the collective memory, which pertain to the aspect of inferiority. It would then no longer be a memory of past experiences, but they would undergo it presently, which would further consolidate this part of the collective memory. Therefore, as well as for further reasons addressed in this book, you will certainly try to turn off all aspects of dominance, try to be as unobtrusive as possible, minimise your invasiveness on the level of visual semiotics, try to show that you have come in peace, be friendly and communicate with all of

---

[17] Groh (2016b).

your perceivable behaviour that you accept and respect the indigenous culture. Anything else would contribute to factors which influence the indigenous people in a destabilising way and influence their behaviour accordingly, so that you could not claim any more that your findings reflect their normal behaviour, or otherwise normal characteristics of the community or features of the culture, like it would also be the case in your absence. In short, the more invasive you are, the less valid are the findings, especially in field research in indigenous contexts.

But we have to bear in mind here that there is no neutral behaviour. Reducing invasiveness does not mean that you should stand there with a poker face that is blank, with no interpretable countenance. Being friendly means to smile, to laugh, to win the hearts of the people and to open your heart to them. It is certainly not too easy to find the right balance, and the complexity of those intercultural, situational and interactional factors has certainly shied off many methodologists from designing and practising field research. Coping with practice is something quite different from coping with methodology at the desk, where you can reduce the research situation down to a formula. To give you an example, on the way to a Dani village in West Papua, we were walking along a river, when the situation became somewhat uncertain, because at the other side of the river, a group of children and adolescents turned up, who greeted us in a rather hostile way by pitching spears towards us. We did not know what was the reason for that or which previous event had incited them to do this. Fortunately, these were only their toy spears, which did not make it across the river, but fell into the water. We reacted naively, as if to some fun, by smiling and waving towards the kids. By the way, some years before, some foreigners had been killed in that area, and allegedly, parts of them had been eaten. So, it did not feel too comfortable to be greeted that way. When we arrived to the village after the conventional announcement by yodelling, there was the customary greeting, but it was not quite clear if the friendliness was only superficial. As we hoped to stay there for the night, this needed to be straightened. We had some tiny sweets with us, and it seemed all right to give them to the children, because this community was acquainted with the market in the nearest town, where they had such sweets. I had some qualms about bringing them, but the Dani guide, who accompanied us, approved it, and it was indeed helpful to ameliorate the atmosphere. I noticed a slightly jealous glance from one of the men, when the children enjoyed their candies. However, he certainly did not want to lose his face by asking for children's sweets. So, I jokingly shook this man's hand, and while giving him a conspirational wink, I secretly passed him one of the little sweets with the handshake. He seemed to be very happy with this solution, so I repeat it, and from then on, the tension was gone, and the atmosphere generally became relaxed in that community, and so we stayed for a couple of days in this village. This example shows that validity regarding field research, and in particular in complex intercultural situations, is not to be understood as something that is static. Situations, in which interactions and communication take place, are characterised by perpetual fluctuation. It is an interplay between each participant in the situation and the others. Like all of the situation's participants, the researcher permanently has to analyse the situation and make decisions with regard to the optimal reaction to the requirements set by the situation. Every moment implies a countless number of hypothetical reactions, each of which would determine the further course of events in another direction. The actual response of each participant to each situation is based on a preselection of possible reactions, which is provided not only by culturally standardised behaviour patterns and individual learning history but also by the relation between each actor and the other persons involved, as well as ensuing cognitions.[18] The dynamics of real-life situations are characterised by unpredictability. There are merely probabilities of possible outcomes, but as this pertains to every take of the interaction, field research validity differs from laboratory validity in the sense that a strict planning of the interactions would be counterproductive and actually hamper a valid outcome. Therefore, contrary to the dogma of previous schools, more recent approaches point out that in participatory field research, communication should not be planned, but that the researcher should let the communication come along naturally (Girtler 2001). However, this general framework does not exclude to integrate more predesigned units of research, such as structured interviews or even the collection of data, which could be evaluated quantitatively.

Commonly, there is the distinction of internal and external validity. Like already said above about validity in general, the aspect of internal validity pertains to the question, if really that is measured, what is supposed to be measured. For example, when you present certain stimuli as independent variables, such as colours or sounds, and you are interested in the response, which would then be the depending variables, then you want to be sure that those responses have really been caused by the independent variables, i.e. the stimuli presented, and not by any confounding variables, which could be any interfering factors. Usually, one tries to achieve the best possible internal validity by maximally controlling the situation, in which the stimuli are presented. But the more the situation is controlled, the more artificial it becomes and thus loses its relevance for reality. And this is the other aspect, namely, external validity, which pertains to the question if the findings of a certain study can be generalised and claimed to be relevant for any comparable but non-artificial situation. This means for field research that we should keep the overall encounter with the other culture as non-artificial as possible, and insert targeted research units only, where we can expect the outcomes not to be spoiled by interfering variables. Shadish et al. (2002) turn the tables by underlining that the causal interference, which are drawn from a field experiment, can be of high internal validity, so that the question should rather be, if the findings from field could be generalised to the laboratory research situation.

A further aspect of validity is content validity, which refers to the degree, by which the procedure fully covers the content of the feature or trait to be measured, and yet another term in this context is the so-called construct validity. This means the degree to which a certain research procedure really measures a trait or a feature in accordance to existing theories or the definitions of constructs. Explained from another point of view, one has to question the results' pertinence to the research

---

[18] Accordingly, this is accompanied by specific activities both in subcortical and in cortical regions (cf. e.g. Nash et al. 2014; Mauss et al. 2007; Hariri et al. 2002).

issue, even when one can be sure of internal validity and statistical soundness. Therefore, one has to keep an eye on the way by which the independent and the dependent variables are operationalised and thus on the relation between the procedure and the theoretical idea, in which it is embedded. Variables should always be as close to real life as possible; ideally, they should be natural part of real life. If construct validity is low, then automatically the generalisability is narrowed, which means that the external validity is also low.

3.4.3 Reliability

Studies are considered to be reliable, when repeated investigations yield the same results. This is why we also speak of retest reliability. We expect that a reliable method works independently of the moment, in which something is measured, and that therefore at different moments in time the results are similar or even identical, provided that other factors, such as the sample, with which the study is carried out, remain constant. Of course, it does not make sense for many psychological studies to repeat the same investigation with exactly the same persons. Remaining the sample constant should in those cases mean that the repeated measure should be carried out with a sample that is comparable and as close and as similar as possible to the previous one.

To compare reliability with validity, we can metaphorically think of a dart board. Reliability would be the precision, by which the darts are thrown. When you would not throw them precisely, then at the end of your turn, all the darts would stick on the board in quite a scattered distribution, while throwing them precisely would finally let them be together in a rather compact bunch. If we now bring validity into play, then this would be the trueness of your targeting, or, to pose it as a question, are you truly targeting at the centre of the dart board? Without that trueness, the darts would end up somewhere at the edge or even outside the board, never mind if they do so in a scattered way or as a bunch. When your throws are both precise and true, then they are accurate. Likewise, we speak of accuracy, when the study is both valid and reliable.

The application of the concept of reliability to field research is a matter of discussion. Basically, the point of this discussion is the question of how to define precision with regard to repeating an investigation. Some researchers prefer to neglect the aspect of reliability with regard to field research or to qualitative studies in general. However, this would be somewhat inconsiderate, because the results of field research might be relevant for eventual interventions that take place as a consequence of the findings. When the aspect of reliability is ignored, then this could lead to cases of false alarm, so that interventions would take place, which interfere with the indigenous people concerned and, in effect, destabilise their social system; or the necessity of interventions could be overlooked, so that the chance of intervention would be missed and the suffering of the indigenous community would continue or even worse.

The aspect of reliability is not only explicitly considered in quantitative studies, but it is also implicitly applied in standardised qualitative procedures. In non-indigenous settings, this is the case, for example, in psychotherapy, where usually a number of sessions take place to make the diagnosis (Bortz and Döring 2003).

When you investigate a phenomenon in a number of ascertainments, which yield quantitative results, then a regression line can be derived from the scattered dots in the graph. With the regression line, you depict the typical relation of variables. However, this line is only calculated from the actual results, and a common calculation of the accuracy of the regression line is the standard error of the estimate. When the measure, with which you carry out your investigation in your field study, is not sufficiently reliable, then the standard error of the estimate will be inflated. As a result, it will become problematic to deal with the means of the results, which you have obtained from the different groups. To enhance the reliability, you could do different things. You could increase the number of items, by which you investigate a phenomenon, or you could carry out the investigation with groups rather than with individuals. Due to the cultural requirements, you would have to work with groups anyway in traditional indigenous settings (see also Sect. 3.4.5 on Ethical Aspects), so that the advice in this case could only be to increase the group size. But the steps taken to increase reliability also have their disadvantages. To increase the number of items could also mean to increase obtrusiveness. Yet, this depends on the type of investigation. When the people find the study very interesting, they might even wish to extend it. For example, we are presently carrying out a cross-cultural study, by which we present standardised smells, each of which is encapsuled in something that looks like marker pen, so that each lifting of the cap brings about a surprise, and the indigenous peoples, who have so far cooperated in this study, have generally liked this study. In other cases, when there is less interest in the items presented, you will have to decide how to proceed, depending on the situation. If people really dislike the items presented, or find them boring, they will probably turn away, so that the number of items will even be reduced. As for statistical evaluation, the aggregation of persons will lead, on the one hand, to a group mean, which is more stable than individual schools, but on the other hand, the number of degrees of freedom is reduced (Cook and Campbell 1979).

To ensure the reliability of interventions, which take place in the fields, you might also want to carry out research, by which you assess this. For example, in our Tourinfo project, we inform indigenous peoples about their rights and options of protecting their culture against destabilising influences. When they are interested in applying measures to protect or restabilise their culture, which they usually are, then it is left to them, if they want to implement effective measures. Nevertheless, it makes sense to visit these communities from time to time, in order to see how they are doing, and, if necessary, to do some touching-up or to amend the intervention. For the assessment of such measures, you will have to keep an eye on the persons who are involved in the implementation, as well as on situational circumstances, which may differ between the times of implementation. These differences between persons and between situations can decrease the reliability of the intervention. To counteract this, it is advisable to standardise every step of the intervention. Although this often cannot fully be the case in complex field settings due to unpredictable influences, the data obtained by the assessment of the implementation can still be interesting in terms of analysing the reasons for the different outcomes. If you have studied the community concerned already before the implementation, then you have another additional moment on the timeline, as you can compare situations longer before the intervention, immediately before or at the time of intervention, and then, later on, you can do the first assessment, and so on. To have data about two different times before the intervention allows you to assess the variance independent of the intervention and to take this into account, when you assess the effect of the intervention (cf. Shadish et al. 2002, on regression artefacts).

3.4.4 Objectivity

The procedures, which are applied in a study to determine the characteristics of interest, should yield unambiguous results. The findings must really and fully pertain to the issue, or object, of the investigation. Furthermore, procedures should function independently of the question, which researcher carries out the study. Different researchers must come to the same results, when they apply the same methods. Objectivity is fully given, when the researcher has no influence on the results. Thus, objectivity can be understood as being contrasting to subjectivity.

As subjectivity refers to bias that comes to bear in the study due to the researchers' feelings, attitudes, preferences and disapprovals, such influence would debilitate the results. Objectivity of research, on the contrary, is the condition of being unbiased and without any of these subjective influences. Objectivity is indispensable for any scientific study (Scert Kerala 2016). It is clear that researchers cannot reach total objectivity, but this ascertainment should never be taken as an excuse, and we should always do our best that our studies are as objective as possible.

For field research in indigenous contexts, this implies the necessity to reduce any influence, which we as persons could have, and since the aspect of culture plays a pivotal role, special weight has to be put on disabling all cultural influence or at least to reduce it to a minimum. At the same time, it has to be taken into consideration that the indigenous peoples visited behave in particular ways, just *because* you are there; otherwise, they would behave differently. People behaving in other ways than usual due to the fact that they are being investigated is a well-known effect from social psychology. They might put on clothes or cover their bodies partially because they don't want to be seen as being primitive. Since this is an effect of dominance and feelings of inferiority, it should be counterbalanced by the researchers. Concrete examples are given in the next chapter of this book (Sects. 4.3 and 4.5.1). But it also happens that parents tell their unmarried daughters to stay in the hut, as long as there are visitors in the village, or even all young women are confined to either the hut or to fieldwork, so that you only see them very briefly, at the best, when the pass by. Furthermore, as an honour to the guests, it could happen that indigenous people put on some decoration, which they usually wouldn't.

By the way, one also has to be thoughtful with regard to the different ways feather headdresses are regarded. It once happened that a man, while we were in a Dani village, tangled up a feather of his headdress in twigs, so that it fell off. He kept on lamenting about this, and my automatic reaction was that I thought, so what, why does he make such a big deal about this feather? But then, it became clear to me that this mishap was at least comparable to a car body damage, if that would be an expensive car. Then, the owner would certainly also be lamenting. The Dani man was privileged to wear that particular feather crown. Not everyone is allowed to do so. You have to earn your right to wear it, which means that you first need to reach the social status, and for that, you have to go through the particular initiation rituals. The feather has a special meaning, and it is not easy to obtain. You have to know where this certain bird can be found, you have to go to that place and you must be able and have the right to hunt it. It might seem objective to neutrally note that this man lost the feather from his feather crown, and then he lamented over several hours. But such a seemingly neutral note would not render the impression that is necessary to understand the situation, which is embedded the cultural system.

Validity should also be reflected in the congruence of evaluations carried out by different evaluators. In qualitative research, evaluation is often done according to predefined categories. The more categories you have, the more probable it is that different evaluators will vary more with regard to allotting the findings of the categories. Consequently, objectivity of the study can be increased by reducing the number of categories. However, a reduction of the number of categories also reduces the information value of the findings. The objectivity of the evaluation process can be increased by formulating unambiguous evaluation criteria, to have several evaluators do the evaluation independently of each other (Clauß and Ebner 1979).

To enable other researchers to carry out the same study again, which will probably be the case in a different place, it is necessary to precisely and transparently describe the methodological procedure. When stimuli are applied, such as colours, smells, sounds or gestures, then they need to be standardised, so that the other researchers will be able to apply the same stimuli in their studies. When the stimuli material can be bought, the brand and all necessary details should be named in the publication.

For the quantitative parts of your field research, it is necessary that the external conditions are kept constant, and for such things as structured interviews, objectivity of application is ensured by the identical questions to be posed each time the structured interview is carried out. For all practical parts of the study, which prevail in field research or even constitute it entirely, the researchers have to adjust themselves, as well as the course of the conversation, to the subjects. Often, it is not possible to verbally stick to interview questions. Rather, they often have to be reformulated and modified, in order to ensure that they are understood to the best possible extent (Bortz and Döring 2003). When carried out during field research in indigenous contexts, interviews are situationally interwoven with the setting, and the researcher has to keep that in mind. "The researcher must adapt to the world of the individuals studied and try to share their concerns and outlooks. Only by doing so can he or she learn anything at all" (Fontana and Frey 1994).

There are several effects that are well-known to social psychology, which can influence objectivity. One is the so-called Rosenthal or Pygmalion effect, by which positive expectations can improve the actual performance of a subordinate person. In the original study, teachers were told by the experimenter that certain pupils of their new class where particularly intelligent, and as an effect, they earned better marks than before, which was explained by characteristics of the teachers' attitudes and special way of communicating with these pupils. The same effect could also occur in the other direction in the sense that someone has particularly negative expectations towards certain others. When such expectations become a threat and thus evident, this can then lead to the stereotype threat among the persons concerned, who fear that their behaviour could confirm the stereotypes, which are directed towards them. Furthermore, the reactions of the persons concerned could lead to either self-fulfilling prophecies or self-defeating prophecies, both of which are based on perceptual, cognitive and motivational processes that either have the effect that the expectation comes true or that the fulfilment of the prediction is prevented.

Since this book, as well as much previous literature, underlines the necessity of participation, integration and immersion with regard to field research in contexts that are different from one's own cultural background, it has to be pointed out that not only these special effects, but also more general effects of identifying oneself with the particular role, can have an effect on one's own performance (e.g. Shih et al. 2002; Ferguson and Bargh 2004; Wheeler et al. 2004; Aarts et al. 2005). If this is an enhancement, which helps us to understand the indigenous context and to gain deeper insight into the indigenous culture, then this is fine. However, since such priming of cognition is a rather complex and systemic issue, we should make sure that we do not get stuck, so to say, in merely seeing things through the other culture's eyes, because then, we could less perform our task of understanding, which involves the metalevel of reflecting *about* the other way of seeing things. Therefore, we have to strive for multi-tasking in the sense of dual perceiving and bicultural thinking. Again, the metalevel seems to be the only way of making us immune against slipping away and of ensuring that we not only are competent in switching between cultural roles but also to gain from having access to, and making use of, both perspectives at the same time, the indigenous one and our academic perspective.

3.4.5 Ethical Aspects

With regard to methodology, ethical aspects set limits to certain procedures, so that some forms of investigations or studies cannot be applied to field research in indigenous contexts. We have to accept that in the same way as there are limits of research in the natural sciences, set by limitations due to the natural laws. Researchers, who are only accustomed to laboratory research or to quantitative research in non-indigenous settings, often have problems to understand this. For example, one has to deal in traditional settings with the situation that data collection cannot be carried out with individuals, as one has to accept the communicational standard of many indigenous communities, which requires that questions are directed to, and interaction takes place with, the collective that is presently there. Concretely this means, that you ask a question, which leads to a discussion among the persons who happen to be there, and after they have agreed upon an answer, they will tell you. Giving examples, a researcher could perform gestures or show colour samples and ask the indigenous people how they would call it. Then, the gestures or the colour samples can be standardised, but you cannot even state the precise number of participants, because they come and go. Some of them might stay with you for all of the time that you ask those questions, while others only do so for a while. Furthermore, you can keep the situation constant only on your behalf, but you cannot control that or what the indigenous persons are discussing about the situation or about different things. You also have to expect that the indigenous people will laugh a lot, which you do not have to understand in a derogatory way, but rather as an expression of enjoyment. While it is easy to determine the sex of indigenous persons, you can often only estimate their age. When you then want to publish your findings in one of the distinguished journals, and your manuscript is given to a reviewer, who is not familiar with research in indigenous settings, then it might be rejected straightaway because of your statements of approximately so-and-so many subjects of approximately this and that age, etc. Therefore, you will always have to point out in such an article the particular situation of indigenous settings and the ethical requirements due to which the respective procedures have been applied.

Implicitly, ethical aspects are prevalent not only in the United Nations Declaration on the Rights of Indigenous Peoples but in many of the works that laid the path to it, as well as in many works that followed. But ethical aspects are also addressed explicitly, for example, in regional reports such as the one by Ermine et al. (2004) on "The Ethics of Research Involving Indigenous Peoples" regarding Canada or the "Guidelines for Ethical Research in Australian Indigenous Studies" by AIATSIS (2012). Basically, these are recommendations concerning the initiation and realisation of research, based on principles of equality and mutuality. It is important to understand that the indigenous peoples are partners in research and that all communication during negotiation and collaboration should equally flow in both directions. There should be full agreement on any action that is carried out during the research. It has to be made sure that each side completely understands what the other side is communicating, in order to ensure fairness regarding any agreement that is reached. Each side must also be able to reject any of the other side's intentions. These considerations pertain not only to preparation and realisation of the research but also to the outcomes and benefits.

It needs to be taken into consideration that indigenous peoples have conceptions of legality that are different from the industrial culture's idea of law, which is of European origin. With regard to field research, it is necessary to find ways in which the two systems can interact in a cooperative way. For example, the observance of both individual and collective rights is important from both sides' perspectives. Therefore, we should seek mutual compliance by clarifying all relevant issues with the individuals concerned and at the same time make sure that there is consent from the community. However, we also need to take account of the hierarchical structure that exists in many indigenous societies. Practicality, this means that indigenous persons' positions have different weight within their society. Usually, the elders are in charge of all decisions that pertain to the community. Any objections of the younger ones are considered irrelevant. But generally, the younger ones do not express any individual opinions, and at least in some cases, it might ethically be questionable when researchers interrogate them to find out about their personal opinion. Even though it might be difficult for the dominant researcher, it should be accepted if they don't have such a personal opinion regarding particular issues like their future work life. In many indigenous social systems, there is already consent about the future vocation of a child or young person, and by insisting with certain questions, one could irritate or even psychological destabilise that person.

From the indigenous rights perspective, researchers are allowed to visit indigenous communities, even if they are in a protected area, when these researchers have been invited by the indigenous community. Again, taking the hierarchy into consideration, it is in most cases not necessary to seek approval from each single person of that community. It is enough to be invited by the elders or, depending on that indigenous culture's legal system, by the chief. Although this might make things easier, it can at times be misused for political reasons. We once wanted to visit a certain indigenous community in Mato Grosso, Brazil, during the time when there was much international protest against a hydroelectric dam project, by which this indigenous people was threatened. Apparently, the Brazilian government did not want to have foreign researchers in that area. After several attempts of proceeding towards applying for a permit by first contacting official authorities had failed, and likewise the efforts via a Brazilian universities and colleagues, we tried to take the direct way of obtaining the chiefs consent, since an invitation by him would have been an equally legal way to enter the area, in which his community lives. After we had arranged an appointment with the chief through another contact person, the chief had disappeared at the fixed date, so that eventually, we gave up our attempts to visit his community. Days later, I was informed that the chief had been found drunk in a pub. Although at first sight, this looked like an unfortunate coincidence, there is a certain probability that in this case, he had been made drunk to prevent us from visiting his community, examining their situation and subsequently reporting about it.

Besides official recommendations regarding ethical standards of carrying out field research in indigenous contexts, there are various regulations of the researchers' national authorities, their universities, departments or faculties, as well as their professional associations. The advice to be given here is first to observe the United Nations Declaration on the Rights of Indigenous Peoples when defining the design of your study and then to carefully check, which ethical commission might be responsible and if any ethical clearance is necessary for the envisaged research. If such clearance is needed, then collate your research design, which is already in line with the UN Indigenous Rights Declaration, with the particular regulations of the ethical commission in charge, in order to avoid any difficulties.

Bearing the situation of indigenous peoples' everyday life in mind, our ethical obligations cannot only be targeted at the way we design our study and the way we behave in the field. By techniques of minimising our invasiveness, at which we shall look in the next section, we already take precautions not to destabilise the indigenous people and the respective culture, which means that we take into account the time after our visit. We want to leave them behind in the most possible stable way. This implies that we not only avoid any destabilisation, but that we also try to do rescue work whenever possible. We shall address that further below as well, since we should also consider to ensure cultural sustainability as part of our ethical obligation. Yet, trying to behave the best possible way in the field is not enough.

We usually do our research in order to communicate about that later on, by writing reports, by publishing articles or books and by giving presentations at conferences, as well as classes and lectures at universities. What will happen to the indigenous people after the disclosure of information concerning their whereabouts or habitual place of residence? We should be very careful about that, because it might incite many others, from backpackers to filmmakers, to invade that indigenous people's land, without caring about any violation of the United Nations Declaration on the Rights of Indigenous Peoples.

Such precautions that we should take are in line with the precautions that researchers from other fields of science take. Geologists' reports about deposits of minerals attract the attention of prospectors, mining companies and individual fortune hunters. Publications about rare species can likewise be disastrous. When particular plants are of commercial use, they might be collected without caring about any collateral damage.[19] Disclose of the last habitat of endangered animals can lead to their final extinction in nature. As for the damage brought about by filmmakers on indigenous peoples, there are many sad examples. In 1979, the film "The Gods Must Be Crazy"[20] was shot in Northern Transvaal, South Africa, and Namibia. The story is centred around a Coca Cola bottle, which is found by an indigenous San person, and which subsequently causes some confusion in the indigenous community. After its release in the following year, the movie became an international box office hit, with two sequels to follow in 1989 and 2004. One decade after the release of the first film, Gordon (1990) remarked about it: "Some films can kill. (...) This movie has substantially contributed towards ensuring that life in Bushmanland will never be the same again" (Gordon 1990, p. 6). The impact of the film on the San people is still an issue in the anthropological discourse (Thomas 2015; Hüncke and Koot 2012). Why is this so? There are several reasons. Firstly, we have to be aware that the shooting of the film is a rather sophisticated business. What the audience later sees on the screen is only what the camera records. But the major impact on the

---

[19] An interesting example of how to deal with endangered species in order to protect them on site and support their survival can be found regarding *Wollemia nobilis*. After this coniferous tree was discovered in Australia, the New South Wales National Parks and Wildlife Services had its seeds and seedlings distributed worldwide commercially while at the same time keeping secret the exact location of their natural habitat.

[20] Uys, J. (1980). *The gods must be crazy* (109 minutes). Bloemfontein: Mimosa Films.

indigenous community comes from activities behind the camera and all the other film crew swarming around in the village. All of them are focused on the job, and it is their common aim to deliver good and enough raw material for the cut. You can be quite sure that they wear jeans, independent of the climate, and of course T-shirts, that they smoke and that they swear when they pull the cables across the place. They don't care about indigenous peoples' rights, and they modify the scenery according to their own taste and interests. Secondly, there is a huge repercussion, as the audience is made aware of the particular indigenous group, which is usually depicted in a very clichéd way, which actuates the desire to go there and see these people. "The Gods Must Be Crazy" was an enormous incentive that stimulated tourism, with the result that the indigenous people had to make the bitter experience of the humiliation to be an exhibit for the inundating tourists. It is practically not feasible to train all these tourists as how to practice culturally sustainable behaviour and how to observe indigenous rights before they arrive. For many stakeholders, from governments through economists to the tour operators, any boost for tourism is most welcomed. There are very few exceptions of films that are set in an indigenous context and promote the indigenous cause, without destabilising the culture. "Emerald Forest"[21] does not portray a real community and yet calls attention to the abuse of indigenous women. In "Rapa Nui",[22] inhabitants of Easter Island actively participated in reconstructing the largely extinguished culture, which incited their general interest in the past, so that now even tourists are encouraged by Easter Islanders to participate in events that seek to revive the old Rapa Nui culture. As Wallace (2009) put it, "the people of an 'extinguished culture' have no alternative but to reinvent themselves" (p. 232). However, generally, detrimental effects can be expected from movies that exploit indigenous culture commercially. In the film "Tanna",[23] indigenous actors were made to behave contrary to their traditions. In their culture, unmarried girls do not touch young men. Yet, as the story, which bears a certain resemblance to Romeo and Juliet, required, the main actress even had to take the main actor in her arms. The global film industry dominates over indigenous culture, and indigenous people have to serve dominant peoples' amusement. As it is usual in such films, it is made sure that the standards of the dominant are not infringed. The playing children wear loincloths, and while many male breasts are shown, it is cautiously avoided to show too much of any female breast. For stills, and especially during her visit to the Venice Film Festival, the actress had to put some raffia before her chest. The result, again, has been a strong boost for tourism to the remote island of Tanna. Looking at these mechanisms, we have to consider that there is a fluent transition from ethnologists to filmmakers, and the output of both groups has an intersection that is manifest in ethnographic films (cf. e.g. Wogan 2006). Other anthropologists, though, as well as researchers from further academic fields, play a preparatory role for film business and for tourism. It cannot be denied that Margaret Mead's depiction of Samoa substantially contributed to the image of a South Sea

---

[21] Boorman, J. (1985), 114 min., Los Angeles: Embassy Pictures.

[22] Reynolds, K. (1994), 107 min., Burbank: Warner Bros.

[23] Butler, M. & Dean, B. (2015), 100 min., Studio City, Cal.: Lightyear Entertainment.

paradise – a deceptive picture, which later had to be decomposed laboriously by Derek Freeman (1983). The impact of that wrong image should not be underestimated. Quite different sections of the industrial culture had been influenced by it for a long time, directly or indirectly, be it the concept of antiauthoritarian education, the Frankfurt School or the hippie movement. When the findings from field research in indigenous contexts are popularised in a romanticised way, then the indigenous peoples are prone to become attractive exhibits for tourists, and the targets of film-makers, who further build on the image that has been created, and thus function as catalysts within the process, in which the indigenous peoples are increasingly exposed to destabilising external influences.

Therefore, when we have returned from field research and carry on, working with the findings and data that we have collected, then, in addition to this analysis, we should also carry out some meta-analysis. What are we doing there at all? Why are we doing it, and for whom are we doing it? What is the purpose, and what kind of benefit are we seeking? After all, it is not about impressing others with the exotic places we have been to, but about gaining knowledge that will help us to understand what is going on in this world. What shall be the use, and will it really be of use? By all means, we must keep away any consequential damages from the indigenous peoples. This is our ethical obligation. We have to consider the mechanisms that we set in motion, when we present or publish our results. Who are the recipients and what will they do with the information? What do we want to convey? Which details are necessary for that? In most cases, the exact location of the indigenous group that we have visited is not necessary to be mentioned at all, as most research questions do not pertain to an exact geographical spot, but rather to more general scientific issues.

Another ethical aspect concerns corruption. It goes without saying that we should never ever give up truth, correctness, veracity, honesty and sincerity, by accepting any personal advantage or endearing ourselves towards sponsors, supporters or protectors. Yet, in many parts of the word, bribes are daily routine, and they are just as expected as any official fare. Often, police and soldiers are barely paid, and the authorities proceed on the premise that they arrange for extra income themselves. When I was academic guest at a Nigerian university, and the department driver brought me from A to B, it was usual that we passed persons with guns in various types of uniforms, who were collecting some loose change to let the cars pass. Sometimes, when leaving one of those checkpoints, one could already see the next one along the road. Mao already made clear that power comes from the gun barrels.[24] So, there's not much use to discuss with these self-declared posts. However, I remember one situation in which I managed to avoid some extra payment. We had to pass a border in West Africa, and it was mandatory for everyone to hold an international vaccination pass with a valid certificate that was proving yellow fever vaccination. Many locals were passing this border without having that certificate.

---

[24] "Political power grows out of the barrel of a gun". Mao Zedong during a party plenary session in 1938   <https://www.marxists.org/reference/archive/mao/selected-works/volume-2/mswv2_12. htm#p1> (accessed 11 Aug. 2017).

The yellow fever vaccination checkpoint consisted of a little table, at which an officer with uniform was sitting, and everyone had to give him a special fee in order to compensate for the missing certificate. Before him on the table, there was a big book, in which he diligently noted down each of the special fees he received. When it was our turn at this yellow fever vaccination checkpoint, we presented our international vaccination passes. But this seemed to be something unprecedented to the officer. It was not part of his protocol. He said that we had to pay the special fee. I did not want to accept that and told him that we did not have to pay it, because we were holding the required passes certifying valid yellow fever vaccinations. The officer did not care about this, but insisted that everyone had to pay the fee. The discussion went on until I told him that I was willing to pay the fee, when he would confirm this on a receipt. The officer stopped and thought for long moment. Then he told us to move on.

3.5   Minimally Invasive Techniques

The previous chapters and sections have laid the foundation for generally understanding mechanisms of interactions between cultures. It has become clear that there are different types of cultures, that they can be categorised within a spectrum and that certain cultures are dominant towards certain others. It has also been elaborated how such dominance arises and why it is problematic. The knowledge of the underlying mechanisms, as well as of the international law perspective, enables us to formulate strategies of counteracting the destructive processes. Not only methodological, but also legal and ethical requirements make it imperative to avoid and to counteract any influences that can have a destabilising effect on indigenous cultures.

We shall now go more into detail in order to not only theoretically reflect about lofty goals but rather substantiate how to translate minimally invasive techniques into action in the indigenous contexts. The deductive chain so far is as follows: The most common cause of destabilisations regarding indigenous peoples can be attributed to the dominant culture's impact on the indigenous cultures. Destabilising indigenous cultures has a number of detrimental effects, including the destruction of indigenous social systems, violations of international law, consequential damages of the environment and, with regard to research, unserviceable data. We, as researchers, are part of the culture from which most of the influences originate that have destabilising effects on indigenous cultures. Therefore, we have to identify possible problematic ascendancies on our part and make sure that they are not applied. To prevent any invasiveness, which could possibly destabilise an indigenous culture, we need to analyse ourselves with scrutiny, in particular by regarding our habitual behaviour patterns.

Invasiveness is not confined to certain delimited acts that we should avoid. Most indigenous peoples of the world have already been subject to external influences from the dominant culture. Not all of these influences are a threat to their respective culture. But some of them are, and in many cases, we can even be witnesses of the decay of cultures that formerly had stable social systems, agreeable living conditions and a perfect interplay with their natural environment. It is up to us to differentiate between harmless and detrimental influences and then to counteract the detrimental ones. When an indigenous person accidentally has found an empty can and then uses it for storing some collected grain, this is not a big problem for the respective culture. But if some agency delivers a charge of several hundred cans to that village, the villagers will no longer produce those little containers from calabashes, and the knowledge of how to produce them will not be passed on to the next generation any more. For a transitory time, the use of the can will be a symbol of progress, of a linkage to the global culture, whereas those, who still use the calabashes, will be considered backward. By this, the traditional culture will implicitly be deprecated, and the use of the can will be a commitment by which the attractiveness of the global culture is underlined. As we can see, acts, values and assessments are interlinked and part of the dynamics of cultural change. Even though a can is just a can and only a minor tessera of the mosaic depicting the present culture, it is nevertheless part of the whole picture. If there would only be the can and nothing but the can, it would not even be worth to be mentioned. But as a matter of fact, the can represents the industrial culture; its use is associated with cognitions, affects and motivations. This can easily be witnesses when travelling through the Congo basin. There are only a few, unpaved roads, and people use the trucks that occasionally pass through as means of transport, densely packed on top of the load. Sometimes a passenger has brought along some canned drink or food from town. Once the can is emptied, it is commonly thrown away from the driving vehicle in high arch, as there is no garbage collection system. If this happens in sight of a settlement, where the road touches the local cultures, then the reaction can be quite instantaneous. While the can is still in the air, the boys, who see it from a distance, jump up and race for it.

The attractiveness of the dominant culture has the general effect that members of indigenous cultures often try to copy its features. Since this is a central mechanism of cultural change, we shall look at it in more detail now. Firstly, we shall try to find a socio-cognitive explanation for this phenomenon. Secondly, we are going to distinguish different cases of such copying behaviour. And thirdly, we shall discuss implications and consequences of this copying for both of the sides involved.

The socio-cognitive mechanism
Wicklund and Gollwitzer (1982) explain in their theory of symbolic self-completion (which we have already addressed in previous chapters of this book under various aspects) that of the goals, which people have, those goals, which are relevant to their identity, have particular implications for their behaviour. As long as persons have not reached their goals, there is a certain tension, resulting from the discrepancy between the envisaged self and the actual self. People bridge this gap with symbols of the identity they are striving for, as long as they feel incomplete with regard to the goal they have set for themselves. Hence the name of this theory. For example, it has been shown that undergraduate students tend to show off in order to pretend expertise by telling others about the high-ranking journals of their subject, which they

read, and they even create an impression by their appearance respective to their subject, so that they identify themselves visually with lawyers, businessmen or whatever they want to become. Interestingly, this impression-making decreases, the more they approach their goal. Graduate students talk less about the journals they read, and they prefer casual from business dress. As they have already demonstrated that they have accumulated the relevant skills, they do not need to show off with symbols, which only have the function of creating a certain impression. Symbolic self-completion is apparently part of a general principle, which can be found in human behaviour, of compensating some lack or shortcoming, and which becomes evident even on the political level. It is those states where the people has nothing to say, and which are undemocratic, that call themselves "people's republic of …" or "democratic republic of …". This socio-cognitive mechanism comes to bear, when people strive for being something different than they are and when they see a chance of becoming so. Marketing makes use of this mechanism when applying the lack-and-satisfaction strategy in advertising or the so-called stigma management when addressing minority groups (Groh 2008). The industrial culture creates the impression of being powerful and attractive.[25] This does not only happen during face-to-face encounters of globalised persons with indigenous persons. It also happens through mass media, not necessarily directly, but by creating a general consent,[26] which then is prevalent and reaches indigenous peoples through any contact persons. At the same time, this consent is part of the mechanism of cultural dominance, in which it plays a key role. In persons exposed to this dominance, directly or indirectly, a feeling of inferiority is created, and they try to escape it by completing the incompleteness, which they feel. To compensate their supposed deficiency, they use symbols that bring them closer to their goal of being complete. To become like the dominant, they copy their behaviour, or sequences or patterns thereof, as far as known to them. This socio-cognitive mechanism is the main force that drives forward cultural change and loss of indigenous identity. It is an automatic, rather than a rational process. Wearing jackets and long trousers in tropical areas is not comfortable when you know the freedom of indigenous life close to nature. However, the process can be overcome rationally, and there are indigenous, as well as non-indigenous, persons who reflect it on metalevels and consciously refuse to be part of it. There are indigenous activists, who advocate the maintenance of their culture on the local level; others are representatives, who are sent by their communities to the regional and national authorities to claim their rights, and again others represent their peoples regularly at UN sessions targeted at indigenous rights. Their efforts are supported by non-indigenous persons organised in NGOs, in the field of education, at the UN and in other political agencies. But reflecting those socio-cognitive mechanisms on the metalevel and then taking the appropriate actions require commitment and dedication. Whereas for indigenous peoples, such commitment is often a matter of cultural survival, it is of course easier for the dominant not to reflect, to let

---

[25] Cf. Mummendey (1990) and Mummendey and Bolten (1985) on the Impression Management Theory.

[26] Cf. Herman and Chomsky (1988).

the automatism go ahead and to continue enjoying their dominant position. The more important it is to observe the UN Declaration on the Rights of Indigenous Peoples, as well as ethical and, when we do research, methodological principles.

Types of cultural copying

Commonly, distinctions are made between different forms of cultural learning (Heine 2012). In imitational learning, role models are copied in their entirety. In emulative learning, the focus is directed on the use of a tool. These learning types can be found to be exerted not only by humans but also by animals (e.g. Boesch and Tomasello 1998). Both types of learning have their advantages and their disadvantages. In imitational learning, irrelevant parts of the behaviour sequence are copied and adopted, along with the relevant ones, while in emulative learning, the mere focus on the function of the tool might have the effect that some behavioural components, which might be of further use, are overlooked. The question, to what extent imitational learning is done in a rather reflected or rather unreflected way, is a matter of discussion (Csibra 2007; Froese and Leavens 2014). However, it seems to be unique to humans to look for prestigious models in order to copy their behaviour (Cheng et al. 2013).

Knowing these mechanisms is relevant for the research methodology, which is to be applied in indigenous contexts. Being perceived as members of the dominant culture implies that aspects such as effectivity are attributed to us, which are connotative with prestige. We can hardly control the imitation mechanism itself, but we can control what we present for copying. It goes without saying that we should avoid any dominant conduct and demeanour. Yet, the mere facts of our cultural background and our ability to arrive to that particular indigenous place leads to attributions, which have the effect that we are relegated to being role models, even if this is neither intended nor approved by us. As we have thoroughly investigated in Chap. 2 of this book, imitability applies to anything that we perceivably do. Especially striking is the behaviour pattern of shrouding our bodies, which is particularly characteristic for our culture. Even, if we cloak certain parts only, but that happens on a systematic and regular basis, then we point out that we consider it to be important that these parts are veiled. The adoption of this behaviour pattern is not only identity-relevant, but it also modifies the indigenous peoples' way of thinking, both on the level of rational evaluating and on the level of affective connotation.

What we are dealing with here is not the cultural learning that takes place within a culture, but it is a cultural learning between one culture and another. As we have examined in detail in Chap. 1, there is a disparity regarding mutual imitation between indigenous and globalised culture due to the dominance gradient. The globalised culture is regarded as being attractive and prestigious by the indigenous culture, much more than this is the case vice versa. When we compare cultural learning that takes place within a culture, with the processes that could be elicited regarding the imitation of globalised behaviour by indigenous persons, then we can name some differences in detail. Instructed learning, which is effectuated by targeted teaching, is, to a large extent, part of the learning processes that are mediated through language. "Teaching, high-fidelity imitation, and language are three linked abilities that work in concert to support cultural transmission in humans", as Legare (2017, p. 7877) put it. But this concertation, in the sense of a triangulation, is only applicable to cultural learning within one culture. Regarding the learning processes between indigenous and globalised culture, the weighting is quite different. As language does not play a prominent role in the transcultural communication between globalised and indigenous culture, emphasis is shifted to the cultural transfer through imitation. Ideally, and in accordance with methodological and ethical research perspectives, it should be prevented that any such imitation takes place at all; but since this is not feasible, we can only reduce it to a minimum, by avoiding to present any templates that could possibly be destabilising, be it for an indigenous person's identity or for the indigenous culture as a whole.

Copying the dominant culture is dangerous for indigenous cultures because behaviour that results from the copying is (like perceived behaviour in general) an act of communication, and what preponderates here are the self-definitions that are made by that copied behaviour or behaviour components. Every single indigenous person, who strives for imitating the dominant culture, is part of exactly the mechanism that can be described very well in terms of the theory of symbolic self-completion as outlined above. The cultural dominance of an external culture creates a feeling of inferiority within the indigenous persons, which they try to evade, as long as they do not realise the value of their own culture by reflecting the cultural constellation from a meta-perspective. The self-definition associated with the copying of behaviour patterns of the dominant culture implies the modification of the respective indigenous persons' identities. Cultures consist of individuals, and the deletion of indigenous identities eventually leads to the disintegration of the indigenous cultures. This is what we are witnessing right now worldwide. Yet, not every copied behaviour sequence ushers in the end of an indigenous culture. I remember a case of New Guinea, where indigenous people put up poles and stretched vines between them, because they had seen white people's telegraph poles with the lines. So, what? As long as this is all they copy, this is no threat to their culture. Certainly, behaviour patterns are not always understood transculturally. For example, there is a story[27] of the first Europeans, who reached a tropical mountain summit, where they emptied a bottle to the honour of their ruler back home, put a letter in it and stuck it with its neck into the ground. The local porters had witnessed this and from then on required this procedure from all following visitors as a necessary ritual. So be prepared if you go climbing. Children in Africa and other less industrialised places can be very ingenious. They bend wire to toy cars and carve a piece of wood to a toy camera, to imitate the tourists. However, such a toy has only limited impact on the indigenous culture, maybe even less than a can left behind by a tourist. The child uses that toy for a while and then forgets about it. Maybe a visitor, who thinks this is a funny object, buys it. But then, the introduction of money is a matter of its own; we shall look into it soon. Generally, closer a particular element is related to a

---

[27] I forgot where this was said to have taken place, but I probably took notice of it in connection with our ascent of the Ruwenzori – cf. note on Stuhlmann and the Bottle Camp in Bere (1952, p. 485).

person's self, the more relevant is the adoption of this cultural element to that person's identity. These elements can be classified and rank-scaled according to their relevance to identity. At the bottom of that scale would be ethnical features, as they can be copied only in a very limited way. Sometimes, body painting can be seen in East Africa that makes indigenous persons look like Europeans, with white skin and high socks. But this only works from a distance, as long as the colour is fresh. Anyone who sees such a painted person from up close knows that this person is not a real European. Next in the ranking would be alimentary habits, but the effects of copying them are also limited. Firstly, it depends on the availability of the particular foods. Secondly, not all food is tolerable for any person; for example, there are ethnic correlates of lactose intolerance (e.g. Shaukat et al. 2010; Khabarova et al. 2012). Thirdly, it is culturally relevant only while it is communicated within the social system; only when others perceive it, like seeing that person eat a yoghurt, it can unfold its defining, and thus identity-relevant, function. Further up the scale would be the use of goods that are produced in the dominant culture. But, similar to alimentary habits, the effect depends on the availability, and the use of those goods needs to be perceived and associated with a person, to be relevant to his or her cultural identity. The use of a dominant, especially colonial, language is relevant to a person's identity, but only to the extent in which it has been acquired. The way of housing is quite relevant – is it a traditional hut, or is it partly or in whole dominant-style? Habitation is a place bound act of communication. But when others meet the inhabitant in a different place, they might be unaware of this person's lodging style. Top-ranking in this scale is the bodily self-presentation. The way a person designs his or her body is something directly linked to that person. The way people show themselves defines how they want to be seen. It is a central expression and the most concrete statement about their identity. Looking at it from a different angle and taking the research line on social embodiment into consideration (Gallagher 2005), we can say that if a person's bodily self-presentation is changed, this has an effect on his or her identity. If it is changed profoundly, then this entails an identity change. We have to reiterate here that cultures consist of individuals. Therefore, if the identities of some individuals of an indigenous culture are modified, then this could lead to the destabilisation of that culture. Even this would be an infringement of Article 8, 2a of the United Nations Declaration on the Rights of Indigenous Peoples. If the identities of all members of an indigenous culture are deleted, then the result is the disintegration of that culture. As we can see, different types of transcultural behaviour copying have different types of consequences. The more the copied pattern concerns the identity, the more critical it is.

Implications and consequences of transcultural copying

If we zoom in to analyse the processes in more detail at the community level, then we find that not only the quality of the copied pattern but also the quantity of copying plays a role. Indigenous persons, who copy behaviour patterns from the dominant culture, modify their identity, and while doing so, they also change their position within the social hierarchy. By defining themselves as belonging to, or as being affiliated with, the dominant culture, those persons might then also look down at the others of the community, the same way as they had felt to be looked down at before by representatives of the dominant culture. In some cases, which are not so rare, the hitherto most respected elders have meanwhile lost their authority towards the younger generation, who is now styled like town people, playing with smartphones and chewing gum. This is only the surface. We are witnessing in these cases a transgenerational breaking-off of the passing on of cultural knowledge, of strategies to sustainably manage habitats, of language, of a variety of lifestyles and of cultural diversity. The consequences for the planet, for ecosystems and for the climate are devastating. Short-term consequences for the economy might seem to be not that bad, as incorporating these people means to have both new working and new consumer potential. For politics, people coming out of the forest or even cutting it down themselves are advantageous in terms of controllability. But these seemingly positive effects are at the cost of the long-term damages. You cannot restore the very complex culture-environment systems, especially not, when the knowledge is gone, when species have become extinct, when erosion and desertification have taken place, when the climate has changed and when the planet is damaged. Is it really worth it? Those, who profit from it, say: "Yes, and we don't care". It is clear that, seen in sufficient context, such a position is irrational. We, as researchers, are, as anyone, liable to observe the law and ethical principles, but moreover, we owe our role to not only follow methodological principles but also to reflect about how we could do, what we do, in the very best way.

Understanding the mechanisms and causal relations between identity-relevant behaviour, the modification of cultural identity due to external, dominant influences and the destabilising effect resulting thereof for the culture concerned makes it imperative for us not to provide any destabilising momentum to indigenous peoples. From the UN declaration, this is clear, anyway. But we are not only required to avoid "[a]ny action which has the aim or effect of depriving them of their integrity as distinct peoples, or of their cultural values or ethnic identities" (Art. 8, 2a), but also to ensure that indigenous peoples can realise their "right to practise and revitalize their cultural traditions and customs" (Art. 11). One way to deal with these requirements would be to simply deny that their identities would be changed, or to claim that they want this themselves, thus ignoring all the cognitive mechanisms triggered by cultural dominance. But such way of dealing would not be just, fair or correct. It would rather be a comfortable play-off, taking advantage of our dominant position, against our better knowledge. The only acceptable way of dealing with the requirements is to minimise our invasiveness.

At this point, someone usually says, then it would be best not to contact indigenous peoples at all and to leave them alone. This might be applicable to a few cases and to those invaders, who are not willing to minimise their invasiveness. These are not only and always loggers, settlers and militias. There might even be tourists and academics, who think that it is enough to accept indigenous cultures in an abstract and theoretical way, without practically translating their respect into action. However, an abstract conception of acceptance that only exists in the heads of those otherwise dominant persons is of no use for indigenous peoples. It would even be paradox, if they would ask the tour guide to translate "We respect your culture" into the indigenous language, while all other communication channels convey a different message. The most prominent is the visual channel; non-acceptance would be communicated by not integrating into the traditional way of presenting oneself. The auditory channel is also important; though it is clear that visitors do not speak the indigenous language, non-acceptance would be mediated by not obeying indigenous norms such as singing or, while approaching, to yodel or to be otherwise loud enough to be perceived. And there are more behaviour patterns by which non-acceptance would be communicated, such as sitting with the people on the ground or generally following their behaviour standards. For all those persons, who are not willing to integrate themselves, their appearance and their behaviour into the indigenous culture's tradition, it would indeed be better if they stay away from indigenous peoples.

Most indigenous peoples are aware of the global culture, which has spread rapidly in the very recent history of the world. They have been or are in contact with the industrial culture, either directly or indirectly. Depending on the circumstances, the dominance they are exposed to has unfold its effects to various degrees. There is resistance of the indigenous peoples. One result of this resistance over the past decades is the Declaration on the Rights of Indigenous Peoples. Despite this outcome, indigenous representatives continue to appear before the UN to demand acceptance and respect. The reason for this is that most indigenous peoples still experience that their rights are not fully respected. Most governments have not invested much effort in even informing their peoples about indigenous rights. The ongoing pressure of the global culture's dominance leads to the step-by-step assimilation of indigenous peoples to the global culture and thus to the deletion of indigenous identities and to the loss of indigenous knowledge and competencies to manage habitats in fully sustainable ways. This is, what many elders realise, why they send representatives to the UN, and what they try to counteract.

In this situation, the idea of "leave them alone altogether" is irrational. Actually, the tourism industry, settlers, extractive industries and governments would very much appreciate if all those who support indigenous rights would stay away. Because then, indigenous peoples could more easily be abused and displayed without respecting their rights, their forests could be cut down more easily, they could be expelled from their lands more easily, and the minerals of their territories could be exploited more easily. In all these cases, leaving them alone would not be an option, as it would not be compatible with our ethical obligations. One thing we have to ensure is that we do not contribute to the destabilisation, but that we counteract it instead.

Let us think, for a moment, not in terms of research, but in terms of tourism. If tourism agency A would withdraw from a certain destination, then the agency B would use that opportunity and take charge of that destination. For us researchers, the situation is comparable. If we stay away, then this might invite those who do not like witnesses around, be it those with extractive interests or even unscrupulous scientists. Although those who behave in destructive ways towards the indigenous peoples usually do not bother to ask them if they may enter their land, we should of course observe the indigenous rights and always seek the agreement and full, free, prior and informed consent of the indigenous peoples. This is not always easy, and sometimes, those who do not want researchers to investigate the situation of indigenous peoples, especially not, if they write reports to the UN, manage to keep them out. This is what we once experienced when we were planning an excursion to indigenous peoples in Mato Grosso.

As for minimising our invasiveness, the classification and rank-scaling of cultural elements' relevance to identity gives orientation. What we should absolutely avoid is the import of body-veiling standards. As we know that within indigenous cultures, who are in occasional contact with the dominant culture, even the few existing veiling norms are often the result of the external, dominant influence exerted on them, we should try to keep the extent of veiling below the actual extent practised. At least, it should be not more than that. But since in most, if not all, cases, veiling norms have been induced into indigenous cultures, it is advisable to keep the extent smaller or not to cover at all, in order to observe Article 11 of the UN declaration, which grants the indigenous peoples' right to revitalise their culture. Especially, as they usually receive dominant input that pushes them into one direction only, namely, towards the globalised covering norms, it is our obligation to counterbalance this pressure. Such would be the obligation of all representatives of the global culture, anyway, as it is our culture that is responsible for all the threats, suffering, destabilisation and destruction of indigenous cultures. But as scientists, we should be good examples, as we are aware of this in a particular way, reflecting things from a metalevel and knowing about the positive chances that we have as role models.

The rank scale of cultural elements, which result from behaviour patterns and therefore are often associated with objects, also gives us orientation with regard to further, not top-ranking positions on the scale. It is clear that we speak another language than indigenous peoples, and that in most cases, our physical appearance, like the colour of our skin, hair and eyes, is different. When, as mentioned, young indigenous men in East Africa imitate white people with body painting, then this certainly has a humorous aspect. Also, when indigenous peoples see a camera or other technical gadgets, this is not automatically a threat to their culture. They will probably never be able to afford such a camera themselves, unless they change cultures. We must admit that they would have the right to do so. Only, if it happens, it must be the result of free choice. But at the moment, there is no such free choice; as for indigenous peoples, their whole life situation is characterised by the pressure of cultural dominance. The decisions, which individuals make under such pressure, are actually attempts to escape from the intolerable situation.

We had mentioned above the case that a tourist might buy a toy camera, carved from wood, or a toy car from an indigenous child, and this brought the problem of money into our focus. Practically speaking, should we give money to traditionally living indigenous peoples? As far as possible, it should be avoided. Sometimes, it is not avoidable, because the indigenous people have already become used to demanding money from strangers, or the intermediary tour guides have accustomed the indigenous people to a share. Nevertheless, the indigenous peoples are usually short-changed by the tour guides. Since they are not too acquainted with the economic system, indigenous peoples often do not have a conception of a price-value ratio as it is common in the global culture. This is true in both directions. They might ask fancy prices for handicrafts, but they also are preyed upon by others. When we were with the Bambuti pygmies in the eastern Congo basin, we found out that a pineapple they had given to us was from a nearby Bantu farm but that they had to do such a great amount of work for the farmer for a single pineapple that was absolutely disproportionate for the worth of that fruit.

One way to circumvent the entanglement of indigenous peoples into the monetary system is to bring presents instead of paying for one's stay and to swap instead of buying things. But here again, the same cautionary rules come to bear, which we shall address in the next chapter of this book (Sect. 4.5.1, on Practical Aspects).

With regard to ethics, it is not enough to minimise one's own invasiveness. Once we know about the destructive mechanisms, we can and should help the indigenous peoples to assert themselves and ensure the observance of their rights. It is clear, from ethical, legal and methodological requirements, that we may not be invasive towards an indigenous culture. But what does that mean in detail? Reducing one's invasiveness to a minimum – what is the measure for this? We shall look at this in the next two sections.

3.5.1 Total Immersion

The term immersion is actually a metaphor, which is used to describe field research techniques, by which researchers put themselves fully inside a cultural setting in order to gain knowledge about that context in the best possible way (Mason 2002). From the perspective of system theory, there are then no longer two communicating systems, but an immersed researcher has become part of the contextual system. Total immersion is a popular concept among ethnomusicologists (e.g. Kippen 2008), as well as in feminist qualitative research (cf. Punch 1994; Kempskie 2005). There are criticists of the theoretical concept of a field (cf. Amit 2000), who also question the technique of immersion, but they consistently understand immersion in the sense of resorting in a cultural setting for an extended period of time. But total immersion is not necessarily linked to long-term stays in indigenous communities. It can be practised just as well during shorter visits to indigenous peoples, which is even to be preferred and advisable due to the aspect of the paramount principle of minimising the invasiveness.

The usage of the combined term total immersion points out the necessity to reduce any apparent semiotic separation between the researchers in the context as far as possible. As already shown in the second chapter of this book, this particularly pertains to visual semiotics. By way of our bodily self-presentation, we make two pivotal definitions, which are (1) how we want to be seen and (2) how we relate ourselves to the context. These two aspects are linked to each other, but they are to be separated as it is possible, in principle, to maintain the definition of how we want to be seen, across contexts, and in disregard of effects on our relation to the context. For example, there are persons who compulsively wear suits and ties, even when the context does not require so. And there are others who refuse to ever wear a suit, let alone a tie, thus marginalising themselves by disregarding rituals of the globalised culture. In these cases, immersion remains incomplete; it is not total.

While these two examples pertain to cross-subcultural situations of the global culture, let us now take a look at cross-cultural situations. When such situations exist in the sense of contrasting encounters of persons from different ends of the cultural spectrum,[28] then again, we can differentiate between persons from the cooler part of the spectrum immersing into the warmer part and vice versa. At this point, effects of cultural dominance become very evident. Due to their feeling of inferiority, persons from the cooler part try to emerge totally into warmer contexts, whereas persons from warmer parts, who go to cooler contexts, often do not care about adaptation at all, even though they then remain but alien elements. The reason for this is that the cooler persons expect humiliation from the warmer contexts, while the warmer persons feel superior to a cooler context. This automatic behaviour is not determined by the absolute position of the involved parties on the spectrum, but it is determined by their relative position with regard to each other. Contrast is not only given when persons from the far ends of the spectrum meet. It is already given when an indigenous person goes to the nearest town or when a globalised person goes to a less globalised context. In both cases of such automatisms, the process of globalisation, which goes along with the deletion of indigenous culture and the industrialisation of formally natural contexts, is further fostered and pushed forward. The whole globalisation actually consists of many of those micro-processes.

Since these are automatisms, total immersion of globalised researchers into indigenous contexts requires the researchers' conscious self-control and regulation of their own behaviour, especially of their visual self-presentation. This conscious adaptation is practised in consequence of the knowledge of cultural dominance with its imbalance of mutual influence and the potential effects.

Lest we think that such insight was academic privilege, it has to be pointed out that the deletion of indigenous culture caused by visual elements from the dominant culture is exactly what indigenous chiefs and elders refer to and criticise. They do not only do so with words, but chiefs of indigenous communities in the Pacific region refuse visitors to appear in their globalised dress, and even the common people of the Swazi and Zulu refuse visitors to participate in their traditional mass assemblies, when these visitors keep on their clothes. On Easter Island, visitors are encouraged to take off their dress and actively participate in the parade, which is part of the cultural revitalisation. In a meeting of indigenous representatives with representatives of globalised organisations in Brazil, where the problem of indigenous culture being deleted by globalised culture was addressed, Tacumã[29] of the Kamayurá made these worrisome processes very clear by appearing fully naked (Morais 2004).

---

[28] The concept of the cultural spectrum has been explained in Chapter 1 of this book.

[29] Tacumã died in 2014 <https://socioambiental.org/pt-br/blog/blog-do-isa/o-adeus-de-takuma> (accessed 26 Oct. 2017).

If the situation was very simple, one could say, the indigenous culture uses a certain set of cultural elements, and the researcher, while being in that context, only uses elements that are exactly from that culture's set and not even a single different element. But that is not feasible. Starting with physiognomy, researchers usually are equipped with different genes, so that they look differently – the skin, the hair, the eyes as well as bodily shapes are outside the range that prevails in the respective culture. Then, the language cannot be adopted in the same way as one can adopt less complex behaviour patterns. Yet, physiognomy and language are not really problematic. It is commonplace for most indigenous peoples that persons from a different community with different genetic background look differently and that persons from other places speak differently. But this cannot be taken as an excuse not to do what is possible. The adaptation to the extent that is achievable is an act of communication. Total immersion does not just pertain to the simple physical state of being there. It is a process of interaction, by which respect is communicated and acceptance is achieved. Making compromise here can be detrimental, because it symbolises reluctance and thus lack of full acceptance towards the cultural context. If, for example, globalised clothes are taken off except for a bra, then this is an act of communication by which the importance of a dominant taboo is underlined, and the induction of this taboo then has destabilising effects, as mechanisms of social embodiment, cognition, emotion and social coherence are triggered. But what to do, when the indigenous people are wearing a particular type of loincloth, and you are not in the possession of exactly such a loincloth? Well, the point here is that a particular body zone is covered and that this taboo should not be expanded. When you cover not more than this, with whatever material, then you signal your orientation towards their present standard. In an indigenous village, which has some contact to the dominant culture, you can often find various degrees of body covering. While the older ones appear more traditional, younger ones often already wear shorts and T-shirts. When you orientate yourself towards the most traditional members of the community, you are on the safe side because then, on the one hand, you do not participate in pushing those people further into globalisation, and on the other hand, you will also be more accepted by the elders, and this is very important in these hierarchically structured societies. However, the extent of body covering,[30] which you find in an indigenous village, is often only the way, in which the indigenous community present themselves towards non-members. This can be maintained for long periods of time or even become a permanent façade. Researchers, who think that they immerse completely by orientating themselves towards the present state, without knowing that this only is a façade, actually cement this façade, when they stay there for an extended time, because then, the people become used to it and are thus separated from their tradition. Therefore, it is safer for the maintenance of the traditional indigenous culture, if you stay below the actual extent of covering, as you find it, and you can gradually explore the lower limit. You might be surprised, eventually, that there is none. This is further explained in Chap. 4 of this book (Sect. 4.5.1).

---

[30] If you want to register the extent of body covering as a research issue to work on, the schematic registration by Jourard (1966) can be referred to, to which Morris (1977) resorted as well.

3.5.2 Rescue Work

There are several aspects that call for researchers in indigenous contexts to apply rescue work. Most indigenous cultures are already destabilised to some degree. A number of articles of the United Nations Declaration on the Rights of Indigenous Peoples should prevent us from banalising this fact as a normal matter of course, or as these peoples' free choice, and from turning a blind eye on the mechanisms of dominance with the social pressure being put on indigenous peoples. The UN Indigenous Rights Declaration clearly points out the obligation to protect indigenous cultures, as well as indigenous peoples' right to revitalise their culture. If we, the researchers, would just be bystanders, then we would let the processes of dominance and the further destruction of indigenous culture just go on, and thus also become guilty, as we do not do anything against it, although we could and although we know about the mechanisms. Like anyone else, researchers are obliged to adhere to the law, and they have ethical obligations. As we cannot not behave, we are always responsible for choices that we make in situations, about which we are aware and in which we are able to make choices. This pertains to general positions, as well as to concrete behaviour in the field.

Because the present state of an indigenous people already in contact with the dominant culture has an antecedent history, in which this people has been pushed some way out of the autochthonous culture, this state is not based on legitimate processes. Signalling that one accepts the present state would communicate the implicit message that it was all right that the dominant influences have brought the indigenous people to the state, in which they are now. Roughly categorised, there are three possible types of encounter:

Type A, globalised visitors display their dominant role by visually presenting the signs of dominance, directly linked to the bodily appearance and thus identified with themselves.

Type B, globalised visitors adapt to the state as it is, or in orientation towards those indigenous persons of the community, who are already the most globalised.

Type C, globalised visitors orientate their bodily self-presentation towards the visual culture of the indigenous people, as it was before the dominant influence.

Type C of the encounter is the type of choice, because only with this one, rescue work can be done, and only this one can be a counterbalance to the destabilising external influences. This counterbalance is necessary in order to enable the indigenous people to exercise their right to revitalisation as granted by Article 11 of the United Nations Declaration on the Rights of Indigenous Peoples.

With type B, this necessary counterbalance cannot be granted. At the best, the present state will be confirmed. But it is doubtful that this can counteract further destabilisation, as the globalising influence is immense, and indigenous peoples lack self-confidence. Their cultural self-confidence should be strengthened until they have reached the same level of it as the globalised culture. This is a long way to go, for which the second type of encounter would probably not be sufficient.

Type A would be fully destructive, as it disregards the indigenous culture and ratifies the global culture's dominant position. Superiority of the global visitors and inferiority of indigenous people are confirmed, as those visitors would behave diametrically opposed to the equivalent situation of indigenous persons visiting the globalised context, to which indigenous peoples adapt as a general rule by covering their bodies, even when the climate is hot. With type A of encounter, visitors would communicate their non-acceptance of the indigenous culture, which they probably see as entertaining exhibits.

It is out of the question that type A is completely unacceptable with regard to the behaviour of visitors in indigenous settings. Type B should only be applied, when there is definitely no more chance of revitalisation. If anybody is reluctant to apply type C in the indigenous context, then it is good if this person stays away from it. There must be other than rational reasons for such a reluctance, as it does not cost anything, it is not connected with much effort, taking off the clothes only takes a moment, and especially in tropical climate, it is much more comfortable and less energy consuming, as you do not have to sweat that much and your skin can pursue its natural function of cooling your body.

What you see as the present state of indigenous peoples, and what is actually the result of external influence, can take different forms. It can be a simple loincloth of industrially manufactured textile, which they have been ordered to buy for decency reasons as defined by the dominant culture. This is the case with the Emberá; men have been told to wear plain, while women have been told to wear flower design. In other cases, they have been ordered by the dominant culture to wear something more exotic. Usually, this is done in orientation to special accessory, which they only wear for particular festivities, but which they have then be told to permanently wear it as their allegedly traditional dress. But this is relatively easy to reveal. For example, when my wife and I came to a Yagua village in Peru for the first time, we were guided there by the chief of a Bora village not too far away. We went through the forest, and when we arrived at the edge of the clearing of the Yagua village, my wife and I waited there, as the Bora chief went ahead to announce our arrival. We could see the huts from where we were standing, and the Yagua could see us from the huts. After the Bora chief had received the O.K. from the Yagua chief, we were taken to the village and into the chief's hut, where we met the chief and his wife, sat together, had a long chat and agreed that we would come the next day to give a workshop on indigenous rights and carry out the olfactory study. Anyway, the chief and his wife had put on some scratchy bunches of bleached brushwood, both at their loins, and the wife in addition in front of her breasts. But we did not have this on and were bare breasted, and after they had realised this, they soon took the scratchy lopping off with some relief. When we came back the next day together with students of mine, and the Yagua saw that the women were bare breasted anyway, then the Yagua knew from the beginning that they did not have to do the brushwood act, so that the Yagua women and women of our team sat together, relaxed, and in a somewhat more authentic and natural way than with that staged exoticism.

We should not miss any chance to do such rescue work. Since representatives of the dominant culture are role models, we have to expect that our behaviour is copied by the indigenous peoples. This is why we need to make sure not to import any behaviour patterns that could have any destabilising effect to indigenous identities. But importing body-veiling norms would have an immediate destructive effect to traditional indigenous identities. This usually happens step by step. First, the loin region is covered, then the female breast, and this process goes on until the persons concerned are not discernible any more from other globalised persons. As many indigenous identities are already destabilised to a certain extent, we have to ensure that we do not destabilise them any further. Instead, we have to support the implementation of their right to revitalise their traditions. On the level of cultural identity, this means that we should use our role to reimport the former standards of bodily appearance. When these are copied by the indigenous peoples, then we have brought back to them what our culture had stolen. Our culture has stolen the nakedness from so many indigenous peoples, and therefore, we have the obligation to bring it back to them. But since the indigenous peoples' naturalness has been replaced by double standards and sexualisation, the reversion of our culture's interference has to be done very thoughtfully and carefully.

Of course, you always have to plan your trips thoroughly and reflect all these behavioural aspects well in advance. To ensure that methods are applied correctly, it is necessary to compose the team with outmost scrutiny. No one should participate without their competence absolutely ensured or with serious previous training and with certainty about their competence after the training. We shall address the issue of education and training in the next chapter of this book (Sect. 4.4), but what can be said already here is that the principle of full, free, prior and informed consent is to be applied well beforehand, even before any field training. Those who want to participate in the training need to fully understand what it is about. Some persons might then choose not to participate. But even those who have passed the training successfully should not automatically be eligible to join the team for the field research in indigenous contexts. Especially, when rescue work is part of the field activities, this implies the perspective of supporting the indigenous people concerned in making use of their right of revitalisation as granted in Article 11 of the United Nations Declaration on the Rights of Indigenous Peoples. Full reconstruction of an indigenous culture's bodily appearance, in orientation towards the situation prior to influences from the dominant culture, almost always comprises public social nudity as the standard and as normality. Regarding the members of the research team, it can be expected that those who are experienced with practising naturism will neither have had any problems during the field training nor with the actual fieldwork itself. However, having no problem with nudity at first sight could also have different reasons. Persons who, in their private life, are nudists merely out of hedonistic motivations could be very detrimental, and they could damage the whole field research. Before composing the team, the slightest hint of any sexual connotation with indigenous or quasi-indigenous nudity should be taken very seriously, and the persons concerned should be excluded. Any idea of giving them a chance to prove themselves in the field is absolutely out of place. Indigenous peoples are no guinea pigs, and indigenous contexts are not the place for checking out if team members would behave correctly or not. To draw a comparison, much effort is invested for training astronauts, and this is done so in order to optimise their functioning and the chances of their own survival. In indigenous contexts, research is always confronted with the question of the survival of whole, irreplaceable cultures. They are always at stake.

References

Aarts, H., Chartrand, T. L., Custers, R., Danner, U., Dik, G., Jefferis, V. E., & Cheng, C. M. (2005). Social stereotypes and automatic goal pursuit. *Social Cognition, 23*(6), 465–490.

AIATSIS. (2012). *Guidelines for ethical research in Australian indigenous studies.* (Revised 2nd ed.). Canberra: Australian Institute of Aboriginal and Torres Strait Islander Studies.

Aldrich, D. P. & Meyer, M. A. (2014). Social capital and community resilience. *American Behavioral Scientist.* Online version: <http://abs.sagepub.com/content/early/2014/10/01/0002 764214550299>, Accessed 27 Aug 2017. https://doi.org/10.1177/0002764214550299

Amit, V. (2000). *Constructing the field. Ethnographic fieldwork in the contemporary world.* London/New York: Routledge.

Bere, R. M. (1952). The exploration of the Ruwenzori. *The Alpine Journal, LVIII*(284), 483–495.

Boesch, C., & Tomasello, M. (1998). Chimpanzee and human cultures. *Current Anthropology, 39*(5), 591–614.

Bortz, J. & Döring, N. (2003). *Forschungsmethoden und Evaluation.* (Reprint of 3rd ed.). Berlin/Heidelberg: Springer

Chakkarath, P. (2013). Indian thoughts on psychological human development. In G. Misra (Ed.), *Psychology and psychoanalysis, Part 3, of history of science, philosophy and culture in Indian civilization* (Vol. XIII, pp. 167–190). New Delhi: Munshiram Manoharlal Publishers.

Champagne, P. (2013). Pierre Bourdieu, Séminaires sur le concept de champ, 1972–1975. *Actes de la recherche en sciences sociales, 5*(200), *Théorie du champ*, 4–37.

Cheng, J. T., Tracy, J. L., Foulsham, T., Kingstone, A., & Henrich, J. (2013). Two ways to the top: Evidence that dominance and prestige are distinct yet viable avenues to social rank and influence. *Journal of Personality and Social Psychology, 104*(1), 103–125. https://doi.org/10.1037/a0030398.

Chomsky, N. (1972). *Language and mind.* New York: Harcourt Brace Jovanovich.

Clauß, G., & Ebner, H. (1979). *Grundlagen der Statistik für Psychologen, Pädagogen und Soziologen.* Thun/Frankfurt on the Main: Verlag Harri Deutsch.

Cook, T. D., & Campbell, D. T. (1979). *Quasi-experimentation. Design & analysis issues for field settings.* Boston: Houghton Mifflin Company.

Csibra, G. (2007). Action mirroring and action understanding: An alternative account. In P. Haggard, Y. Rosetti, & M. Kawate (Eds.), *Sensorimotor foundations of higher cognition: Attention and performance* (Vol. 22, pp. 435–480). Oxford: Oxford University Press.

Daniel, B. (2010). Concepts of adversity, risk, vulnerability and resilience: A discussion in the context of the 'child protection system'. *Social Policy & Society, 9*(2), 231–241. https://doi.org/10.1017/S1474746409990364.

Eckensberger, L. H. (2015). Integrating the emic (indigenous) with the etic (universal)–a case of squaring the circle or for adopting a culture inclusive action theory perspective. *Journal for the Theory of Social Behaviour, 45*(1), 108–140. https://doi.org/10.1111/jtsb.12057.

Ermine, W., Sinclair, R., & Jeffery, B. (2004). *The ethics of research involving indigenous peoples. Report of the indigenous peoples Health Research Centre to the interagency advisory panel on research ethics.* Saskatoon: Indigenous Peoples Health Research Centre.

Eshel, Y. & Kimhi, S. (2016). Community resilience of civilians at war: A new perspective. *Community Mental Health Journal, 52*, 109–117. https://doi.org/10.1007/s10597-015-9948-3. Published online 2015, available at <https://www.researchgate.net/publication/283050154_Community_Resilience_of_Civilians_at_War_A_New_Perspective> (Accessed 27 Aug 2017).

Ferguson, M. J., & Bargh, J. A. (2004). How social perception can automatically influence behavior. *Trends in Cognitive Sciences, 8*(1), 33–39.

Feyerabend, P. (1975). *Against method*. London: New Left Books.

Fontana, A., & Frey, J. (1994). Interviewing. The art of science. In N. K. Denzin & Y. S. Lincoln (Eds.), *The sage handbook of qualitative research* (pp. 361–376). Thousand Oaks/London/New Delhi: Sage Publications.

Freeman, D. (1983). *Margaret mead and Samoa. The making and unmaking of an anthropological myth*. Cambridge, MA/London: Harvard University Press.

Froese, T. & Leavens, D. A. (2014). The direct perception hypothesis: Perceiving the intention of another's action hinders its precise imitation. *Frontiers in Psychology, 5*, 65. https://doi.org/10.3389/fpsyg.2014.00065. Article URL <http://frontiersin.org/Journal/Abstract.aspx?s=228&name=comparative%20psychology&ART_DOI=10.3389/fpsyg.2014.00065> (Accessed 1 Aug 2017).

Gallagher, S. (2005). *How the body shapes the mind*. Oxford: Oxford University Press.

Girtler, R. (2001). *Methoden der Feldforschung* (4th ed.). Vienna: Böhlau.

Glaser, B. G. & Strauss, A. L. (1967). *The discovery of grounded theory. Strategies for qualitative research* (Reprint, 2006). New Brunswick/London: Aldine Transaction.

Gordon, R. (1990). The prospects for anthropological tourism in Bushmanland. *Cultural Survival Quarterly, 14*(1), 6–8.

Greenfield, P. M. (2000). Three approaches to the psychology of culture: Where do they come from? Where can they go? *Asian Journal of Social Psychology, 3*(3), 223–240.

Greenfield, P. M. (2004). *Weaving generations together. Evolving creativity in the Maya of Chiapas*. Santa Fe: School of American Research Press.

Groh, A. (2002). Humanontogenese in kulturelen Kontexten – Gesteninterpretation in Südostasien. *Zeitschrift für Humanontogenetik, 5*(1), 66–83.

Groh, A. (2008). *Marketing & Manipulation*. Aachen: Shaker.

Groh, A. (2016a). Culture, language, and thought: Field studies on colour concepts. *Journal of Cognition and Culture, 16*(1–2), 83–106. https://doi.org/10.1163/15685373-12342169.

Groh, A. (2016b). The impact of mobile phones on indigenous social structures: A cross-cultural comparative study. *Journal of Communication, 7*(2), 344–356.

Guba, E. G., & Lincoln, Y. S. (1994). Competing paradigms in qualitative research. In N. K. Denzin & Y. S. Lincoln (Eds.), *The sage handbook of qualitative research* (pp. 105–117). Thousand Oaks/London/New Delhi: Sage Publications.

Hariri, A. R., Tessitore, A., Mattay, V. S., Fera, F., & Weinberger, D. R. (2002). The amygdala response to emotional stimuli: A comparison of faces and scenes. *NeuroImage, 17*, 317–323. https://doi.org/10.1006/nimg.2002.1179.

Heine, S. J. (2012). *Cultural psychology* (2nd ed.). New York/London: W. W. Norton.

Herman, E. S., & Chomsky, N. (1988). *Manufacturing consent. The political economy of the mass media*. New York: Pantheon Books.

Hofstede, G. (1980, 2001). *Culture's consequences* (1st ed.). *International differences in work related values*. Newbury Park/London/New Delhi: Sage Publications, 1980; *Comparing values, behaviors, institutions and organizations across nations* (2nd ed.). Thousand Oaks/London/New Delhi: Sage Publications, 2001.

Hüncke, A., & Koot, S. (2012). The presentation of bushmen in cultural tourism: Tourists' images of bushmen and the tourism provider's presentation of (Hai//om) bushmen at Treesleeper camp, Namibia. *Critical Arts: South-North Cultural and Media Studies, 26*(5), 671–689.

Jourard, S. M. (1966). An exploratory study of body accessibility. *British Journal of Social and Clinical Psychology, 5*, 221–231.

Kelly, C. (2013). *Using attribution theory to understand resilience for looked after children*. Ann Arbor: ProQuest.

Kempskie, N. (2005). *The sociologist: A dramatized exploration of feminist roles and research methods*. Paper presented at the American Sociological Association Conference 2005. Available online at: <https://my.alliant.edu/ICS/icsfs/Kempskie-TheSociologistADramatizedExploratio nofFem.pdf?target=ca07543f-e331-427d-8f47-7e6e056c0402> (Accessed 29 Aug 2017).

Khabarova, Y., Grigoryeva, V., Tuomisto, S., Karhunen, P. J., Mattila, K., & Isokoski, M. (2012). High prevalence of lactase non-persistence among indigenous nomadic Nenets, north-west Russia. *International Journal of Circumpolar Health*, *71*, 17898. Published online 25 Apr. 2012. <http://tandfonline.com/doi/full/10.3402/ijch.v71i0.17898> (Accessed 18 Aug 2017). https://doi.org/10.3402/ijch.v71i0.17898

Kim, U., Yang, K.-S., & Hwang, K.-K. (Eds.). (2006). *Indigenous and cultural psychology: Understanding people in context*. New York: Springer.

Kippen, J. (2008). Working with the masters. In G. Barz & T. J. Cooley (Eds.), *Shadows in the field. New perspectives for fieldwork in ethnomusicology* (2nd ed., pp. 125–140). Oxford, New York: Oxford University Press.

Knorr-Cetina, K. (1981). *The manufacture of knowledge. An essay on the constructivist and contextual nature of science*. Oxford: Pergamon Press.

Kuhn, T. S. (1962). *The structure of scientific revolutions* (2nd ed.: 1970). Chicago: University of Chicago Press.

Legare, C. H. (2017). Cumulative cultural learning: Development and diversity. *Proceedings of the National Academy of Sciences*, *114*(30), 7877–7883. Available at: <https://static1.squarespace.com/static/53485734e4b0fffc0dcc64c2/t/597a4879db29d6d5dc3658f9/1501186171924/cumulative–cultural–learning–development–and–diversity.pdf> (Accessed 1 Aug 2017).

Lévi-Strauss, C. (1949). *Les Structures élémentaires de la parenté*. Paris: Presses Universitaires de France (Engl.: *The elementary structures of kinship*. Boston: Beacon Press, 1969).

Lévi-Strauss, C. (1958). *Anthropologie structurale*. Paris: Librairie Plon (Engl.: *Structural anthropology*. Harmondsworth: Penguin Books, 1977).

Lévi-Strauss, C. (1973). *Anthropologie structurale deux*. Paris: Librairie Plon (Engl.: *Structural anthropology* (Vol. 2). New York: Basic Books, 1976).

Lewin, K. (1951). *Field theory in social science: Selected theoretical papers*. New York: Harper & Brothers.

Libet, B., Wright, E. W., Jr., Feinstein, B., & Pearl, D. K. (1979). Subjective referral of the timing for a conscious sensory experience – A functional role for the somatosensory specific projection system in man. *Brain, 102*, 193–224. https://doi.org/10.1093/brain/102.1.193.

Lindström, B., & Eriksson, M. (2005). Salutogenesis. *Journal of Epidemiology and Community Health, 59*, 440–442. https://doi.org/10.1136/jech.2005.034777.

Mason, J. (2002). *Qualitative researching* (2nd ed.). London/Thousand Oaks/New Delhi: Sage Publications.

Mauss, I. B.; Bunge, S. A. & Gross, J. J. (2007). Automatic emotion regulation. *Social and Personality Psychology Compass*, *1*, doi:https://doi.org/10.1111/j.1751-9004.2007.00005.x. Available online at: <http://bungelab.berkeley.edu/wp-content/uploads/2014/05/Mauss_SPPC_2007.pdf> (Accessed 26 Aug 2017).

Mayring, P. (2000). Qualitative content analysis. *Forum Qualitative Sozialforschung/Forum: Qualitative Social Research* [online journal], June 2000. Available at: <https://utsc.utoronto.ca/~kmacd/IDSC10/Readings/text%20analysis/CA.pdf> (Accessed 29 Aug 2017).

Morais, J. (2004). Os novos índios. Available online at: <http://planetajota.jor.br/xingu.php> (Accessed 29 Aug 2017).

Morris, D. (1977). *Manwatching. A field guide to human behaviour*. New York: Abrams.

Mummendey, H. D. (1990). *Psychologie der Selbstdarstellung*. Göttingen/Toronto/Zürich: Hogrefe.

Mummendey, H.-D., & Bolten, H.-G. (1985). Die impression–management–Theorie. In D. Frey & M. Irle (Eds.), *Theorien der Sozialpsychologie, Motivations– Und Informationsverarbeitungstheorien* (Vol. 3, pp. 57–77). Bern/Stuttgart/Toronto: Verlag Hans Huber.

Narayanan, A. (2009). Resilience, metacognition and complexity. *Journal of the Indian Academy of Applied Psychology, 35*(Special Issue), 112–118.

Nash, K., Prentice, M., Hirsh, J., McGregor, I., & Inzlicht, M. (2014). Muted neural response to distress among securely attached people. *Scan, 9*, 1239–1245. https://doi.org/10.1093/scan/nst099.

Olsson, C. A., Lyndal Bond, L., Burns, J. M., Vella-Brodrick, D. A., & Sawyer, S. M. (2003). Adolescent resilience: A concept analysis. *Journal of Adolescence, 26*, 1–11.

Punch, M. (1994). Politics and ethics in qualitative research. In N. K. Denzin & Y. S. Lincoln (Eds.), *The sage handbook of qualitative research* (pp. 83–97). Thousand Oaks/London/New Delhi: Sage Publications.

Ritchie, J., Lewis, J., & Elam, G. (2003). Designing and selecting samples. In J. Ritchie & J. Lewis (Eds.), *Qualitative research practice. A guide for social science students and researchers* (pp. 77–108). London/Thousand Oaks/New Delhi: Sage Publications.

Rutter, M. (2006). Implications of resilience concepts for scientific understanding. *Annals of the New York Academy of Sciences, 1094*, 1–12. https://doi.org/10.1196/annals.1376.002.

Ryan, G. W., & Bernard, H. R. (1994). Data management and analysis methods. In N. K. Denzin & Y. S. Lincoln (Eds.), *The sage handbook of qualitative research* (pp. 769–802). Thousand Oaks/London/New Delhi: Sage Publications.

Scert Kerala. (2016). *Anthropological research methods and techniques*. Available online at: http://scert.kerala.gov.in/images/2015/Plustwo/antrapology%20final.pdf (Accessed 28 Aug 2017).

Schachter, S., & Singer, J. E. (1962). Cognitive, social, and physiological determinants of emotional states. *Psychology Review, 69*(5), 379–399.

Schülein, J. A., & Reitze, S. (2010). *Wissenschaftstheorie für Einsteiger*. Stuttgart: UTB GmbH.

Schultze-Kraft, M., Birman, D., Rusconi, M., Allefeld, C., Görgen, K., Dähne, S., Blankertz, B., & Haynes, J.-D. (2016). The point of no return in vetoing self–initiated movements. *Proceedings of the National Academy of Sciences of the United States of America, 113*(4), 1080–1085.

Shadish, W. R., Cook, T. D., & Campbell, D. T. (2002). *Experimental and quasi-experimental designs for generalized causal inference*. Boston/New York: Houghton Mifflin Company.

Shaukat, A., Levitt, M. D., Taylor, B. C., MacDonald, R., Shamliyan, T. A., Kane, R. L., & Wilt, T. J. (2010). Systematic review: Effective management strategies for lactose intolerance. *Annals of Internal Medicine, 152*(12), 797–803. https://doi.org/10.7326/0003-4819-152-12-201006150-00241.

Shean, M. (2015). *Current theories relating to resilience and young people: A literature review*. Melbourne: Victorian Health Promotion Foundation.

Shih, M., Ambady, N., Richeson, J. A., Fujita, K., & Gray, H. M. (2002). Stereotype performance boosts: The impact of self-relevance and the manner of stereotype activation. *Journal of Personality and Social Psychology, 83*(3), 638–647.

Spengler, O. (1926). *The decline of the west* (Vol. 1: *Form and actuality*). New York: Alfred A. Knopff (Orig.: *Der Untergang des Abendlandes. Umrisse einer Morphologie der Weltgeschichte*. (Vol. 1: *Gestalt und Wirklichkeit*). Wien: Braumüller, 1918. Revised ed. Munich: C. H. Beck, 1923).

Spengler, O. (1928). *The decline of the west*. (Vol. II: *Perspectives of world–history*). New York: Alfred A. Knopff (Orig.: *Der Untergang des Abendlandes. Umrisse einer Morphologie der Weltgeschichte*. (Vol. 2: *Welthistorische Perspektiven*). Munich: C. H. Beck, 1922).

Thomas, R. (2015). "He wants to know how all those people got in there": Surveying the gods must be crazy through a post- and neo-colonial telescope. *Public Journal of Semiotics, 6*(2), 32–42.

United Nations General Assembly. (2014). *Promotion and protection of the rights of indigenous peoples in disaster risk reduction, prevention and preparedness initiatives*. Study by the Expert Mechanism on the Rights of Indigenous Peoples. (A/HRC/EMRIP/2014/2).

Vos, M., & Sullivan, H. T. (2014). Community resilience in crises: Technology and social media enablers. *Human Technology, 10*(2), 61–67.

Wallace, T. P. (2009). *Wealth, energy and human values: The dynamics of decaying civilizations from ancient Greece to America*. Bloomington: AuthorHouse.

Watzlawick, P. (1977). *How real is real?: Confusion, disinformation, communication*. New York: Vintage Books.

Watzlawick, P., Beavin, J. H., & Jackson, D. D. (1967). *Pragmatics of human communication. A study of interactional patterns, pathologies, and paradoxes*. New York: Norton.

Wheeler, S. C., DeMarree, K. G., & Petty, R. E. (2004). Understanding prime-to-behavior effects: Insights from the active-self account. *Social Cognition, 32*(Special Issue), 109–123.

Wicklund, R. A. (1990). *Zero-variable theories and the psychology of the explainer*. New York: Springer.

Wicklund, R. A., & Gollwitzer, P. M. (1982). *Symbolic self-completion*. Hillsdale: Lawrence Erlbaum.

Wogan, P. (2006). Laughing at first contact. *Visual Anthropology Review, 22*(1), 14–33. https://doi.org/10.1525/var.2006.22.1.14.

Chapter 4
Field Research in Indigenous Contexts

Abstract In this final chapter, the theoretical considerations of the previous chapters are applied to real-life situations. Thus, the perspectives gained on what cultures are; if, when and why they change; how they can become dominant; and what globalisation means now help to find the best practices for planning and carrying out field research in indigenous contexts. This is done on the basis of relevant articles for the United Nations Declaration on the Rights of Indigenous Peoples, which are examined under the aspect of our topic. Since comprehensive preparation for field research in indigenous contexts is indispensable, it is set out in detail how to conduct education and training, aiming at optimum transcultural competency of the researchers-to-be, as well as of others, who want to be fit for sustainable intercultural work. While preparing the field research, it is necessary to understand the semiotic functions of the indigenous people's descriptions in already available texts and pictures. Such descriptions need to be scrutinised critically, taking the relevant psychological mechanisms of their origination into consideration. Also, the socio-cognitive functioning of scientists is analysed, resorting to functional models of intercultural processes. From such meta-perspectives and a Theory of Mind approach, the role of the researchers' culture of origin can be taken into account with regard to their perspective-taking, the effects of their expectations and cultural distance, so that irrationalities can be avoided. Finally, practical issues are addressed, including healthcare, and advice is given as how to concretely behave in particular circumstances in indigenous settings.

Keywords Planning · Mentalisation · Functional models · Ethnography · Teaching · Intercultural competency · Expedition conduct

As we have worked out the legal basis and the methodological aspects in the previous chapters, we shall now address the issue of translating these considerations into action. We cannot do this without again bringing ethics into play. Like anyone, researchers should avoid destabilising other persons or their cultures – even without an Indigenous Rights Declaration, this should be clear. Nonetheless, researchers usually come from the dominant culture, and the indigenous peoples represent

© Springer International Publishing AG 2018
A. Groh, *Research Methods in Indigenous Contexts*,
https://doi.org/10.1007/978-3-319-72776-9_4

dominated cultures. However, it cannot be ruled out that there are some researchers who might feel somewhat uncomfortable to integrate themselves into the indigenous culture and to adapt to it. Provisions have to be taken to prevent those persons with such problems to, from their dominant position, give way to their feelings and blind out the necessity of minimally invasive behaviour.

Therefore, one section of this chapter is dedicated to comprehensive education and targeted training of those who are planning to do field research in indigenous contexts, as this is indispensable for any responsible preparation. The training of transcultural competency should start with theoretically addressing the three significant aspects – law, methodology and ethics. Then, these aspects should be applied to the perspective of cultural theory, so that the trainees can locate themselves within the transcultural constellation from a meta-perspective. Before going into the fields, the appropriate behaviour should be trained in quasi-indigenous settings. Equipped with the conceptual structure and with practical experience, the trained researchers should then be able to apply their competence in the field. There, the learning process will certainly go on, but for obvious reasons, this process has to start before going to any real indigenous context, as we cannot take the risk of destabilising an indigenous culture by dominant persons, who are not yet sufficiently competent. However, after having acquired the necessary competence and after having applied it, the field researcher will experience even a personal gain, have a widened horizon and appreciate the access to new spheres of human culture.

"You're a race of scientific criminals".[1]

The indigenous person, who said this, was Minik, an Inuit from Greenland. He had been deported as an 8-year-old boy to New York by researchers, together with five other Inuit. Most of them died, among them his parents, and so, Minik grew up as an orphan in New York. In 1909, at the age of 20, he was allowed to take a ship back to Greenland. At this occasion, he said this sentence, which should give us some pause to think about what we are doing at all and how we could avoid being or becoming a scientific criminal.

By generalising and talking of a "race", Minik was certainly addressing the whites and their culture. Instead of simply rejecting this categorisation as the exaggerated reaction of a traumatised young man, we should rather take the opportunity of self-critically asking ourselves which features in particular could elicit such a way of looking at us.

When Minik said this, his father's bones were on display at the American Museum of Natural History. Minik had found this out only when he was already 16 years old. Until then, he had thought that his father had been buried. But he had been fooled after his father's death, as the burial was a mere fake. He had to realise and face the truth that he and the rest of the group were not really seen as humans with the same dignity as attributed by the whites to themselves. Instead, the anthropologists of the museum, headed, by the way, by Franz Boas, Margaret Mead's

---

[1] Meier (2013); Chartier (2003), p. 184.

mentor,[2] saw the indigenous persons as living objects for their research. After the sentence quoted, Minik went on: "I know I'll never get my father's bones out of the American Museum of Natural History. I am glad enough to get away before they grab my brains and stuff them into a jar!"[3]

Not only Minik's story but likewise other perspectives taken, like the pseudo-external perspective taken by Paasche (1921), render the impression that our culture is preoccupied and even obsessed with measuring things. This feature has reached quite large dimensions by the Big Data Business of IT behaviour analytics (cf. Mau 2017). If this would just be a minor whim of our culture, others could live with it easily. But for many members of the globalised society, this obsession of measuring and quantifying is a belief system, in which they invest much more fervour than they do in religion. This trait already becomes problematic when it collides with ethical values, which can happen very quickly. As soon as the collection of data becomes more important for a researcher than respecting the people involved, even the dignity perspective, which is very central to the Universal Declaration of Human Rights (United Nations General Assembly 1948), might be ignored, and, depending on the circumstances, articles of the United Nations Declaration on the Rights of Indigenous Peoples could be violated. Minik's statement is not irrelevant to us. Researchers in indigenous contexts are much more prone to trespass against human and/or indigenous rights issues than many other scientists in different contexts. Let us, therefore, always strive after the best practices to avoid any mistakes.

4.1 The Scientist as a Psychological Being

As researchers, we want to carry out our studies objectively, unbiased and without seeing things through howsoever coloured glasses. But first and foremost, we are human beings, like the others, who are, in our case, the indigenous people. So, there are humans studying other humans. As such, we underlie psychological laws, principles, regularities and mechanisms, just as all other humans do. In order to minimise misperceptions, misinterpretations and misconceptions due to these functions, we need to be aware of them and reflect about possible consequences, scenarios and options.

Socio-cognitive theories are quite helpful in this respect. They serve very well the purpose of modelling interpersonal constellations, which then can unveil what is happening on the psychological level of the persons involved. Lewin's (1951) Field Theory can be seen as the primordial conceptualisation of the socio-cognitive approaches. To avoid any confusion, it has to be pointed out that the term "field", here, does not refer to fields like an indigenous camp or settlement, but to the cognitive field. Every one of us carries an internal representation of the world in his or her mind. When we perceive or think about something, we focus on particular details,

---

[2] Cf. Chap. 1 of this book (Sect. 1.2).
[3] Meier (2013); Chartier (2003), p. 193.

but we know that the rest of the world is still there, although that rest might be irrelevant to us for the moment. It actually does not even matter much if we are perceiving something or if we are thinking about something,[4] because every perception is transferred into a cognitive unit, anyway. As such, it is cognitively constituted in the same manner as any other cognitive unit that we actively deal with in our cognitions. In other words: the perception becomes a thought and thus equivalent to other thoughts, which do not result out of current sensory perceptions, for example, through our eyes or ears.

The cognitive field comprises both the externally induced and the internally available cognitive units.[5] The physical field, in which we are situated momentarily, is represented in the cognitive field, as well as other issues that matter to us, including goals and values. Our self is located in the centre of the cognitive field, and all cognitive units are related to our self. These relations can be positive or negative, and they can be strong or weak. When we are thirsty, and we know that there is a nice drink waiting for us to quench the thirst, we have an appetence towards this drink. When we go to take this drink and then realise a big tarantula sitting next to it, we might feel an aversion towards this animal. These two forces, appetence and aversion, counteract each other. Although the appetence towards the drink becomes more apparent and stronger, the more we come closer to it and the more it becomes present in our field of vision, the aversion towards the tarantula also becomes stronger, the more we approach to it. At some point, these two forces might annihilate each other, so that we halt and think about what to do next.

Actually, these positive or negative, strong or weak relations apply to all cognitive units that are present to us in our cognitive field. There are other persons, wherever they physically are, who are relevant to the situation in which we presently are, and we have ideas about what they are expecting from us, what we owe to them or what we want to do to impress them. There are commitments we have made with regard to what we want to accomplish. There are behavioural standards and methods that we want to pursue. All these factors push us and pull us all the time, so that our actual behaviour results from the "sum of the forces bearing on the individual", as Wicklund (1990, p. 123) put it.

If we unreflectedly give way to any impulse that then manifests itself in our behaviour, it might well be the case that this behaviour is not compatible with the context. Each one of us researchers was born into a culture and has been socialised in a culture, so that we have internalised culture-specific behaviour patterns, including patterns of cognitively valuing or devaluing, categorising and interpreting things that we see or otherwise perceive.

---

[4]Already long before fMRI studies, Farah et al. (1988) have demonstrated in an impressive EEG experiment that brain activity measured at immediate perception is compared with the brain activity when the subjects had to imagine the same perception. Thereby, although with quite different methods, she confirmed considerations that had been presented earlier by the philosopher Edmund Husserl (1948) on the constituting of the aesthetic (i.e. perceived) object (see also Ingarden 1985).

[5]At this point, it seems reasonable to leave unconscious processes out of focus. Nevertheless, they might play an important role (cf. Dixon 1971; Dijksterhuis et al. 2005).

To be prepared for field research in indigenous contexts, it is of central importance that we are aware of the different socio-cognitive systems and that we control our behaviour to an extent that we can deactivate those habitual patterns that are inappropriate in the indigenous culture.

Researchers are humans and therefore are subject to all socio-cognitive phenomena like anyone else. But it is also a socio-cognitive phenomenon that we can overcome those phenomena and are no longer subject to them, if we reflect about them and our roles from a metalevel. As long as we are aware of these mechanisms, we can decide about our behaviour consciously. Therefore, it is helpful to ponder upon these phenomena and the relevant studies. One finding from socio-cognitive research is quite important for any researcher, who is dealing with people: Persons, who are uncertain about their own competence regarding their self-defined realms, neglect the perspectives of other persons (Gollwitzer and Wicklund 1985). Consequently, those who are not quite sure if they should go into a particular area of research, or be a researcher at all, should first find out what really matters to them, and what their vocation is, before they go on with any other decisions.

4.1.1 Researchers and Their Culture of Origin

Research that focuses on humans and their behaviour wants to find explanations for the perceived phenomena and usually claims universality for the results found. This means that it is claimed that the phenomena and explanations are applicable to the human being as such, independent of any cultural background. But even with regard to relatively simple phenomena of visual perception, such universality has been proven by some studies to be wrong. To give an example, the Müller-Lyer illusion was seen as a universal. If we draw two lines, which are identical and therefore have equal length, and equip one line with arrow tips, and the other one with arrow tips that are turned around, then we have the impression that the lines are of different length. This phenomenon is explained by the fact that we are used to see edges in different angles and therefore intuitively understand each of the two combinations of lines as a representation of the three-dimensional space. For globalised laboratory researchers, it might seem plausible that the Müller-Lyer illusion could be explained by processes determined by the physiological structures of the human visual cortex. However, it has been found that persons from indigenous backgrounds are largely immune to the Müller-Lyer illusion (McCauley and Henrich 2006). When you show them these lines, they tell you that they are of equal length, as they actually are. Apparently, the phenomenon is something culture-specific. We, the members of the industrial culture, live in artificial environments with straight lines, right angles and even surfaces. You won't find such things in nature. If you look closely at two leaves from the same tree or bush, you will find that they are not identical, but each one has individual features. The standardisation of our artificial environment has made our perceptual system lazy, so that we can be fooled by the Müller-Lyer illusion. The leaves of bushes and trees are but a green mass for us, and we might find it hard to believe that indigenous peoples can not only see that someone has walked through the forest but also which direction that person went, how tall and how heavy that person was and if and how that person carried something, as well as the weight of the carried object. The ability to read such traces can be compared to our ability to read letters. We do this very easily and almost automatically, which, in turn, is hard to understand for illiterate persons. Especially the precise meaning attributed to arrangements of little signs might be hard to believe. Plarre (2005) has found during her research in West Papua that the attempt to copy the globalised person's behaviour of writing led to the drawing of lines, which roughly resemble the lines of writing, and that the indigenous persons, who "wrote" such lines, then acted as if they were reading them. The other way around, our attempts of participating in indigenous activities might leave similar impressions. But in each case, mutual acceptance is the prerequisite for an intercultural relation that is free of tensions.

As scientific researchers, we are conditioned to function within industrialised contexts. But when we do research in indigenous cultures and their environments, chances are absolutely high that our behavioural and cognitive patterns are inappropriate for these contexts. We see the indigenous people, and automatisms take effect that we have acquired in the context that we are accustomed with. These assessments are, very likely, fully appropriate in the culture where we are socialised. They are based on associations and probabilities, and they rely on a large database stored in our individual minds. We have had experiences with other persons' behaviour and consequences that we can expect, and we have been told by our social peers how we shall valuate certain behaviour patterns, if we shall appreciate or reject them. These are mechanisms that function in our society. But they might be totally inapplicable elsewhere; our appraisal and rating might be wrong.

This does not necessarily only be the case in very traditional cultures, which are very different from our globalised cultural background. We have to bear in mind that in the present progress of globalisation, the processes of change are occurring quite quickly, and they even become faster and faster (Baudrillard 1986), some of them increasing perhaps exponentially.[6] This concretely means that people with indigenous backgrounds might appear globalised, but this could only be the surface. They have grown up in a traditional setting and have then given in to the social pressure of the industrial culture by visually adapting their personal appearance to the global standard, and they might have adopted some external cultural elements, which serve as status symbols. To give an example, I once happened to be in an indigenous village near Gamboa, where an Emberá-Wounaan community lives. From there, you only have to row over by boat, and then you are already in the industrial world, where you could hop on a bus and be in the city in less than an hour. The hut next to the chief's hut was not used at that time, and so the chief invited me to stay overnight in this unused hut. In that community, they did not follow a strict post-marital pattern of patrilocal residence. The chief's wife had a hut on her own on the other side of the path, opposite the chief's hut, which was much larger than his and equipped

---

[6] It could be worthwhile to investigate these changes under the aspect of fractality. Such approaches, though, only play marginal roles in present theoretical research (e.g. Svane et al. 2016).

with some modern technical devices. During the day, the chief spent some time in his wife's hut, because that was the place where also the kids were and where the wife was cooking for the family. They had electricity and a TV set, and while I was sitting there, there was a children's film on TV, in which animals were speaking with humans. It seemed that the chief really believed that there were talking animals out there in the globalised world. I tried to explain that this was only a trick, with the audio track added to the pictures. But I had the impression that he did not quite believe me and thought that I was talking nonsense, because he could see with his own eyes and hear with his own ears that the animals in the film were talking to humans. I was very surprised by his conception, but the reason for this surprise was, in turn, my own conception. Meeting this chief, who was wearing globalised dress and who was acquainted with the industrial culture, with electricity and with TV, had misled me to the generalising conclusion that his cognitions regarding that film were the same as those of other globalised TV watchers. But from his perspective, the assumption that the globalised animals were really talking made sense. During his life, he had to learn many astonishing things about the dominant culture. As he knew mobile phones, he could be certain that it was not a thought-out story that the dominant people can talk over long distances with the help of little gadgets. He knew about other technical devices, and he knew about medicine and certainly a number of further impressive elements of the globalised culture. Since he had experienced that these are all true, it was easy to accept that there were also talking animals.

Yet, we cannot simply say that we may not apply perspectives of our own culture of origin to persons with indigenous backgrounds, who appear to be globalised. We have to take a closer look in order to avoid further mistakes. The younger people in the same village had not experienced the former traditional culture to an extent as the middle-aged chief and all the older people still had experienced it, which became clear from the different reactions, when we sat together in the morning and discussed about the options of maintaining indigenous lifestyle.

Generally speaking, we can escape from our automatic inferences and way of thinking, as well as from the behaviour patterns that we have internalised during our own socialisation and in which we are trapped to a certain extent, by reflecting them on metalevels (we shall go into more detail below in Sect. 4.2) and then consciously governing our behaviour. It might require some effort to overcome these automatisms and certain barriers set by our culture's behavioural standards, but when we reflect these things with enough scrutiny, then the difficulties dwindle, the more we rely on logic. Together with experience and routine, meta-reflections make consequent acting a matter of plausibility.

4.1.2 Rationality and Irrationality

We can often encounter irrational interactions in everyday life. Transaction analysis (overview: Solomon 2003) categorises types of communication in adult-, parent- and child-self. While the adult type of communication is rational, the parent type communicates from a presumably superior position, which entails the communication partner to be pushed in the inferior child position. Once such a constellation has been arranged, it is easy for the parent communicator to manipulate the other side. However, it is relatively simple for the one, who is prone to be pushed into a child's position, to exactly address this by saying, "Stick to the facts!" or "Be objective!" In other words, he or she takes the communication up to a metalevel, from where both communication partners have to look at it to identify what exactly is nonfactual or not objective and what would be the factual and objective alternatives. Whereas irrationality in everyday communication usually takes place in relatively small communicational units, indigenous peoples are exposed to irrationalities of the dominant industrial culture on a global, large scale. Here is an example:

Vitamin D (cholecalciferol, also known as D3) is vital for our osseous structure, as well as for the cardiovascular, immune and muscular systems. With an insufficient blood level of vitamin D (25-hydroxycholecalciferol), a person's risk of cancer and osteoporosis could increase. Unlike other vitamins, we barely obtain vitamin D from the food, but it is produced in our body. However, the precondition for this is that the skin receives sunlight, in order to synthesise vitamin D. This does not mean extreme exposure to sunlight, but rather indirect bright daylight or rather scattered sunshine. Due to the cultural practice of covering the body, a large proportion of persons from the industrial culture suffer from lack of vitamin D. In middle-aged persons, the lack of vitamin D could remain largely unnoticed, as severe symptoms, like those of cancer or osteoporosis, might only start at a later age. But lack of vitamin D could also cause mental health problems, such as depression. Often, patients are then treated for other causes than lack of vitamin D. As for the percentage of persons concerned by a lack of vitamin D, the views differ a lot in current research, but some assumptions go up to 50 or even 80% in the industrial culture. Anyway, there is large consent that vitamin D should be substituted (Pfotenhauer and Shubrook 2017).

The synthetisation of vitamin D is a process, which is provided by the natural condition of daylight shining on the human skin. Covering the human skin is an unnatural condition, which prevents this vital process. Due to the effects of cultural dominance, the cultural practice of veiling the human body is now being spread worldwide and implemented in other cultures, where the lack of vitamin D is increasingly becoming a problem (Khadilkar et al. 2017).

Cultural dominance is stronger than rationality. Indigenous peoples living close to nature do it correctly. Furthermore, those living in rainforests also have an environment that is perfectly suited for the human body's needs, because they have daylight reaching their skin without the sun shining directly on them. Actually, it would only be logical if we would learn from them. But this is not even taken into consideration. Rather, the environment, which is the world's best for the natural human body, is being destroyed, and we prefer to have our pharmaceutical industry produce vitamin D artificially and then take this purified chemical substance. Moreover, we are exporting both unnatural ideas – the one of covering the body and the one of substituting the resulting lack with industrially processed vitamin D – instead of considering to encourage these peoples to maintain their closeness to nature and to take them as our role models. Yet, cultural dominance works the other way around, by us being their role models, even if it does not make sense.

The benefit of indigenous peoples' social nudity goes far beyond the synthetisation of vitamin D. In the industrial society, non-sexual social nudity correlates with prosocial behaviour, such as social adjustment; happy and long marriages; low incidence of sexual, child and spouse abuse; healthy lifestyle; and support of sexual equality (Hill 1996). On the individual level, globalised persons, who practice non-sexual social nudity, have greater life satisfaction, a more positive body image and higher self-esteem than persons who do not practice this (West 2017). Here, again, we have to acknowledge that indigenous peoples close to nature do it correctly, whereas our behaviour should raise the question, if there is any connection between our cultural practices and the problems produced by the industrial, globalised culture. Since the present data suggest a correlation of lack of vitamin D, caused by the veiling of the body, with depression and other mental problems, and since they furthermore suggest a negative correlation of body covering with prosocial behaviour and well-being, it would be worthwhile to further investigate this interrelationship with regard to our collective behaviour.

So, how do we cope with irrationality? If we rely on automatisms, then we have to expect that the mechanisms of cultural dominance manifest themselves in irrationality. The only way we can counteract is to argue with evidence and with logic. This is not always easy and requires sufficient and plausible input (Frey 1981). Generally, it is useful to help those who are stuck in irrationality, to regard things from a metalevel, in order to enable them to understand their own role within the often very complex situation. For those who realise their own irrationality and who want to consciously overcome it, but still feel that there are some insistent hindrances, Rational Emotive Therapy (also called Rational Emotive Behaviour Therapy, REBT) might be helpful. Basically, in this approach, the actual state of the client is defined, then the state to be reached is defined, and then the therapist discusses with the client how to move from the actual state to the other in the most realistic way. When such persons, who are determined to overcome their irrational hindrances, would like to do this in connection with the field research education and training as described below (Sect. 4.4.1), the trainers should make sure that these persons have already made sufficient progress, before they start the training. Furthermore, the trainers might want to integrate targeted behaviour modification techniques (overview: Miltenberger 2012) into the training.

4.2 Meta-perspectives

Let us now look at some of the rhetorical strategies which people use, who are not willing to apply minimally invasive immersion techniques when doing field research in indigenous contexts. Actually, these strategies are simple defence mechanisms, which are well-known in social and cognitive sciences. One of the often applied strategies is *downward comparison*: the destruction that has already happened is used to justify one's own contribution to further destruction, with non-sequitur statements like "The situation cannot be improved anyway". Likewise common is the *diffusion of responsibility*; in this case, incompatible behaviour is defended, "because others do the same". Then, there is *devaluation* in the sense that culturally compatible behaviour is devaluated by denying any effect, accompanied by sentences like "That wouldn't change anything". Also popular is *denial*, by which the mechanisms of the destructive influence are denied. If, then, in the further discussion, the denial itself is denied, this will be a difficult blockade for an actual solution, as we know from psychotherapy. Irrational fear plays a prominent role. So, it is no wonder that we can also find *anxiety defence*: the idea of adaptation to, and immersion into, any traditional indigenous culture is associated with abasement and is, in reaction to that projected feeling, warded off with mockery and jeer. In this case, we can even apply Freud's (1905) concept of jokes to this quite interesting reaction. Freud reasoned that the unconscious tried to avoid conflicts, while at the same time trying to gain pleasure from a short-term easing of repression; by solidarising, people could use this mechanism also to oppose meaningful content. Sometimes, in conference presentations on minimally invasive immersion techniques in field research to indigenous contexts, even seasoned scientists, grown-up men, blush and giggle like schoolboys and are apparently unable to rationally reflect about the role of the body and indigenous nudity but rather disturb their colleagues sitting next to them, who want to be attentive, by nudging them and speaking to them. Furthermore, we can find *distraction*: culturally compatible behaviour is only exercised with regard to some rather unimportant points, which are then used as alibi, whereas, at the same time, destructive behaviour is exercised in some central points. *Mislabelling* takes place when some interventions, such as building roads or electrification, are labelled as "culturally sustainable", although they deeply destabilise the particular culture. Another strategy that can be found is the *blocking out* of the constellation of dominance; then it can happen that adaptation is rejected because it was "fake", because one didn't want to "give up one's personality", "simulate" or "play a role". It is well known in communication research that it is impossible *not* to play a role, and interestingly, the same people, who claim that they did not want to play a role, have no problem to avail themselves of unusual forms of self-presentation (Goffman 1959; Brown 2007), when they go snorkelling or diving in the sea, riding their bikes or climbing in the mountains. Apparently, these people do not have a problem with playing roles as such, but rather with the integration into the visual context of certain indigenous cultures. These traditional ways of bodily appearance have negative connotations to some globalised persons to an extent that the complete adoption of this appearance is considered to be rejected categorically. However, these reactions result from misconceptions, as standards are applied to indigenous cultures, which are not applicable in those contexts.

Theory of Mind

The theory that comes to bear here is the Theory of Mind (e.g. Gweon and Saxe 2013; Happé 2003; Meltzoff 1999), as it is often named, or also, depending on the perspective; mentalisation, as it pertains to mental processes (Fonagy 1999); or, more generally, empathy. What is meant by this is a certain capability that is characteristic for humans, namely, the ability to imagine what others are thinking, including their feelings, values, motivations and intended reactions. It means our skill to put ourselves in someone else's position and to see things from that other person's perspective. Of course, there is a wide range of accuracy of these guesses. When we have lived together with other persons, or maybe even have grown up in their presence, then we have learned from experience to predict these persons' behaviour, including their verbal communications, with a certain probability, from their preceding behaviour sequences. With regard to other persons of our culture, the probability might be lower, because we are less experienced with their behaviour, and therefore our guesses about what they have in mind might be not that exact. Nevertheless, as we live together in the same culture, where we share common standards, our assumptions are still largely true. Otherwise, many interactions in our culture would not function. There are several mechanisms supporting this. We are trained to respond to specific situations, in which we receive certain perceptual input, in a particular way. During our socialisation, we have internalised these reactions to an extent, which also include the performance of cognitive procedures related to these behaviour patterns. This goes along with empathy, as we condition each other, and we mutually show reactions that fall within the range of standardised behaviour, thereby further consolidating our culture's standards.

Perspective-Taking and Cultural Distance

Yet, the accuracy of our ideas about other people's cognitions decreases with cultural distance. Within the globalised culture, there are many subcultures, and already here, we can find various standards, which are connected to distinct cognitive patterns. Globalised persons with different subcultural backgrounds have problems to communicate with each other, or to imagine what the other person is thinking, and there is mutual misinterpretation of behaviour patterns. If we apply the Polysystem Theory of Even-Zohar (1990), we can say that these people are from different layers of the social stratification. For example, academics in a restaurant sometimes do not realise the communicational barriers between themselves and personnel. There, a scientist might make a joke, but the joke is too sophisticated, and when the waiter laughs, then that scientist does not realise that the waiter only does so out of politeness. To give another example, a story that enjoys some prominence is that of American soldiers, who had been stationed in England, where they flirted with local girls (Watzlawick et al. 1967). The soldiers said they were very much caught by surprise how passionate the girls were, but the English girls said the same about the soldiers. The thing was that both sides had different courtship patterns. For the Americans, deep kisses were already normal at an early stage, whereas for the English, such kisses were only part of the late stage, immediately before sexual activities. So, when the American soldiers kissed the English girls, the latter thought that the G.I.s already wanted to have sex and reacted accordingly. As we can see, misinterpretations increase with the cultural distance. When even persons from different sections of the globalised culture are mistaken regarding the assumption what the other person has in mind, then we must take into account that such misapprehensions are even more pronounced, when the other person is from an entirely different culture. Being aware of that, reflecting about one's own role within this mechanism and about such things like probabilities, confidence levels, vagueness and projections means to perform metacognition regarding the Theory of Mind (Papaleontiou-Louca 2008).

For research situations in indigenous contexts, these aspects regarding perspective-taking specifically mean that we have to challenge our assumptions about the others' thoughts, estimations and reactions. Especially, we have to scrutinise our implicit assumptions, which we frequently make in an unreflected way, automatically and by taking things for granted. We have been brought up in the industrial, globalised culture. Thus, we have been trained from childhood on within the framework of this culture's standards to apply particular cognitive patterns, and due to our pronounced experience with our fellow humans within the globalised society, we might be quite good at estimating the presence of certain cognitions that they have. But this only pertains to our culture. As long as we have not been brought up in exactly the indigenous culture we are visiting, it is very likely that we are often wide off the mark regarding our assumptions about what these indigenous persons are thinking and intending, how they are valuing things and how they will react. The best thing we can do about these shortcomings is to observate our own thoughts and reactions, in particular the automatic decisions, motivations, emotions, affects and attributions, and to analyse them, thereby searching for possible sources of error. On the one hand, these sources of error pertain to us, as we apply our standards and interpret things in our culturally specific way, in the sense that we assume that something should be seen in a particular way. On the other hand, there are erroneous assumptions pertaining to the indigenous persons by merely projecting on them, in an automatised way, our own standards of thinking, evaluating, deciding and reacting.

Factors of Mentalisation Competence

Anyway, there are some prerequisites for a person to adequately perform such metacognition in particular, as well as to be highly accurate in assuming other persons' cognitions (Fonagy 1999). It is a key competence for social functioning. Yet, this "capacity to conceive of mental states as explanations of behavior in oneself and in others (…) is acquired in the context of early attachment relationships. Disturbances of attachment relationships will therefore disrupt the normal emergence of these key social-cognitive capacities and create profound vulnerabilities in the context of social relationships" (Fonagy and Target 2006, p. 544). This essential skill is "a form of mostly preconscious imaginative mental activity, namely, perceiving and interpreting human behavior in terms of intentional mental states" (ibid.), comprising "needs, desires, feelings, beliefs, goals, purposes, and reasons" (ibid.). Along with other deficiencies, this skill is impaired, if there had been insufficient attachment in a person's childhood. Lack of a close, healthy relationship, in which a child can develop basic trust, enjoy security, unconditional love, cosiness and comfort, results in social and interpersonal problems, as well as in psychological disorders in later stages of life. Cross-cultural research on attachment highlights differences in caregiving and child-rearing (e.g. Pearson and Child 2007), while generally both universal and contextual factors are identified (Mesman et al. 2016) regarding parent-child relations. In many indigenous cultures, babies have permanent skin-to-skin contact with their mothers. Even at night, they are in her arms or right next to her. They can drink from her breasts whenever they want. As they grow up, they can always rely on their mother, and as they detach by and by, they can equally trust on their community. This interpersonal closeness is seen as a basic requirement for healthy psychological and emotional human development, and thus, in turn, the lack of such closeness, prevalent as deficiencies in parent-child relationships in general and bodily parent-child contact in particular, accounts for according problems in the industrial culture (Liedloff 1975). In fact, the findings of cross-cultural developmental research, which indicate that there is neither a defiant age of the young children nor an awkward puberty age of the teenagers in indigenous cultures (overview: Heine 2012), should give us cause for concern. I can personally confirm such difference between globalised and indigenous cultures from my field research with quite a number of indigenous groups. However, when drawing implications from cross-cultural developmental research, we need to do this in a differentiated way. The terrible two and the awkward age might attract our intention, but the reason for this is that these are phenomena that are manifest at the surface, which we hardly can ignore. Nevertheless, this is only one side of the coin. On the other side are those implications that pertain to our own way of thinking and feeling and in particular to our ability to have empathy as addressed above. This other side of the coin is easily overlooked. The reason for that is also twofold. On the one hand, we are ourselves subject to these causalities[7]; here, rather unconscious mechanisms might be at work that hinder us from reflecting. On the other hand, we might also feel uncomfortable in our role, in the case that there has been such lack of closeness in our own childhood, so that further reflections would be dissonant or even painful. So, what are the consequences of such considerations? Are we just a sport of fate, completely at its mercy, or can we do something about it? Yes, we can. First of all, we are not necessarily exposed to the influences of our childhood and the factors of our own development. Secondly, there are large interindividual differences regarding resilience, that is, the capability to cope with adverse life conditions (Rutter 2006; see also previous chapter of this book, Sect. 3.3.1). Resilience can be enhanced, though training programmes vary in effectiveness (Vanhove et al. 2015). Thirdly, we are not talking about mental illnesses but about influencing factors. As intelligent, healthy grown-ups, we have the ability to reflect about these mechanisms and our roles, and we should also be able to overcome potential cognitive hindrances by analysing situations and then rationally and autonomously controlling and determining our behaviour and reactions. It is very important that we are always honest regarding ourselves

---

[7] Heine (2012) points to the fact that North Americans, unlike people in other parts of the world, put their babies in a separate room at night, and he poses the question if this might be an explanation for certain psychological or behavioural peculiarities of North Americans. One might add here that acceptance vs. non-acceptance of breastfeeding, particularly in public, is a similar matter, as it directly concerns the babies' being in touch with the mother.

and never turn a blind eye on our own role. Once the causal relations are clear to us, we have to figure out the most logical way to proceed and then translate this into action. When we encounter any irrationalities along the way, we have to address them. They can be overcome in an honest and clear discourse. These are quite general directions indeed, but they are just as well helpful in the present context.

Effects of Expectations

It is our purpose to avoid mistakes regarding our assumptions about the indigenous peoples, when we meet them in the fields. This is a rather central concern, because such errors could be highly consequential. False perceptions would not only lead to wrong conclusions, but they would also determine our decisions and behaviour in the further course of the project. That, in turn, would elicit reactions from people visited, which would then be part of an overall derailed research. Furthermore, such misunderstandings would then be reflected in our input into the academic discourse, where they would manifest themselves by finding their way into publications. This would then have an effect on subsequent research, as the wrong impressions would be taken up by other researchers, so that repercussions of our misunderstandings would even reach the indigenous people we visited, as well as further indigenous peoples. Due to the imbalance of dominance, the external influence would come into effect by relegating the indigenous peoples into certain roles. This would not necessarily happen by directly imposing these roles on them, but rather subtle, through expectations, which we would pass on to them. In consequence, this would lead to a behaviour modification of the indigenous peoples according to our ideas. There are many such examples of formerly authentic indigenous settings, which have been transformed into "indigenous Disneylands" for the sake of tourism, that we have witnessed in Africa and Latin America. Unfortunately, we found similar tendencies in West Papua regarding research, since the Dani had come into the focus of cross-cultural studies. Especially in the 1970s, those studies had been carried out by quite invasive researchers.[8] Even decades later, the neighbouring tribe of the Lani tried to present themselves as Dani, apparently in order to appear more interesting. It was relatively easy, though, to reveal these attempts of pretending false identities on the linguistic level, by simply asking certain words from the Dani vocabulary, which the Lani did not know.

Whereas expectations from indigenous peoples towards the dominant culture might lead to disappointment on the indigenous side, but have no significant effect on the dominant side, expectations from representatives of the dominant culture towards indigenous peoples can result in profound changes. Such expectations of the dominant do not necessarily need to be stated expressively. They can also be conveyed in a rather subtle way. As long as they do not actively reflect about it, the dominant might not even be aware themselves that they have these expectations. However, expectations are also communicated nonverbally. They can be expressed by mimics, by glances, by a smile or by a sceptical look and also by more complex general reactions of appreciation versus rejection. As already addressed the previous chapters of this book, the way we present ourselves is of central importance. Immersive behaviour of

---

[8] Cf. Groh (2016).

us, the researchers, who visit indigenous peoples, is essential from ethical and methodological perspectives, as well as in observance of indigenous peoples' rights in terms of not giving any input that might possibly destabilise their cultures. By orientating our own visual appearance towards the traditional visual appearance of the respective indigenous people, we communicate appreciation of their culture. In those frequent cases that there has already been dominant influence, we should orientate our visual appearance towards the tradition before that influence. This is possible at least as long there are still witnesses of that time alive in the particular indigenous place that we visit. Other than in the globalised culture, old people in indigenous cultures are usually honoured, and these elders also generally rank highly in the particular society's hierarchy. If they still have the traditional appearance, we do well to join them in that respect. This always has many positive effects. These elders appreciate that very much, and also the younger ones of that indigenous group pay much more respect to anyone, who shows respect to the elders in particular and to their culture in general. Apart from the aspect that we neither want to violate the indigenous rights nor infringe ethical or methodological principles, we need to be mindful of our interactional roles in such a situation of contact between the dominant, globalised culture and the dominated, indigenous culture.

Modelling Intercultural Processes
In an abstract model, Posner (1989) allegorised cultures as circles with centres and peripheries and the contact of cultures as the partial overlapping of these circles, in which only the peripheries but not the centres overlap. When we take up this metaphor and zoom closer to the part with the overlap, we come to the following schematic view (Fig. 4.1)[9]:

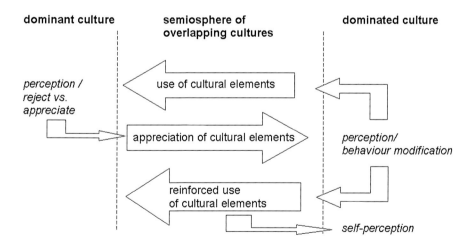

Fig. 4.1 Transference and countertransference in cultural contact

---

[9] Precursors of this section's functional models can be found in Groh (1997) and (Groh 2008).

This figure illustrates some of the processes that have been explained in the previous section. Global culture and indigenous culture are in contact in the central part of the picture. It is designated as semiosphere, because all relevant interaction happens in the form of sign processes (semiotics is the science of the signs). Everything that is perceived and to which a meaning is attributed can be characterised as a sign. Persons from different cultural backgrounds perceive each other. This happens primarily through the visual perceptual channel but also through many, if not all, other perceptual channels, to various degrees, depending on the circumstances. The globalised visitors, who see the indigenous people, could potentially show either rejection or appreciation by their own behaviour. When the globalised visitors pay respect to the indigenous culture by adopting their traditional visual appearance, then this is not only a sign of appreciation towards the indigenous culture, sent by the globalised visitors, but it also has an effect on the indigenous side. This effect is, in a first step, the perception of the globalised visitors' behaviour, which then leads, in the second step, to a reinforcement of the indigenous people's traditional behaviour; in the case that there have already been destabilising influences, this would be a restabilising behaviour modification.

I might add here that the positive effect could even be enhanced. I once arrived in a village of the Wounaan people in Panama. They had not expected me, and I had not been there before. It so happened that the elders were just having a meeting in the traditional community house and that I had been with the neighbouring Emberá people before, who had painted my body with traditional ornaments. Although there were no doors, my body painting was quite "door opening", and I was very warmly welcomed and immediately invited by the elders to their session.

Finally, the schematic view also shows that on the side of the indigenous people, another important process takes place, which is self-perception. When the dominant people have used their position of being role models in the positive sense of communicating their acceptance of the traditional indigenous culture by orientating their behaviour towards it and thus reinforcing it, then the indigenous persons are not only encouraged and strengthened in their self-esteem, but they also perceive themselves as bearers of their own culture. With the dominant visitors having adopted that very traditional appearance, too, the indigenous people now don't have to fear to be laughed at or to be regarded as savages, of whom the visitors would take pictures for their amusement. The indigenous people don't have to hide their indigeneity any more. They don't have to quickly put on T-shirts and shorts, in order to kowtow to globalisation when visitors arrive.

Due to their dominant position, globalised persons often do not understand the significance of their own behaviour towards indigenous peoples. This misconception regarding the effects of their own behaviour can be explained from the fact that they usually interact with other globalised persons, so that there is no cultural bias with an imbalance of dominance between them. Therefore, such abstract modelling makes sense to clarify the intercultural constellations. Regarding contacts with indigenous peoples, it is helpful to consider our roles on such a schematised level. When you orientate your visual appearance towards the traditional indigenous culture, then you do rescue work, as you strengthen the cultural identities and self-confidence of indigenous people. Thus, you do not impede, but rather support the implementation of Article 11 in particular and the United Nations Declaration on the Rights of Indigenous Peoples as a whole.

For the clarification of our own role, let us zoom even closer to the contact situation, to examine our individual perceptions. We might have the simple assumption that our perceptions are something objective or neutral and thus perhaps comparable to video recordings. However, they are not. It is long known from perception research (e.g. Baddeley 1976, 2004; Moray 2017) that selective processes already determine the ongoing perception. After stimuli have reached the organism, there are many interfering factors along the further way of processing. Subcortical regions have influence on our reaction in the sense of directing our attention to a stimulus or ignoring it, or categorising it as good or bad, or possibly becoming alert. Higher cognitive functions exert evaluations and decisions pertaining to more complex aspects such as dissonance reduction or social desirability. These are all highly automatised processes. Only targeted reflections are carried out consciously, and only then are we aware of our valuations and decisions regarding our perceptions and reactions to them. Due to the unconscious processes, biases come to bear as the perception is filtered before we consciously reflect about it. Nevertheless, we *can* be aware of these processes and reflect about them, thus reducing possible irrationalities of our reactions.

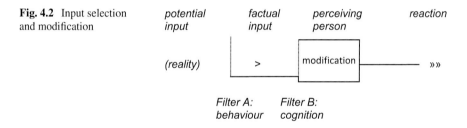

Fig. 4.2 Input selection and modification

Figure 4.2 shows the described processes in their context. It is to be read from left to right. We all undoubtedly live in a reality, and anything that is perceivable from that reality is a potential input. Filter A determines which stimuli reach the person. First of all, this depends on the person's behaviour. When someone is supposed to investigate the situation of a certain indigenous group, then there are various possible ways to do so. Perhaps such researchers, who have just arrived at the capital of the country, in which this ethnic group lives, take the chance of an invitation to an ambassador's garden party to be informed of this people's situation and then decide that this is already sufficient information to write a report. Actually, this would not be a good and responsible fulfilment of the job. Others might go to the capital's university to meet some students with that particular ethnic background and interview them. They would do the job a bit better than the party-goers. Then, there might be those who go to the part of the country, where the ethnic group lives, to see the actual life situation of the majority of that people. They have the potential to do the best job, provided that they abide by the rules, which we are discussing in this book. Yet, they could spoil it by behaving in a way that destabilises the indigenous group. If, for example, they do not minimise their invasiveness, then they might trigger some behaviour patterns of the indigenous people, which they practice in order to protect themselves. Such protective behaviour patterns are common among indigenous peoples, as most of them have had quite negative experiences with dominant people. As shown with the examples above, the foremost practice of these patterns aims at suggesting that they were not that indigenous any more, that they had abandoned traditions and that they were already part of the global culture. Semiotically, this can be described as sending signals, which qualify such meanings, by presenting signs of cultural affiliation. Practically, this is done visually by covering the body according to the standards set by the global culture. If the visitors are not aware of this mechanism, they are prone to be taken in by it. In that case, they would join the game without realising it and thus contribute to the further destabilisation of the indigenous culture. When indigenous people practise this protective behaviour pattern for more than one generation, then their culture is likely to be lost, as the young ones learn that they need to be ashamed of their background, that traditions should be hidden and that it is much easier and more rewarding to play the role of being part of the global culture. But if the visitors have realised this mechanism and act, accordingly, in an integrative way, then they will gain a much more authentic insight into the culture, which means, in terms of the functional model, that Filter A would be more permeable.

After the selection through behaviour has taken place, the factual input reaches the person. Here, the various cognitive factors come into play, preceded and accompanied by unconscious subcortical and cortical processes. These processes are not only determined by internal operations and regulations but also by external circumstances. The researchers might have had a long trip and therefore be tired or be less attentive for some other reasons. Or their attention might be very much focused on something, which they had never seen before. This could be quite different things, such as plants or animals, objects or cultural techniques. I remember that when we stayed with the Punan people on Borneo for the first time, I was very much impressed by the way the ladies were stamping grain. Each of them had a huge wooden pounder, with which they were stamping in a rhythm. After the first had started, the second joined in by first stamping the pounder outside the bowl-like excavation of the wooden utensil, in which the grain was, until they had a common regular rhythm, and only then she also stamped the grain, in an alternating beat with the first one. Then the third arrived and also hit the wood outside the grain pit first, between the others' strokes, but this irregular beat quickly became a rhythm of a regular triplex beat, at which all three then stamped the grain. There are many intriguing things in indigenous settings that, like in this example, catch your concentration, so that temporarily you won't pay much attention to other things. This means that the activity of Filter B varies significantly on the timeline.

It is a matter of dispute how much of the stimuli that have reached a person's senses are actually stored in that person's memory. Ever since Wilder Penfield's (1952) famous experiments, we know that continuous recordings of our perceptions take place in our brain.[10] The problem is not the storage, but rather the retrieval of the data. We sometimes have difficulties to consciously recall memories, and even if we do so, we can be wrong to a certain extent, depending on underlying circumstances (Baddeley 2004). The reason for this is that other memories are interfering with the memories that we want to collect, and there are also other mechanisms at work, such as expectations and dissonance reduction. Processes that are important for our considerations are those of modifications of the memories that are carried out due to social desirability and one's own cultural standards. Social desirability and cultural standards cannot always be separated, because persons, who have been brought up in a particular culture, have internalised that culture's standards, which they also project on other people of their culture, in the sense that they suppose that these other people have the same standards, as well as certain expectations in line with these standards. The term "social desirability" refers to the assumption that certain behaviour in the widest sense is desired by the society. The behaviour that is supposed to be expected can comprise various forms of communication or production. It could, for example, be the content or the tenor of a written article. It could be opinions and attitudes that are conveyed somehow. But social desirability and one's own standards will not necessarily have to be congruent. It could well be the case that some persons have stricter standards than what they think society expects from them. However, non-congruence does not have to be present in the sense of a person having stricter standards than the rest of his culture. Whatever standards persons have, they might assume different external expectations that they are supposed to fulfil. Journalists, for example, need to be in good terms with their editor, if they don't want to lose their job, and the editor has to fulfil the readers' or media consumers' expectations. There is a chain, or rather network, of dependencies and deference to the interests of others (Herman and Chomsky 1988). Some people might think that scientists are not concerned by such factors that modify, distort or even blot out information. However, this would be a somewhat naive assumption. Scientists are humans and as such are part of social mechanisms, in which they take their share.

The effect of supposed or real expectations of others can be seen as a slight form of social pressure. There is vast research on this issue, triggered by experiments such as the famous study on conformity by Asch (1951) or the much more drastic so-called Milgram experiment (Milgram 1963). Asch (1951) demonstrated that people join the opinion of their group, even when that opinion is apparently nonsense, while Milgram (1963) showed in his noted study that persons submit to authorities to a degree that they actually carry out orders, which will cause pain, serious harm or even death to another person, provided that the authority of the context is awe-inspiring. However, these are no automatisms in the sense of linear determinations, like the more awe-inspiring, the more willing are people to submit to authorities. Milgram (1974) scrutinised his findings with regard to the determinants of the subjects' behaviour. Apparently, persons, who have sufficiently reflected

---

[10]They are stored in neural cell complexes of the right temporal lobe, and detailed recall can be evoked by electric stimulation.

about authorities and the effect which obedience to destructive orders can have on other people, are somewhat immune to such authoritative pressure, which means that they simply do not obey any orders, when they expect that carrying out these orders could result in any other person's harm. Such persons, who reflect and then consequently refuse to hurt others, see their own responsibility for what they are doing as being of major importance. In contrast to them, those who blindly follow authorities, either as single actors, such as Eichmann, or in a group, such as the soldiers of My Lai, can be extremely destructive and yet argue that they only carry out what they have been told to do.

The Milgram experiment shows us the interrelationships between motivational factors and resulting behaviour in a very dramatic way. Nevertheless, behavioural sciences have learned from it some lessons that are very important with regard to general coherences. For us as researchers in indigenous contexts, this means that we do not automatically have to carry out any scientific routine or take academic perspectives that seem to be fashionable, in fulfilment of what Kuhn (1962) and Knorr-Cetina (1981) have warned of. Rather, we can evade such mechanisms by virtue of our reflections. This brings us to the final part of Fig. 4.2, which is the reaction that results from the filtering and modification. This reaction is anything that is elicited by the perceptual input. It manifests in the immediate behaviour, in the situation concerned, following the perception, and it extends to later substantiations like reports, articles or any other accounts given, which relate to that input.

The separate consideration of determinants of behavioural factors, cognitive factors and a resulting modification, which is then manifested in the person's reaction, is done here for the sake of explanatory modelling. Of course, behaviour results from cognitions, which also are intertwined with motivations that then result in reactions. And, as we know from research on social embodiment, things work the other way around as well, which means that cognitions also result from behaviour and in particular from the bodily state – one's own, as well as the perceived bodily state of others. Furthermore, it is difficult to separate the concepts of behaviour, cognition and motivation, not only from each other but also from the selective processes that engage in perception. But our aim here is to understand these factors and therefore to categorise them, so that we know what we are dealing with. In the issue, we want to be optimally prepared for field research in indigenous contexts, which differs from other research settings in so many ways.

In reality, information is often conveyed through a chain of communicating persons. Within each and all of them, filters are active in the way that we have just looked at in Fig. 4.2. Therefore, we have to consider that the information that we pass on to the next person in the chain is an input to this person, which is treated like other perceptual inputs. The behavioural filter, which was Filter A in Fig. 4.2, comes into effect by the way in which your information, that you have passed on, is received by the next person. If you have sent an email, for example, then the recipient might either read it carefully, just quickly skim it or not open it at all. When the email is opened, then the intensity by which it is read determines the further cognitive processing. Here, the cognitive filter, which was Filter B in Fig. 4.2, interferes, and after further contingent modifications, information is passed on, which is then treated by the next person in the chain as perceptual input, and so forth. We can lay hold of the different interfering agencies in a compact way by summarising them as "sources of disturbance", which modify the information that passes through the chain. First in the chain is the person in the field, in direct contact with the indigenous setting, and all the following persons in the chain are transmitters of information.

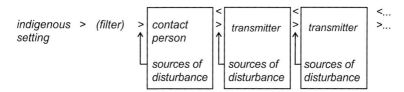

Fig. 4.3 Chain of information transfer

It has to be noted that the information, which passes through the chain, is changing along its way, as it is modified by everyone in the chain. Here, effects come to bear, which already Bartlett (1932) has investigated. He found with regard to stories, which originate from a different culture setting, that the texts become shorter, as they are passed on, and they are also made more coherent according to the expectations of the transmitters, who, furthermore, assimilate them to their own cultural conventions by omitting details that are not customary to them, but they retain more familiar aspects and might even extend them in a clichéd way. While Bartlett (1932) focused on phenomena in connection with one informational unit, which was sent in only one direction through the chain, the reality, in which researchers live and work, is more complex. Information passes through such chains in both directions. Therefore, in Fig. 4.3, arrows are consequently pointing back and forth. From the researchers' point of view, the collective of their own culture is perceived in the way of a generalised other, as George Herbert Mead (1934) put it, all the more so, as it is largely beyond one's own control, what happens to the input, which one has fed into the academic discourse. Consequently, researchers experience a relation between the collective and themselves, as shown in Fig. 4.4:

Fig. 4.4 Reciprocity of researcher and culture of origin

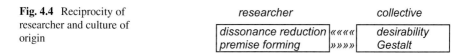

Researchers make projections on the collective, in particular regarding social desirability. These projections exist in the form of the ideas the researchers have regarding the collective's expectations, and they determine what kind of information they send in the direction of the collective. The researchers' image of the collective results from their subjective perceptions. From the sum of these individual perceptions, each researcher makes conclusions, and based on these, the researcher's image of the collective is composed in the sense of a Gestalt effect.[11] Those perceptions, which the researchers experience, are caused by the information, which comes from the collective. This information is not just a projection, but it is actually manifest in the communications, which reach the researchers, for example, in the form of editorial specifications, which are given to their notice to be observed, or various other feedback from along the way that a researcher's input makes through to the recipients inclusive of the participants in an eventual discourse.

When we include the indigenous culture into these considerations, then we can say that researchers are mediators between two cultures, by passing information about indigenous cultures on to their own culture, as shown in Fig. 4.5.

Fig. 4.5 The role of researchers as mediators between cultures

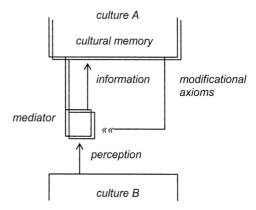

Culture A with the cultural memory, as well as the researcher-mediator, and their connection are depicted in Fig. 4.5 with double lines, as they are a coherent social system, with the researcher-mediator being attached to culture A by the communicational cord. In the field, researchers are perceiving the other culture. However, their perception is subject to certain modifications, which are determined by their own cultural standards. The information that is passed on by the researchers to their own culture has undergone such modifications. Once this modified information has reached the researchers' culture, it contributes to the cultural memory, in the form of concepts, which this culture has about other cultures. Here, cultural memory can be understood in the sense of Jan Assmann's (1992) approach, which we have briefly outlined in the first chapter of this book.

Clarifying all these mechanisms helps us to consequently apply minimally invasive research techniques in orientation towards the presumed authentic tradition. Although it is only a logical consequence from a rational perspective, researchers, like anyone else, are under the influence of their own cultural background. However, they are very much experienced in applying rational reasoning in order to overcome

---

[11] Since the Gestalt psychology approach states that the whole is composed from the sum of its elements, one has to point to the fact that it is not possible to perceive the collective as a whole. Therefore, to be more precise, it seems necessary to assume completion mechanisms, which manage to achieve the conception of the whole from the limited extent of subjective perceptions, such as in the Associative Models proposed by Kohonen (1988) and by Palm (1982).

irrational affective obstacles. Yet, especially those who have not carried out any immersive field research so far might find it somewhat difficult at first to overcome their internal barriers. Some might feel such barriers especially with regard to the very concrete, physical integration into traditional visual indigenous culture. So, how can we help them and which impulses can we give them for their thoughts? Well, this is what the next passage summarises in a largely pragmatic way:

Practical Advice

Being socialised in the industrial culture, with the feeling of being the dominant one, who is used to determine the situation, you might have an automatic reflex of aversion with regard to fully immersing in traditional indigenous culture.[12] You could overcome such an irrational reflex with rationality. Think about the options. Going there without adaptation, sending all the signals of globalisation, would push the indigenous peoples, whom you visit, further into destabilisation and the loss of their culture. You would thus violate Article 8, 2 (a) of the UN Declaration on the Rights of Indigenous Peoples. If you would adapt only partially by making some compromises, like keeping a bra on, then you would reinforce exactly those impacts that destabilise indigenous cultures in a particularly effective way, as these very taboo-related cultural elements have an extreme impact on the indigenous identities. If the present state already bears signs of the dominant influence, then, if you orientate yourself at that status quo, you would endorse that influence. This would mean that you would not only deny respect and acceptance of the indigenous people's authentic culture but you would even block their exercise of the right to revitalise their traditions, as granted by Article 11 of the UN declaration. You cannot not behave; your behaviour is an act of communication, and the input you give has a strong influence, because as representative of the dominant culture, you are a role model, if you like it or not. Therefore, the only rational way is to try to reconstruct the appearance as it was before the external influence. Which body parts, if any, were covered? And then don't cover more than that. You cannot spoil much if you cover less, because that would only mean that with regard to the cultural spectrum,[13] you move a bit more into the cooler part. But you can spoil a lot, if you cover more, because then you push progress forward, furthering the introduction of dominant standards, which eventually leads to the destruction of cultures. Unfortunately, this is, by no means, an exaggeration. When we look into history and into the particular courses of the processes that have led to the loss of all the indigenous cultures that have become victims of the European expansion so far, we can see the systematics of the mechanisms. When we analyse them from psychological and semiotic perspectives, we can find the causal connection in the way that it is the body-related influences, which lead to the deletion of identities and, as a consequence, to the deterioration of the indigenous cultures. But the last authentic indigenous cultures

---

[12] Even Margaret Mead, without such full immersion into the traditional culture, wrote about "the nerve-wracking conditions of living with half a dozen people in the same room, in a house without walls, always sitting on the floor and sleeping in constant expectation of having a pig or a chicken thrust itself upon one's notice" (Mead 1977, p. 29).

[13] As for the concept of the cultural spectrum, see Chap. 1 of this book.

that are left on this planet are much too precious; accepting their disintegration or even their destruction would be unacceptable for many reasons.

The Role of Religion

To continue from the previous passage, one thing that comes to mind is that routinely religion is blamed for the body-covering norms. However, the situation is much more complex, and such an assignment of guilt would be an oversimplification. It is true that strict body-covering norms can be found in various institutionalised religions or their subcultures, but such norms can also be found in communist systems that proudly claim to have overcome religion. And when you think of Internet policies of almost hysterically blurring, or putting black bars across, depictions of indigenous bodies and even certain parts of prehistoric stone statuettes, then one would need a very flexible definition of religion to subsume that behaviour under such categorisation. Evidently, the only clear correlation to be seen is that of body-covering norms with the elaboration of social systems, in terms of a structuring of the society, the complexity of regulations and the delegation of responsibilities to entities within the structure of the society. From the perspective of the social embodiment approach, the shrouding of the body has a psychological function which, on behalf of the social system, reflects the non-acceptance of the human being as it is and the replacement of the natural state by a system of regulations; on behalf of the individual, it symbolises the internalisation of the system's norms and the submission thereunder. Once this submission is fully internalised, then it does not feel to the individual as something caused by external force and against the own will; rather, the individual identifies with these norms and defends them. It has to be pointed out here that these mechanisms are not the expression of a particular religion but that they are at work in different societies of different sizes, which are based upon belief systems that are geared to control its members.

Today, indigenous peoples in contact with the non-indigenous society can generally determine themselves which religion they want to follow. There are exceptions from this rule, for example, in the African Savannah and Sahel zone, where people are forced to convert to Islam. In other places, such as former Burma, which is now Myanmar, indigenous peoples have decided to convert to Islam without such force. Due to the nature of present-day Islam, it is hardly possible for the indigenous culture to be maintained under it, as it collides on the level of visual semiotics with the religious regulations. In India, it is predominantly persons from lower castes, who decide to convert to Christianity or Islam, as such conversion helps them to escape from the social pressure exerted by the higher castes of Hinduism. In Latin America, where Catholicism has existed for centuries with syncretic elements of paganism, Evangelical or Pentecostal movements are gaining ground among indigenous peoples. Worldwide, there seems to be a correlation in the sense that once indigenous peoples are in contact with the non-indigenous society, then the more traditional the indigenous lifestyle is, the more likely it is that preference is given to Christianity, if they become aware of it, rather than to other religions, which might be available in other contexts.

More than 200 years after the enlightenment, 150 years after the end of slavery in most countries where it was practised and 50 years after the official end of the colonial era, many indigenous peoples adhere to Christianity, and others are adopting it. This needs some explanation. Apparently, indigenous peoples generally find it easy to identify themselves with biblical concepts, in the sense that, on the one hand, they find their tribal situation reflected in the Old Testament, while on the other hand they accept the facilitation of faith, as it is given in the New Testament. Interestingly, indigenous peoples even turn to Christianity in otherwise non-Christian contexts, as presently in Southeast Asia, where there is communism and what is left over of Buddhism. As so-called Jungle Christians, they face prosecution.[14] Their situation of turning to Christianity, under these conditions and by their own will, is contrary to the common conception of indigenous peoples being forced into the Christian faith.

Nevertheless, today's indigenous peoples, who are Christians voluntarily, might seek exchange with you, when you meet them in the fields. If you haven't been to Africa, Latin America or Asia before, you might be surprised about the people's unconstrained relation with religion. You will have to travel from the airport, where you have landed, to the indigenous community, and all along the way, you will see religious references written on buses and taxis, on kiosks and posters, because that is an integral and essential part of people's lives. They might ask you *what* your religion is, and not *if* you have a religion at all. They take it for granted that you have a belief. When you cooperate with colleagues at universities in these countries and you sit with them for lunch break, it is normal that they have a long and intensive prayer before they start eating, in which they also pray for you, for your family, for your protection and for your safe travels. And they might invite you to say grace, and they expect that you do it in the same way. I have been an external examiner at different African universities, and it is normal that the graduands first and foremost thank God at the beginning of their theses. And when you have left the modern world behind and you are with indigenous peoples, it is clear to them that the world has come to exist by creation. You cannot expect any sympathy if you would contradict that. Actually, it is some of the industrial culture's positions that are exotic and deviant from the thousands of other cultures' views in the world. At the UN, it is common that sessions pertaining to indigenous issues do not start before there has been an opening prayer held by an indigenous representative and that they do not end before such a closing prayer has been held.

Yet, indigenous persons, who follow Christianity, are sometimes irritated by the amalgamation of various standards, and they cannot be blamed for this, since they experience some inconsistency on the side of their non-indigenous fellow Christians. The good news is often confounded with dominant cultural standards, which have no theological legitimacy. This is not only true for Christianity but for other religions as well. The body-veiling norms are contradictory to the original, intended state of creation, to which it is referred. Indigenous peoples close to nature can

---

[14]Cf. http://s-a-c-s.net/uno/papers-and-reports-to-the-un/, 2017 Report on Indigenous Rights Situations in Southeast Asia (accessed 21 Aug. 2017).

actually identify themselves very easily with the paradisiacal state. In modern terms, paradise could be described like a great naturist resort. It is clear that people are longing for this. When indigenous peoples become more acquainted with external views, the contradictions between these perspectives and the practiced lifestyle become quite evident. When they approach you, hoping that you will ease their confusion, you can do so by making them aware of Genesis 2:25 and also of Genesis 1:31 and perhaps also of Isaiah 25:7.

As already addressed in Chap. 2 of this book (Sect. 2.4) and with reference to the United Nations Conference on the Freedom of Information (1948), intellectual exchange may neither be prevented nor obstructed. Missionary work is covered by these aspects, but the problem is that often, together with the spiritual exchange of ideas, cultural elements from the dominant industrial society are transferred into indigenous societies, where they unfold their destabilising effects. To give you an example, a filmmaker once reported to me a scene that she had witnessed in an indigenous community of the Xingú National Park.[15] The FUNAI maintains bases with radio stations in the park, and the staff not only disregard the indigenous life-style, but they also bring along their families, who stay there with them. One day, she saw an indigenous woman walking by one of the houses of the base. From the window, the wife of one of the base's personnel could see her and was calling this indigenous woman. Those representatives of the dominant culture usually invent names for the indigenous persons, such as "Maria", because in their opinion, the indigenous names are too complicated. So, this lady was calling the indigenous woman and told her that she had dreamt the previous night that the Lord Jesus had stood on top of the house and he had been weeping. "And do you know, why he had been weeping? He had been weeping because you are still walking naked". Of course, the indigenous woman did not want that the Lord Jesus was weeping because of her, and she had certainly put on clothes after she had heard about the lady's dream.

When you do research in indigenous contexts, you might be confronted with many stories like this one. However, rather than reacting by presenting any counter-ideology, it should be clarified that the globalised cultural standards are to be sepa-rated from theological content and that, within any intellectual exchange, the freedom of choice needs to be ensured. Christian missionary work generally asserts the claim to provide a theological offer to the benefit of humankind and normally also to give humanitarian aid. All that is fine. Yet, the reality is that missionaries often are less missionaries of faith than they are missionaries of globalisation. While there are a few missionaries, who are rather exemplary exceptions, as they orientate themselves towards the integration into the indigenous society, like Christ did by birth, there are many others who, instead of preaching, try to bring progress to "underdeveloped" peoples. But this is not what they are supposed to do. Neither researchers, nor missionaries, nor anyone else are supposed to destroy cultures.[16]

---

[15] Rebecca Sommer, personal account.

[16] Theologically, passages towards the end of Revelation (Rev. 21;24; Rev. 21:26; Rev. 22:2) can be understood in the sense that the nations are intended to exist further. In the original Greek text, the word ἔθνη (ethne) is used. Consequently, the deletion of cultures would counteract this intended state of the perfect future world.

It has to be acknowledged, though, that in certain countries, there are less tortures and Human Rights violations in those areas with missionary stations, because such cases would immediately be reported to international organisations. Generally, individual local pastors seem to be more easily misused by totalitarian regimes as instruments to control the people than foreign missionaries in stations, where they have a medical unit and telecommunication, and only pay a visit every few weeks to the indigenous communities. Anyway, researchers in the fields have to face religious issues, even if they are not part of their actual research question. And they have to react, when facing these issues. As we cannot *not* behave, we cannot *not* react. Trying to ignore something would also be a reaction of communicational value. Therefore, always react to situations in all conscience, truthful, helpful and to the best of your knowledge. You can take as a guideline that freedom of information must be ensured and so must be the freedom of choice.

4.3   Transcultural Competency

Transcultural competency basically pertains to skills to behave appropriately across cultural borders. For us, this simply means to carry out research correctly, when we are in an indigenous setting. To be on the safe side, we should be oriented towards the traditional indigenous culture prior to external influences. With regard to Article 8, 2 (a) of the United Nations Declaration on the Rights of Indigenous Peoples, we have to make sure to avoid everything that could possibly have any destabilising effect on the indigenous culture or their members' identity. As it is impossible not to behave, the question can only be *how* to behave. Another aspect that demands our orientation towards the traditional indigenous culture prior to external influences is given by Article 11 of the United Nations Declaration on the Rights of Indigenous Peoples. It is unfortunately true that many governments do not care about this UN declaration or they hardly do more than lip service to it. The same applies to travel agencies, even when they call themselves "respectful", "culturally friendly" and the like. They feel primarily obliged to their paying customers. Likewise, settlers, loggers and prospectors are generally not interested in respecting indigenous peoples at all. It is the common experience of indigenous peoples that their culture is regarded as backwards and primitive, and the solution offered to them in order not to be rejected any more is that they submit to globalisation. *Be like us and we will accept you. All you need is development. The glorious industrial culture will give you the blessings of civilisation.* So, the usual input, which indigenous peoples receive, pushes them towards globalisation. If we, as researchers, obliged to ethics, willing to adhere to the law and interested in correct methodology, take Article 11 seriously, we will acknowledge indigenous peoples' right to revitalise their culture. But how can they do that, if they only receive input that pushes them towards globalisation? How can such an extreme bias be counteracted? Well, at least on our part, we are giving such a counterweight if we consequently apply minimally invasive techniques in orientation towards the traditional indigenous culture prior to external influences.

It is helpful to do thorough research in archives, examine the earliest reports about the people we are about to visit and evaluate images and photo material, in order to reconstruct the original visual culture. As pointed out in Chap. 2 of this book (Sect. 2.4), body semiotics are of central importance with regard to cultural identity. This key point needs to be combined with the perspective of the United Nations Conference on the Freedom of Information. Consequently, intellectual exchange may not be restricted, but it has to be ensured that there is no social or other pressure unbalancing the intellectual exchange. Communicating acceptance and respect by drawing on total immersion into the authentic visual culture is a safeguard against the imbalance of dominance.

Two things are important with regard to ethnological and anthropological material that we have found in our research while preparing our visit to the indigenous people in the field. Especially with regard to photo material, it would be just and fair to take some copies with us and give them to the elders. It is their people depicted, after all. Handing over these pictures also provides a basis for communication about their culture and possible changes that might have occurred since the pictures have been taken. Often, indigenous peoples are not really aware of what their culture looked like a few decades ago. In particular, when they want to exercise their right to revitalisation as granted in Article 11 of the UN declaration, they might be really happy to receive some orientation. The exception to the rule of handing photo material to the indigenous culture where it had been taken is a restriction by Australian Aborigines, namely, that only pictures of their people's living persons may be shown (cf. Chap. 2 of this book, Sect. 2.4.2). I know of a television studio run by Aborigines, where routinely the archive is screened for pictures of persons, who meanwhile have deceased, and these pictures are then deleted. Therefore, before handing over pictures in Australia, it is advisable to first consult with the elders how to proceed.

Another thing to consider regarding pictures and other historical material of indigenous cultures is that the material itself is often biased. Bearing philosophy of science perspectives in mind, one could even say that such material is always biased, as every description or presentation is done from a particular perspective. In that respect, there is no full objectivity. Of course, this also pertains to the book that you are just reading. So, what is the consequence? Giving up, resigning to give any description, is not an option. It is clear that we should do our best to always give descriptions as correct and as objective as possible. This means that we should scrutinise both our own descriptions and those of others, bearing in mind the various sources of error.

What is important for our topic is the aspect of depicting authenticity. And in that respect, biases vary gradually. How much they do so depends on the interests, intentions and standards that the originator of the photo or other description has integrated into the work. Such integration can happen consciously and unconsciously, and we cannot expect much outcome from separating the one from the other.[17] Each

---

[17] Even when people are asked, consequences could hardly be drawn from any assertion if something was done intentionally or unintentionally nor are there ways to reliably check these assertions (Watzlawick et al. 1967).

and every one of us has been raised within a particular culture and its specific sub-cultures. During this socialisation process, we have internalised values, behaviour patterns and cognitive styles, which do not match in all respects with those of other cultures.

As mentioned before, already Bartlett (1932) has investigated the handling of information that originates from another culture. Things that are strange to us are often omitted or adapted to our own culture, or, if deemed suitable, some of them are intensified in the sense of exoticism. Therefore, we should ask ourselves, do we have any affectively tainted reaction to what we perceive of another culture? Do we like or dislike it? Because such feelings might determine whether we ignore it, hide it or give it particular prominence.

These mechanisms can add up with regard to our handling of historical depictions, as they have happened with certain probability on behalf of those who first took these ethnological or anthropological photographs or otherwise made the respective records. Then again, those selective processes take place when some of these historical depictions are picked out to be presented in a new context, like a book, a conference presentation or a lecture, while others are not. Also, in the new context, they are then going to be reinterpreted and put in the perspective that the presenters prefer.

Selective processes can sum up during first-time compilations of depictions, too. They can be explained in a filter model of additive interference (see above, Fig. 4.3). It does not necessarily have to be a researcher, who presents the first-hand depiction, it can just as well be a journalist or someone else, who reports about another culture. Both researchers and journalists are often adjusted to a certain lifestyle. Due to this predisposition, they avoid situations, which are below a self-defined standard of living. In these cases, contacts with indigenous peoples, whose lifestyle is below this self-defined level, might be excluded.

Avoiding immersion often goes along with other behaviour that is distant to the reality of indigenous contexts. Applying for working visa to do research is fine. But there are situations, into which such a working visa won't bring you, especially in those countries, where an official guide from the government would accompany you, watching every step you are doing, obstructing your fieldwork and even keeping you away from the indigenous peoples. So, try to stay legal and look for alternatives. It is, for example, absolutely correct and fully legal for researchers to enter countries as private persons with tourist visa and later report about that visit in articles or conference presentations. Any of those investigations, in which data are gathered by normal communication, don't need to be authorised by an official institution, although people should only be involved with their full, free, prior and informed consent. The point here is that if you do research through an official institution of the respective country, then those in charge of you probably won't show you the places that they do not want you to see. But as a tourist, you might be free to go there. For example, during a stopover in Malinau, a town in the interior of East Kalimantan, we heard of a place across the river called Respen, which was not shown on the map. Locals told us not only about its existence but also that we would find Punan people there. However, it was quite difficult to reach that place, although it was not far away. Most locals were reluctant to bring us across with a boat. When we finally reached Respen, we found something that looked like a town, but it actually was a large camp of forced acculturation. We certainly would not have been brought to that place by officials of an institution loyal to the government in charge of these actions.

Another aspect of the dealing with circumstances concerns principles of one's own behaviour. Researchers, who take part in an organised project, also might miss some insights. Here is an example: indigenous peoples have more or less been extinct in Patagonia. But contrary to the belief that there is no more indigenous life in that part of south Argentina, I met an indigenous family there. This was due to the fact that I was hitchhiking, and one night, I found a place to sleep in a building shell. In the dark of the night, they arrived and slept there, too, right next to me, a man, a woman, and an approximately 1-year-old child. They were gone by dawn. If I had stayed in a hotel, I would not have met them, as they led a hidden life, surviving underground.

In other cases, the situation is determined by the information seekers' predisposition, as, usually, they are representatives of the dominant culture. If the encounter does not take place in a minimally invasive way, then the influence exerted on those visited already has an effect on their behaviour and thus on the information or data gathered.

As we know from perception research (e.g. Moray 2017), distortions of information occur in vision and hearing and thus along the chain of passing them on, according to the expectations persons have. Such distortions already take place when the first person witnesses something. As Plous (1993) points out, "it is nearly impossible for people to avoid biases in perception. Instead, people selectively perceive what they expect and hope to see" (p. 15). Regarding this, the best thing we can do is to strive for becoming aware of these distorting processes and for minimising them as far as possible.

When persons pass on the information that is based upon their skewed perception, as may be the case, then again expectations are crucial. Here, however, these persons' expectations do not primarily concern the information input, but the effect of the output. They have ideas about the recipients' expectations or about the limitations of these expectations, that is, what the recipients don't want to see or hear. What comes to bear here is the social desirability bias. This effect is well known in social sciences. It is not a negligible, small effect, but rather a major force that determines communication within[18] a society. Persons want to be liked, and because of this motivation, at least among psychologically healthy persons, communication generally implies the communicators' reflections on what recipients think about them. How important this effect is can be derived from the fact that identity is largely based upon our ideas of how others perceive us. Through such perspective-taking

---

[18] Social desirability bias is likewise very much effective in communication between cultures, as we always have expectations of what the others expect. Our expectations, which we project onto the others, depend on our culture-specific socialisation and therefore could be mistaken when the others, who we perceive, are of a different culture.

and the wish to be liked, social norms, rules and standards become conventions within a society, as people try to fulfil the expectations of others. And of course, scientists, like their fellow humans, want to be liked, too. All of us, normally, want to maintain, by creating it towards others, a self-image of being smart and approvable. We should be cautious that not another mechanism, symbolic self-completion, comes to bear when we in fact do not have the competence but try to compensate our lack of expertise (Braun 1990). A prominent example can be found in Freeman's (1983) evaluation of Margaret Mead's self-description.

When persons have to convey information that they expect to be disapproved by the recipients, then there is a problem. On the one hand, there is the wish to meet the others' expectations, and on the other hand, there is the need to adhere to the truth. How inconvenient truth is handled affects that particular information all along its way. That way might be short, if the information is intercepted already in the beginning. Otherwise, it is affected by each one, who is part of the information chain and who has expectations regarding what the next communication partner wants to hear or to see. These expectations shape what is experienced as information from the very first input and then along the chain at every relay station, in both directions. Everyone has expectations regarding any input, as well as towards any recipient, to whom they pass on something. Stereotypes are permanently in effect (Cohen 1981), and they have an influence in both directions at the relay stations of the chain.

The first witness in a chain conveying information about an indigenous culture to the global culture might be someone who then gives a written description of the particular social group he or she visited or who takes pictures of persons from this group. In a written description, he or she might circumvent features of this society, which do not match his/her and/or the audience's expectations. For example, as I am writing this, I am sitting in a UN session on indigenous rights,[19] and the last agenda item here was on indigenous health with a focus on children and youth. Another item during the past days pertained to indigenous peoples and disabilities. Although the infanticide, the killing of children with illnesses or handicaps, as it is common practice among certain indigenous peoples in Brazil, is a serious violation of Human Rights, this issue was not even touched by the indigenous representatives. This is a typical example of dissonance reduction, as the notion of indigenous people killing their own ill or disabled people is incompatible with the general idea of appreciating indigenous culture. Such systematic blinding out is then part of the image that is created or maintained.

The first input into the information chain can also be a photograph taken of indigenous persons. Such pictures are always sections cut out of the whole scenery, and it is natural that the way this section is chosen already directs the sensation and excludes the not shown impressions. But it is not uncommon that the manipulation of information goes way beyond that. In Tarakan, a tour guide told me that he had brought some Swiss tourists to an indigenous group some distance upriver in the interior of Borneo. The Swiss ladies wanted to take pictures of the indigenous persons but insisted that

---

[19] 9th session of the Expert Mechanism on the Rights of Indigenous Peoples, Geneva, 11–15 July 2016.

it would be unacceptable to show them as they were, with too much skin visible, including bare breasts. Those tourists had brought blankets and forced the indigenous persons to wrap themselves in these blankets. Then, the Swiss were satisfied and took the pictures. The tour guide showed these pictures to me.

Respectfulness towards indigenous peoples does not only mean not to force them into our standards. As we cannot not behave, and as there is a dominance gradient, we have to avoid the transference of behaviour patterns. But even that is not an easy thing. Here is an example to clarify this: our first encounter with Punan people took place in East Kalimantan. In preparation, I had done some literature screening – there were not many reports – and I had asked inhabitants of the last town before the vast jungle area. Thankfully, someone had organised a boat with an outboard engine, steered by two Berusu boatmen. Way upstream, we suddenly saw something bizarre. Amidst the jungle, there were men standing up there on top of the steep bank, with long black trousers and white shirts with long sleeves. The Berusu said these were Punan. I said no; as far as I am informed, Punan look differently. But the Berusu insisted, and so we went ashore and climbed up the bank. Further inland, invisible from the river, there was a longhouse, into which we were invited. We had agreed in our team to take off our clothes when we were with indigenous peoples, in order to minimise our influence. We adhered to this rule, and for a while, there was a somewhat bizarre situation again – at least it might have been from industrialised persons' perspective: while the Punan were fully dressed, we were not. But interestingly, they did not show any reaction to our appearance. Rather, they acted as if this was the most natural thing on earth. It was quite apparent that the Berusu looked down upon the Punan, being proud of being civilised and exerting their dominance towards them. After a few hours, the Berusu made clear that they did not feel like spending any more time with these uncivilised people and suggested that we went further upstream, where they knew a nice spot for fishing. I said, fine, you go to that place, and we agreed that they would come to pick us up after a couple of days. So, they left, and once the sound of the engine had faded away, there suddenly was a gasp of relief among the Punan as they took off their clothes. Now, they had smiling faces, which they did not have before, and one could feel that some tension had gone and given way for relaxation. We stayed with them and could witness their daily routine, but one morning, they put on their clothes again and sat on the ground with stony faces. I thought to myself, did we do anything wrong? Then I understood: it was the day when we had agreed with the Berusu that they would come and pick us up. Indeed, they arrived after a while, but the Punan must have heard them long before we did. And then I understood one more thing: the day we arrived, they had, of course, also heard the outboard engine long before we came to their place. This was the reason why they had put on clothes and stood there like a reception committee. The reason for that behaviour was also clear: no one likes to be treated with scorn and mocked at as being "uncivilised" and "savage". The Punan certainly had some unpleasant experiences with soldiers, settlers and others, who behaved in a dominant way towards them. We had seen how they had been treated by the Berusu.

Now, let us analyse the possible outcomes of the initial encounter situation a little further: how would ordinary tourists, even backpackers, have reacted if they had met the fully clothed Punan? It is very probable that they would have remained fully clothed, as they were themselves. And how would the situation have gone on then? Both sides would have remained clothed, sweating and perhaps smelling, and sooner or later, the tourists would have left. Then, the Punan had taken off their clothes with great relief. But the tourists would not have seen it.

   If we had not stuck to the rule that we had agreed upon in our team, namely, to take off the clothes when meeting the indigenous people, then the Punan would have stayed covered, as they did not want to be looked upon as being primitive. And we would have come to the false conclusion that it is normal for the Punan to wear clothes. It certainly was of particular importance that we had female team members. Most indigenous peoples are certainly accustomed to see bare chests of male soldiers, settlers, tourists and other dominant invaders. So, they would not have returned to their usual style, either, if we had been a purely male team. It became evident that our female team members played an important role in encouraging the indigenous women not to be ashamed of their traditional appearance.

   Indeed, travellers almost always behave dominantly when visiting indigenous peoples. And researchers often are no exception from that rule. This leads to false and distorted impressions of the respective culture, and, much worse, it accelerates the deletion of the indigenous culture. Setting dominant standards in indigenous cultures modifies the indigenous identities, so that, in effect, the indigenous culture disintegrates. This is why Article 8 of the UN Declaration on the Rights of indigenous peoples – and especially subparagraph 2 (a) – has such an importance. Time is long overdue to put an end to the violations of this vital part of the international law.

   As we have seen, it is important to be aware about the inter- and transcultural mechanisms that take place under the influence of the dominance slope, as well as about the situation prior to the external, globalising influence. Otherwise, there is the risk of misinterpreting the situation and the risk that the dominant remain within their own standards, with which they are familiar and feel comfortable but which destabilise the indigenous culture. But those are risks that we cannot take.

   Because of the dominant culture's tendency to modify information about other cultures according to the dominant standards, simple research of archives is not enough. In semiotic terms, we need to know the code as how to interpret reports, records and pictures. We need to understand the situations in which the reports came about and know about cultural dominance and the biases within the mutual interactions and influences, as well as about misunderstandings, selective perceptions, modifications and manipulations. Conquerors, tourists and even researchers have often encountered indigenous peoples with an implicit conviction of being superior. Such a basic attitude shapes all subsequent perceptions and construals. On the level of overt behaviour, influence is mainly exerted in one direction, from the dominant towards the dominated. Regarding the other direction, the dominant hardly pick up any impulse from the dominated, unless it is something new that further strengthens the dominants' position. Also, the dominant hardly ever call their own standards into question, so that misunderstandings are the consequences. A typical error is the sexual interpretation of indigenous nudity. The example given of the tourists, who told the Punan to wrap up themselves in blankets, before they took pictures of them, illustrates this mechanism very well and so does the example of the FUNAI giving bikini tops to indigenous women and girls before shooting a promotion film (see above, Chap. 2 of this book). So, if we see depictions of indigenous peoples, we have to "read" them carefully, bearing all that in mind. On the part of the head of a research team, he or she is responsible of coaching the other team members, since we cannot expect that all of them become acquainted with the socio-cognitive mechanisms to the necessary extent themselves. Likewise, measures of precaution have to be taken with regard to tourists or any other visitors to indigenous peoples, to prevent destabilising influences. Although Article 8, 2 (a) of the UN Declaration on the Rights of Indigenous Peoples obligates states to take such preventive measures, it is clear that everyone is required to refrain from "any action which has the aim or effect" of such a destabilising influence on indigenous peoples and that "effective mechanisms", which states shall provide, include the prosecution of anyone who violates these protective regulations.

Misrepresentations occur in academic publications just like in nonacademic depictions, although Article 15 of the United Nations Declaration on the Rights of Indigenous Peoples demands correct reflection of indigenous culture in education and public information. When we try to describe such phenomena of misrepresentation in terms of communication models, as we have done above, then we can say that the distortions can sum up to an extent that depictions ending up in books, journals or other media can be quite different from the original version. A fine example can be found in Heine (1987), who reported that when he visited the Ik, an indigenous people in the mountains of Uganda, he had the impression that this was an entirely different people than the one described in literature. The degree to which distortion takes place does not only depend on the length of the communication chain but also on decisions made by each of those who transfer the information.

So, how can we escape those mechanisms or at least minimise them? Again, the answer is that we have to be aware of them and reflect about them from a metalevel. We can then consciously decide that, for example, we do not want to shape what we pass on according to what we think an audience wants to hear or read. This might have the consequence that readers or other recipients will not appreciate what is passed on to them or even feel offended. But as scientists we have a particular obligation to adhere to the truth. Therefore, we have to take such disadvantages into account and take precautions by thorough explications.

However, in order to make the best possible decisions, we need to be informed, too. And this brings us into the same problematic situations as well. When, for example, we find some anthropological or ethnological pictures in an archive, we have to take misrepresentations and distortions into account and try to subtract them out. Think about the circumstances, in which the pictures were taken, think about the persons who took these pictures and think about the social roles of these persons. Think both ways: how did these persons want the indigenous people to be seen and which kind of picture did they want to pass on to their own, dominant culture back home? Also take a sceptical look on details of the pictures. When the indigenous persons depicted are wearing loincloths, what kind of fabric is it? Is it industrial textile or something which they have produced themselves? Sometimes, a closer look can reveal astonishing manipulations of the alleged authenticity (see Yali example below, Sect. 4.4.1).

If you are uncertain about your transcultural competency and hesitant about immersing into a traditional indigenous culture, then it would be advisable to stay away from it. However, those who have no problem with total immersion should be encouraged to even go beyond a mere status quo aspect of minimised invasiveness and enhance cultural sustainability by doing rescue work (see previous chapter of this book, Sect. 3.5.2). Even if there is only one old member left in the indigenous community, who still displays the traditional appearance, then we can take this up and endorse this indigenous person's confidence by joining in and thus help to keep the door open to make use of the indigenous peoples' right to revitalise their traditional culture, as granted by Article 11 of the United Nations Declaration on the Rights of Indigenous Peoples. And even if traditions have already been modified, we should bear in mind that indigenous traditional life often goes on covertly and invisible to outsiders, as long as they don't do the first step of appearing the traditional way.

Those who are experienced with total immersion and transcultural rescue work should then also be encouraged to pass their skills on to the next generation. Of what use would it be to keep it for yourself? Young academics are increasingly under pressure of globalised standards and of surveillance exerted through social media. They are very anxious not to violate any of those post-modern principles. However, traditional indigenous lifestyle is not compatible with these standards. Therefore, young people would be horrified by the prospect that anyone of their globalised friends would find out about their appearance, in case that they had been immersed into a traditional culture, having violated the strict zeitgeist rules that dictate the globalised society which body parts are to be covered. In due consideration of this young people's internal conflict, who, on the one hand, feel a vocation to understand culture and maybe even to help indigenous peoples, but who, on the other hand, are involved in networks of social relations that they do not want to forfeit, it must be a central issue of targeted education and training to allay these fears. Anyone who makes the rational decision to do meaningful work in indigenous contexts should receive the necessary support to overcome irrational inhibitions.

4.4 Education and Training

There are various reasons as to why it is necessary to design education and training appropriately, so that research in indigenous contexts is carried out properly. International law requires the protection of indigenous peoples, along with their cultures. From a systemic perspective, indigenous cultures represent vital resources of knowledge and behaviour patterns, especially with regard to the relations of humans to particular, non-artificial environments. Especially those natural environments with the highest densities of species, which at the same time are the most endangered ones on this planet, are inhabited by indigenous peoples, who are adapted to these environments and specialised in managing them in a sustainable way. It is exceedingly necessary not to destabilise these indigenous peoples, which would be an infringement of Article 8, anyway. And this does not only mean targeted destruction. "Any action which has the aim or effect" – yes: even the unintentional effect – of destabilising an indigenous culture would be such an infringement (Article 8, 2 a).

So, with good reason, we should strive to give the best possible education and training to students, who study relevant subjects, as well as to anyone, who plans to work in indigenous contexts, and of course to all team members when preparing any research in indigenous contexts.

One basic advice is to always bear in mind the theoretical aspects of the cultural continuum as explained in Chap. 1 of this book. Cultures can be located within a spectrum from the very traditional to the very globalised end; some authors have metaphorised these ends with cold and hot (cf.: Lévi-Strauss 1962; Erdheim 1988). What is called progress can be understood as the moving, along the spectrum, from cooler to warmer parts. In class, the spectrum can be visualised by the colour spectrum, like the rainbow colours, from blue to red.

Indigenous peoples not only have the right to maintain their cultures (Articles 5 and 15 of the United Nations Declaration on the Rights of Indigenous Peoples), they also have the right to revitalise their culture (Article 11), in the case that they have lost traditions due to external influence. In order to keep this option open, we may not push indigenous peoples towards globalisation. There is the danger of destabilising indigenous cultures by presenting our lifestyle. As there is an imbalance of dominance, persons from the globalised culture are role models, even if they reject that idea. If they like it or not, their behaviour is not only perceived by the indigenous peoples, but it has a destabilising influence on the indigenous culture, unless the invasiveness is minimised. Such destabilisation needs to be avoided. So, basically, what has to be mediated in education and training is minimally invasive behaviour when carrying out research in indigenous contexts.

Indigenous contexts differ very much from globalised contexts. When we give field training as university teachers, we need to be aware that the contrast between the habitual context, in which the students live, and traditional settings of indigenous culture is larger than any contrast between different subcultures within the globalised society. Therefore, students should be prepared stepwise for indigenous settings. The aim is not to give them a cultural shock but to make them qualified to work in indigenous contexts.

Another reason for stepwise procedures is that not everyone is apt for such fieldwork. Furthermore, people sometimes overestimate themselves, so that they think they would be able to overcome their internal hindrances, but in concrete relevant situations, they cannot function properly. Also, the students might have wrong concepts, which are either idealised or negatively biased. Such misconceptions cannot be foreseen, nor can lecturers exactly know what is in the students' minds. Words, even when they are well chosen and precise, cannot fully describe the real world out there. The students might think they understand what is said, but their internal representation is something different from the situation that has been described. With stepwise procedures, the students bridge the distance between the two cultural realities gradually. At each stage, they have to acquire some competence. In this way, they don't have to learn and perform all at once. Rather, this is a process of incremental knowledge transfer and gradual competence acquisition.

Full, free, prior and informed consent is necessary, here, too. Besides the ethical principle, there is the practical aspect that students, who are not apt for this kind of research, can withdraw from the seminar without losing their face. At the outset, they can decide if they want to participate at all, and later on, anytime in the course of the seminar, they can still opt out. Misconceptions, as well as overestimations, can be addressed effectively in this way, and it can be prevented that students find themselves in situations with which they cannot cope.

A. Announcement and Description of the Programme

As the first step, it is necessary to describe clearly and factually the content and the aim of the seminar. Already here, some students will decide that they are not suitable for such a course, when they read that they shall be trained for field research in traditional indigenous settings, in which it is necessary to be able to behave normally in the respective traditional ways without clothes. Some persons might have prejudices concerning indigenous peoples, and others might have difficulties with nudity. However, the schedule of the seminar should not only focus on indigenous settings at the extreme end of the spectrum. Since the globalised students are positioned at the other far end of the spectrum, it is necessary to train them with due emphasis for those traditional indigenous settings, but such a seminar should actually cover the whole spectrum. You might want to object that this education and training should focus on indigenous contexts, why should then students be trained for globalised contexts? Well, indigenous issues are indeed dealt with in even extremely globalised contexts. I am used to taking the class, which I train for field research, to UN sessions on indigenous peoples' rights, and I do that parallel to the actual field training, which takes place in a quasi-indigenous setting. This has some advantages. For one thing, the students are trained to switch between highly contrasting situations. In this way, they learn to adapt quickly to different requirements. For another thing, they learn to understand in such a UN session the relevance of indigenous cultures for the globalised culture, as well as the devastating impact, which the dominant culture has on indigenous cultures. By this, they can gain some insight into the political structures in charge, and they can reflect about responsibility and future options. Furthermore, these sessions imply the possibility for cross-cultural research. There are indigenous representatives from many different regions of the world, who can participate in questionnaire studies or surveys, if they wish so. The students can be fully involved in this data collection, so that they can also become acquainted with this kind of research on indigenous issues. By the way, the UN is quite an interesting field to be studied, too. If you don't have the opportunity to take your students to UN sessions, you could likewise take them to relevant conferences. Whatever the schedule is, it all should be communicated to the students in the first step, and before the actual teaching starts, so that they have the freedom to decide if they want to participate or not. Even with regard to this decision, they should have the chance to decide for only parts of the seminar or for the entire course. But as this education and training is designed in the form of stages, which build on one another, it would not be possible to skip any of the stages.

B. Theoretical Part

The second step should then be a theoretical part, in which the students receive input regarding cultural theories, cultural psychology, cultural semiotics and other aspects of cultural and social sciences that are relevant to the topic. Sufficient scope should be dedicated to the international law, especially to Human Rights and Indigenous Rights. Methodological aspects need to be addressed, as well as ethical principles. Research situations in indigenous settings should be exemplified by pictures. As the proverb goes, a picture says more than a thousand words. Likewise, pictures should be shown from previous field training, so that the students know what awaits them. These pictures should be well chosen, in order to prevent any misunderstanding. Nudity should in no way render wrong impressions; by no means should they have the slightest touch of any pin-up style. Students must be absolutely sure that the training takes place in a serious, decent way and in a secure setting. The field research, for which the students are educated and trained, should be a real prospect for them. It would not make much sense to acquire practical skills for a hypothetical situation.

Allot enough time for the explication of the intercultural mechanisms, especially to the differences of indigenous versus globalised culture and to the model that explains culture change. Basically, the content for the theoretical part can be derived from the different chapters of this book. Upon ending the theoretical part, explain to the participants in detail what they have to expect from the further steps of this seminar.

C. Practical Training

After the theoretical part, the practical part should follow swiftly, so that the content learned has not faded away. If it takes place outside the campus, which is most probably the case, you should obtain the students' confirmation of consent and disclaimer of liability in written form. Since it is of high importance to ensure the acquisition of full competence by the students, the theoretical part should be divided in a first, introductory, and then the larger part with intensive field training. After all, the students shall be certified that they are skilled for working in indigenous contexts, which are not just any random places. Indigenous contexts are very sensitive to destabilising influences. Therefore, any destabilisation by the newcomers has to be ruled out.

C.a. Mindfulness Exercises

The introductory part of the practical training needs to be thoroughly structured. Begin with mindfulness exercises. If you have a physiotherapy course nearby, meet with the students there. Otherwise, the park or lawn on the campus would also do. Explain to the students that indigenous peoples are very much aware of their natural environment, that their attention is directed to the outside and that they are very vigilant. These exercises are contrary to some esoteric practices of turning the attention inwards. Rather, while standing still, the students will have to be very much aware even of perceptions, to which they usually do not pay any attention. Feel the wind. Listen to the sounds. You could ask them to listen for 2 min, and then each one has to tell what they have heard – birds, cars, an aeroplane or the rustling of the wind. Ask them, if they can name the trees they see and tell which birds are singing.

Next, they have to take off their shoes and socks and walk barefoot. You can tell them that this is the preparation of being fully nude in the next part. What follows now is the caterpillar exercise. Everyone puts their hands on the shoulders of the person front, and you, as the instructor, go first. Tell them to close their eyes, and then you walk carefully over different surfaces, as they usually have them at physiotherapy courses – grass, sand, gravel, stone and bark. By this, they will have to feel the ground very consciously with their feet. After this, explain the indigenous peoples' capability of reading nature, which might only be comparable to our skill of reading texts. We do this almost unconsciously. When we open the refrigerator and take out some juice, we don't really read it, but we see it automatically. Likewise, indigenous persons can see who has walked by. They can tell you the size and weight of the person, because they see it from the leaves that had been touched and bend, and from the soil, the grass or other plants on the ground that had been stepped on. They know how long it takes for the grass to straighten up again and for leaves to bend back into the original position. They can also tell you if the person had carried something, how heavy that was and on which shoulder it had been carried, from the differences of the imprints left by the feet, which we probably won't even see. After this, divide the students into two groups, and each group has to choose a piece of ground of approximately 10 × 10 m. These pieces should lay apart, preferably with bushes in between, so that the two groups cannot see each other. Each group then has to learn the ground – memorise details, such as a little piece of bark, a tiny twig, a small stone or a leaf lying on the ground. When they are done, they have to change places and make ten minor modifications by moving any of these little objects. After that, each group goes back to their piece of ground, and they have to try to find out which changes had been made, one group after the other. While one group is searching for the changes, the other group has to stand aside and say yes or no when they claim to have found a modification. If it is too difficult, little hints might be given, until all ten modifications have been found.

C.b. Impulse for Relating Practice to General Framework

Before you go on to the next part, you might want to insert an agenda item which helps to prevent that the students direct their attention inwards by focusing on their bodily experiences, due to our culture's standardised emphasis of the self and of one's own feelings. A good place to go to would be a memorial that commemorates culture-related injustice and suffering, such as the Holocaust or atrocities committed against ethnic minorities. If you have any memorial nearby that commemorates atrocities against indigenous peoples, this would, on the one hand, be easily linkable to the overall topic of the seminar, but on the other hand, you would then have to put more effort in making clear the general mechanisms of cultural dominance. It would not be reasonable to render the impression that the indigenous peoples' situation of being exposed to external dominance was something segregated, which could easily be set apart. Rather, the participants of the seminar should be made competent to integrate their future work with indigenous peoples into the framework of cultural theories. Otherwise, they would hardly be capable of understanding the inter- and transcultural mechanisms at work.

C.c. First Exercises in a Naturist Context

For the next part of the introductory section of the practical training, you need a secure place. Many of the naturist resorts that are affiliated to the International Naturist Federation (INF) are ideal for several reasons. First of all, a place like this is safeguarded. Such resorts are heavily fenced and not observable from outside. To enter, you need to be a registered holder of an INF card. This is important for security reasons. Should anyone ever misbehave, for example, in an exhibitionist way, then this person would be blocked immediately, for lifetime, and worldwide from all INF-affiliated resorts. Moreover, that person would have to face legal prosecution, depending on the delinquency. Owing to these regulations, trainers and students can feel safe. Of course, at this introductory section of the practical training, the students must still have the chance to withdraw. Since registration for an INF card costs some money, it would make sense to wait with this registration until they have passed these first exercises in a naturist context. Most resorts have regulations, which make it possible that members can stand bail for first-time visitors, who still have to decide about their membership. As it is useful for trainers, anyway, to have an INF card, they could guarantee for the students. There might be other, regional naturist associations, which are not affiliated to the INF. In order to decide if you should use one of these other resorts for the seminar, it is advisable to enquire thoroughly beforehand about the integrity of that club. In Europe, there are also textile free spas, which are respectable and which are constantly supervised by a sufficient number of attendants. But these spas should be second choice only, if there is no naturist resort nearby, because another reason to choose such a resort is that they usually provide a quasi-indigenous setting. In many of these resorts, members have little huts, where they might stay during their summer vacation. This is a situation comparable to indigenous villages. The students are supposed to learn how to interact with persons in such situations that are different from the usual settings of the industrial culture. They shall learn not to be irritated by other persons' nudity but to apply the concept of total immersion by being naked themselves, thus being part of the context, and yet to behave in a fully normal way. It would be irresponsible to do such a training in a real indigenous village, because there still is the risk that some student does not behave correctly. We may not run such a risk at the expense of indigenous peoples. Bearing Article 8, 2 (a) of the United Nations Declaration on the Rights of Indigenous Peoples in mind, no action may be carried out that could possibly have the effect of destabilising indigenous culture. Therefore, the training for field research in indigenous contexts needs to be done in quasi-indigenous contexts with the closest possible similarity to real indigenous settings. Respectable naturist resorts are the best choice for that.

I have been doing such training since almost 20 years now, and according to my experience, the students, who enrol for such a seminar, are of quite heterogeneous, even contrasting, backgrounds. Those who have grown up in families where they are used to seeing each other naked, and who spend their holidays on naturist beaches, cannot understand that others make such a big deal about nudity. Those others, in turn, cannot understand why the first ones cannot understand them. If the tense students are determined to successfully pass the seminar, they have decided that out of a rational decision, and it certainly costs them a lot of effort to see it through. But as we know from cognition research, they will also feel much gratification afterwards.

Naturists put much weight on cleanliness. This means that everyone has to take a shower upon entering and before leaving. Of course, changing rooms and showers is mixed. Usually, naturist also has the regulation that, whenever you sit down or lie down, you have to place a towel underneath for hygienic reasons. This means that you have to carry a towel all the time. In the real indigenous village, you're not supposed to do that, but here, the naturists are our indigenous people to train with, and we have to observe their regulations. When in Rome, do as the Romans do. Naturist resorts can be quite different from each other with regard to their regulations. Some are rather orthodox, with alcohol, tobacco and meat being prohibited on the grounds. You probably won't be able to enter those with your students, because only mixed couples or families are admitted. Others are quite liberal; you can find some people there with towels wrapped around their bodies or even a few clothed persons. You will have to tell your students that they should not orientate towards those deviationists but that the seminar takes place in that resort because, there, the correct behaviour in an indigenous village can be trained. Some students might ask you, why full nudity is necessary and why they couldn't keep on their shorts or a bra. I actually never had this question in all my years of doing this field training, but I could imagine that it might be asked in America. The answer would be that the training needs to cover the full cultural spectrum, which reaches from fully nude to fully clothed. It wouldn't make sense to exclude certain situations of indigenous settings. It is not necessary to particularly train the competence of covering the body, because members of the globalised culture know how to do that very well. But researchers need to be optimally prepared, in order to reduce the probability that, when they are in the field, they encounter any situation that is beyond their competence. And as for bras, they are totally uncommon in traditional indigenous cultures, and by the way, they are also relatively new to the industrial culture.[20] Directly or indirectly supporting their introduction into indigenous societies would entail damage of female self-confidence, as well as further destabilisations of the social system due to sexualisation of the female breast. Generally, the mechanisms known from research on Social embodiment strongly advise against interfering with the traditional indigenous body concept. In the case of a discussion about these points, you would do well to underscore that nobody has to go to indigenous societies, but whoever decides for going there should accept their standards, just as we expect everyone, who comes to our place, to accept our standards. If somebody would insist on maintaining the globalised standards, he or she should stay away from indigenous societies and would also not be suited to participate in the seminar. Yet, such a discussion would be unlikely when the description prior to the beginning of the course has been given clearly and sincerely.

---

[20] The US American Mary Phelps Jacob received the bra patent in 1914, but the idea was not very successful, so that she soon sold the patent. Wearing bras is now rather a psychological phenomenon in parts of the globalised world, and it is worth a mention that the attempts to dismiss bra-related health risks as myth seem to have been defensive reflexes, as recent studies have confirmed such risks (e.g. Silva Rios et al. 2016; Othieno-Abinya et al. 2015).

As for some of the students, this might be the first occasion of social nudity; you need to directly address the level of manifest behaviour, and of course be a good example, that in these settings, we stand normally and we look normally, as in everyday life. We don't stand in any tense way, but we are relaxed. Our arms hang loosely next to our bodies, we don't hold our hands or anything else in front of our bodies. We don't stare at anyone's body parts, but rather have normal patterns of eye movements. At this point, it is a good time to say some words about culture and gaze patterns. These are not universal, but they are acquired during early socialisation. Children of blind parents noticeably differ from the common gaze patterns of their context culture. In many cultures, it is normal in dyadic communication that the person, who starts to say something, looks into the eyes of the other, in order to ensure that the counterpart directs the attention towards the speaker. Then, the speaker looks away from the other person's face. This enables the counterpart to read the fine facial expressions of the speaker. Towards the end of the take, the speaker looks again into the eyes of the counterpart, in order to ensure that the other person is still paying attention. Then, it is turn status, which means the other that person starts to speak now, and the gaze patterns reverse accordingly. But we don't find these patterns in all cultures. In some societies, it is not allowed to look into the chief's or king's eyes. In others, it is not even decent to look to another person's eyes at all. In some cultures, there are further status- or gender-specific rules. I recently met a representative from a North American indigenous community at the UN in Geneva, and he told me that he found it not very decent within the industrial culture that people look into each other's eyes while they are speaking with each other. He said that he felt uncomfortable when globalised persons stared in his eyes, when they were speaking with him. I asked him, where persons from his community were looking when they were speaking with each other, and he answered, and demonstrated, that they looked down or looked around, in order to show respect towards the counterpart.

Starting with such explanations might be integrated into the routine of the arrival at the resort or after you have left the changing room and showers. Going to the registration desk to pay the fee for the day and perhaps sitting down at the buffet among the naturists to have some lunch will further dispel any concerns of the students. They will see that the naturists are normal and friendly people, far from being sexualised perverts or swingers. They will even find that naturists are particularly decent and that there are no salacious remarks or whistles, as you can sometimes find them at textile resorts or beaches.

C.c.a. First Communication Exercise

You can then go with the students to a big lawn, as they usually have it in naturist resorts and find a place that is big enough for you all to stand in a circle without disturbing other people. Tell the students to put down all of their bags, towels, watches, jewellery and anything else, so that nothing is left than the natural human being. Then tell them to form a circle, which is so big that they cannot touch each other, even when they stretch their arms. As you are part of that circle, all of you stretch your arms and move apart until you have such a circle were no one is crowded by a neighbour. Here, you can explain to the students that there is hardly any bodily touch in indigenous societies. The only exception are children, who are very much in skin-to-skin contact with grown-ups, as well as among themselves. In traditional indigenous societies, grown-ups neither hold hands in public nor do they kiss each other publicly. Anthropologists sometimes wonder how their children come into existence. It is good if you keep on weaving such explanations and references into the exercises, so that the students can understand their meaning and link them to field research in indigenous contexts.

Once you're all standing in the big circle, with an ideal number of 10–15 participants, you can start with the first communication training. You stand the centre of the circle and introduce yourself with a few words by saying what has brought you to this kind of research, for which you are training the students. Then, you ask the person next to you to do the same, then the next and so on. Ask them to briefly see their name, where they come from, what they are studying and why they have enrolled for this course. This will further put the participants in a situation of normal interaction, though now they have to present themselves before the group instead of just being part of the mass. When all have introduced themselves, the next exercise will contrast to that one and yet have something in common with the first.

C.c.b. Second Communication Exercise

The participants have to split up, single out and scatter. They shall go out into the nature and make sure that they are alone. Tell them to be aware of the sun on their skin and the wind touching their bodies. They shall feel the grass with the soles of their feet, breathe the fresh air and realise that they are now part of nature, with no separation in between. Explain to them the advantage of feeling happy in such a state. Indigenous peoples are very sensitive, and they would notice it, if researchers had only adapted reluctantly. They would see that the integration was only staged and that the researchers would actually disapprove their going indigenous. When the students are alone in nature, they shall look for a piece of nature, which they can take as a metaphor for themselves, like a leaf, a seedpod or a twig, and bring it when they return after a few minutes. When the circle is complete again, first ask the participants how they are feeling. Usually, the impact of nature and the experience of being an immediate part of it has a very positive effect and calms the students down. Now, say a few words about embodiment, and then you all go "Hooray!" together, stretching your arms up high and smiling. Explain that this has a positive influence on the well-being, as this gesture of freedom and happiness will be reflected in the feeling and state of mind.

The participants shall then one by one go the centre, show the piece of nature that they have brought and explain why this metaphorises them. This exercise contrasts to the previous, because each student first has to be alone in nature, but it also parallels the previous, as there still is communication. However, the participants first have to perceive nature intensively, similar to what they had done during the first mindfulness exercise, but without a barrier now, and then they have to share their nature experience with the others.

C.c.c. Third Communication Exercise

Now, as the students had to prove their communication skills already twice, the requirement is further increased. So far, they have only communicated within their group. In an indigenous village, they would have to communicate with persons unknown to them. Therefore, the participants now have to go out one by one again and communicate with the substitute indigenous persons, which are the naturists in the resort. To prevent the students from doing teamwork, let them go single and wait, until that participant is out of sight, before it is the next one's turn. They shall have a brief conversation of 2 or 3 min about any trivial issue. For example, they can ask someone what time it is, if there is a clock somewhere in the resort, as they were not wearing a watch; they can ask the person for the nearest bus station and also if that person knows about the bus schedule; when there is a volleyball court, they can ask where one could borrow a ball; and so forth; there are thousands of possible topics. It is better for the students to approach the person of the same sex, or a couple, or a family, in order to avoid any misunderstanding. In indigenous contexts, there is often the rule that one is not supposed to approach a single person of the opposite sex.

C.c.d. Simulate the Data Collection Situation

When the students return from this exercise, they have accomplished the most important part of the communication training in this introductory section. Have them briefly report about these chats before you turn to the next exercise. By now, the participants have usually adapted to the setting, and they might remark this in a very positive way. They are much more relaxed now than in the beginning and probably won't form a circle any more, but stand or sit on the ground. Before the situation becomes too casual, you should start with simulating an investigation, which you have already carried out in an indigenous context. For example, I go through the items of a cross-cultural gesture study,[21] which we have done a while ago. I explain to the students that in traditional indigenous settings, we have to present the gestures ourselves, because we do not want to bring technical equipment and show them clips with the clothed actors, which would probably distract the indigenous people's attention and have undesirable influence. Therefore, we need to know each gesture's exact course of movements to present the gestures in a standardised way. We all do the gestures together then, with me giving some brief explications. I also bring the equipment of our cross-cultural study on colour concepts[22] and let the students do the culture-free tests for colour blindness, explaining the situation in indigenous villages and the indigenous people's eagerness to do this test, as we have usually found it. With such examples from real research, you bring the participants another step closer to the actual research situation in indigenous settings. This simulation of data collection in indigenous contexts is the end of the practical part's introductory exercises.

---

[21] Groh (2002).
[22] Groh (2016).

In naturist resorts, there are often sports programmes offered for collective activities, such as aqua aerobics. If something like this happens to be offered while you are there with the class, it is good to join in. Remember, this is the quasi-indigenous setting, in which you train for the real field work. Participatory research means that you take part in the community's activities. If there is no such offer, but they have a swimming pool, as they usually have, let the students have a dip. It is important that they are put at ease. At the end of this day, they will perhaps tell you that they have gained entirely new perspectives and express their appreciation, as this course is different from any other seminar they ever had.

Up to here, the seminar has been something like a preparatory workshop, with a theoretical and a practical part. You can do that workshop within 2 days. However, one should not expect that such a brief workshop will fully enable students to be researchers in indigenous contexts. The acquired competence needs to be consolidated, otherwise it will fade out.

D. Consolidation Phase

Correct behaviour in indigenous contexts is one thing. It would not make much sense to leave it at that. After the fieldwork, researchers have to introduce their findings to colleagues, contribute to conferences and participate in the academic discourse. The context, in which this has to be done, is distinctly globalised. Students, who are being educated and trained for field research in indigenous contexts, also have to be prepared for all those other activities that are connected to, and which follow up, the actual fieldwork. In fact, minimally invasive field research implies only short visits to the indigenous peoples, and the researchers spend most of their time with those other activities of doing literature research, evaluating data, writing papers, collecting control data, doing surveys, working with indigenous peoples in non-indigenous contexts, preparing and coordinating applied projects, writing applications, holding presentations and giving talks at conferences, as well as coaching and consulting stakeholders. The students of this seminar also need to be prepared for that.

In this consolidation phase, the participants shall be involved in real-life situations of such work. This is the main phase of the seminar, and 10 days should be allotted to it. However, as the different parts of this course build up on each other incrementally, it is necessary that all participants of the consolidation phase have successfully passed all previous steps, as knowledge and skills, which have been imparted therein, are indispensable prerequisites for fully understanding the content of the consolidation phase.

As it has been pointed out before, the seminar aims at enabling the students to function across the whole cultural spectrum, from one end to the other. The initial practical exercises have so far focused on the most traditional, indigenous end of the spectrum. Although it is necessary to lay particular weight on the students' functioning in that part of the spectrum, it is not clear yet if they are apt to also behave properly at the other extreme end. It is well possible that some participants have appreciated the quasi-indigenous training units because they favour countercultural or bohemian lifestyles and therefore find it cool to walk naked, but they are unable to function in highly globalised contexts, where formal dress and otherwise appropriate forms of communication are required. Some of them might even refuse to wear a suit. They would have to be excluded from further attending the seminar, just as those who had problems with nudity were excluded from proceeding to the naturist resort. The requirement of wearing a suit is comparable to the necessity of using diving equipment when you do a course for deep-sea diving. Those who refuse to use that equipment would also be excluded. But usually, the students understand that the seminar aims at enabling them to switch quickly and easily between situations. The best way of training this is to make them switch between the most extreme situations of the cultural spectrum.

Whereas the training of properly functioning in traditional indigenous cultures can only be carried out in a quasi-indigenous setting, and not in a real indigenous village, for obvious reasons that have been explained above, the training of functioning in the contrasting situations can and should be trained in a real, highly globalised setting. For one thing, there is no reason to fear that social systems at the very dominant, far end of the cultural spectrum could be destabilised by students who are not behaving quite correctly within that setting. For another thing, students profit far more from real-life situations than they do from any simulation. With regard to indigenous settings, the simulation cannot be avoided for the training, but with regard to the highly globalised context, it can.

So, how can we design this main part of the seminar in a way that the students can gain maximum benefit from it? If you have access to the UN, then you might have the chance to take the students to this highest political body of the world, where sessions with a focus on indigenous peoples take place regularly. Otherwise, there are plenty of high-ranking, international conferences all over the world, with topics that are relevant to indigenous issues or to intercultural aspect in general. For example, the larger psychology conferences often have a section on cultural psychology. But there are also very specialised international conferences, such as those hosted by the International Society for Hunter Gatherer Research, the World Congress of African Linguistics or the Multidisciplinary Conference on Indigenous Peoples, which all take place regularly in changing locations. If you are a researcher and lecturer, you might be a presenter at one of those conferences yourself. This is a good opportunity to bring your students along. Anyway, find such a meeting, which has a highly formal setting, and incorporate it in your seminar.

Parallel to choosing this highly globalised event, look for a naturist resort nearby, which is secure and reliable as described above. This combination is necessary in order to enable the switching between these two settings, in the way that the students have to take accommodation in the resort, and from there go to the sessions during the days of the conference week. As the correct behaviour in the quasi-indigenous setting is what they have to train most, much more weight has to be laid on it. This can best be accomplished by allotting more time to it. Therefore, the students should arrive in the naturist resort previous to the conference, so that they have at least 3 days of retreat there. By now, you should be able to rely on them, as they all have successfully passed the preparatory workshop. You could even leave them alone during this time, if you have a confidable tutor to supervise them. The resort of choice should of course offer accommodation in the form of a dormitory or a campground, and there should be a sufficiently equipped kitchen or other facilities, which enable the students to cook and cater themselves, unless there is a cafeteria in the resort that is affordable for the students. Regarding expenses, they will already have paid for the INF card or equivalent registration, as well as for accommodation or camping fees.

For various reasons, the stay in the naturist resort is the ideal preparation for the students' participations in real field research in the future. After their arrival, they should spend the first 3 days free from textiles without interruption. Other than after the few hours of naturism during the preparatory part, the participants will then become used to it much more. After these days, they might even complain when they have to put on clothes again, that they constrain, cut in, scratch and make them sweat. Indeed, when putting on clothing after several days of freedom, one feels like a chimpanzee forced into a suit, and one has to wonder why our culture pursues such habits that are actually inappropriate for our species. But by reaching such a point of very practical critique of globalisation, they have indeed come to a meta-level, from which they can compare cultures, not only theoretically from the desk but from concretely being in it, thus knowing what they talk about. This will help them to understand that these are roles, and by playing these roles consciously, they will no longer be subject to them. Furthermore, the participants are being prepared for field research in indigenous contexts, because they have to organise themselves. Depending on the local conditions, they might have to buy food in advance, and they will have to function as a team. Although it is obvious, you should instruct them beforehand that they behave decently in the naturist resort and that they abide by the rules. Usually, naturists set great value upon cleanliness and hygiene. They want that all facilities are used properly and left in a good manner. For example, the floor has to be wiped immediately after a shower has been taken, the kitchen has to be cleaned up immediately after eating, dishes must be washed and everything has to be put in its place. All such duties should be arranged among the participants. It is good to ask the resort staff upon arrival and have things explained by someone in charge. It also should be clarified beforehand who is the contact person in the resort in case that there are any questions.

Tell the students beforehand that this *is* an excursion and that they should regard the naturist residents in their huts of the resort in the same way as it would be appropriate towards the people of the village during field research. This way, the students will have communication training under real-life conditions. The resemblance between the naturist residents in their huts of the resort and a traditional indigenous community is the closest similarity that can be reached during field research training taking place in the globalised culture. The students should behave friendly and communicatively, greet everyone, make contacts and approach the people in an unobtrusive way. When you are running any cross-cultural study, this is a good chance for the students to train data collection, and the data obtained in such a resort are indeed an interesting sample.

It is necessary, though, to provide the students with a well-structured schedule for these 3 days. As there is usually a swimming pool in such a resort, they should go swimming at sunrise and at sunset. This is a good preparation for participatory field research, as it is common for many indigenous peoples, for example, in Latin America, to do exactly that in the mornings and in the evenings. By the way, it should be mandatory for any participant in excursions to indigenous peoples to be able to swim. It would be irresponsible to take a non-swimmer on such field research. Most indigenous peoples live close to rivers, lakes or the sea, and even if they don't, you might have to cross waters on the way to them. You never know which kind of transport you will have to resort to, and not only dugouts are easily capsizable.

Tasks should be allocated to the students before they go to the resort for papers to be presented by each of them during the retreat. This should be part of the schedule for these 3 days, and the class with talks and discussions should be supervised by the tutor, who is the overseer, anyway, during these days. Many naturist resorts also offer archery. If this is the case in that particular resort, you should make use of it, because it is a meaningful addition to the schedule, it helps to integrate the participants into the quasi-indigenous contexts, and moreover, knowing how to apply bow and arrow can be very useful in fully indigenous contexts.

When you arrive after these 3 days, you will find that they have constituted themselves as a team. You can then proceed with the conference week. By taking accommodation in the resort yourself, you will be able to monitor the conduct of the participants. This is necessary, as at the end of the seminar, you need to either certify their acquisition of competence and thus take responsibility for giving them green light to participate in excursions to indigenous contexts or to tell them that they need further improvement. Therefore, be vigilant about uncertainness regarding their integration into the quasi-indigenous context. The task to stay textile free in this context is simple and clear and easy to follow, as long as the weather does not definitely prevent it. If there are any participants, who seem to have problems with that, as they are putting on clothes or use towels in a similar way, they might not be eligible for a field trip to traditional indigenous communities. The indigenous people would realise immediately any hesitancy and understand that as reluctance towards accepting their traditional lifestyle. Likewise, keep an eye on the respectability of the participants' appearance at the conference. Make sure that they not only go there in formal dress but also that they behave and communicate in a respectful way. It might happen that there are other people at the conference, who are wearing casual dress, and the students might refer to them and ask why they are required to appear so formally themselves. You can answer that you use the opportunity of the conference to make them fully competent along the whole cultural spectrum, even to this very formalised high end of it. Like in the case of some other guests at naturist resorts, who were not completely free of textiles, you can tell your students not to orientate themselves towards those who do not fully comply with rules and that you want them to prove their ability to function in both ends of the cultural spectrum.

At the conference, you should also use every opportunity that would help the participants of your seminar to acquire skills. When I take my students to UN sessions, I place them, in a rotation scheme, with those in charge of organisational tasks. To them, the students can give a hand. Due to the rotation scheme, each student of the group has the chance to look behind the scenes. Furthermore, I obtain permission from the secretariat to have a table outside the session hall, where information about our institution's research and about our projects is on display and publications are presented, so that the indigenous representatives and the colleagues of the session can have a look, can take some of the information and can also take part in running surveys, questionnaire studies and targeted interviews, if they wish so. By this way, my students, who attend the table in a rotational scheme as well, are again fully immersed into this context. They have to be polite and communicate in a professional manner, and they have to carry out that data collection. For the rest of the time, they can sit on the sidelines of the session hall and listen to the agenda items. In a further rotation, I take one student for half a day each into the session as an assistant.

When you use the opportunity of a conference to let students of your seminar collect data for surveys and questionnaire studies, it goes without saying that you have to instruct them before they start with it and that you also supervise them while they are carrying out the data collection.

This suggested education and training programme is the result of a maturation process over the years. In the beginning, I only offered the final phase to the students, which is the attending of a UN session in connection with taking accommodation on a naturist resort. But this requires very intensive coaching in order to also convey the theoretical framework during that time. When the groups had become larger after a few years, it turned out that some students did not quite comprehend the meaning of the field training and some did not fully behave according to the naturists' rules. Therefore, I added the preparatory workshop, which, at first, took place on one day only. I had to do some more fine-tuning, which is the allocation of theoretical part and practical part of the preparatory workshop on two separate days, which gives the students more opportunity to digest and comprehend the content, and the other thing was to add the days in advance of the UN session week, so that the participants can better immerse themselves in the quasi-indigenous setting, which is actually the most important aspect of the seminar.

Explaining the reasons for the didactic procedure to the students very thoroughly is most important. Otherwise, there might be students, who neither comprehend the precarious situation of indigenous peoples nor the significance of the seminar's content and who might make fun of it in a misconceived way, and such gossip could, in the worst case, spoil not only your reputation but thus also deprive future students of the chance to become researchers, who are particularly sensitised for indigenous issues. As the full competence for working in indigenous contexts also includes the professional handling of social nudity, I can give you the serious advice to make sure that the content of the seminar is never misunderstood. Generally speaking, the integrity and good reputation of the lecturer-trainer are vitally important. The best things to do to ensure this is that other professors of the department participate in the seminar and that the seminar itself takes place in an absolutely reputable way, so that no one can take offence at it, but that students, who have completed it, will rather promote it in the very best way.

Overall, such a seminar comprises as much relevant teaching as possible. It does not make much sense to separate the different parts, unless you only want to present the theoretical perspective. But as for the practical training for field research, it is advisable that you keep it all together.

It is not always necessary to prepare team-members-to-be with such an extensive seminar. In central and northern Europe, we have a well-established sauna culture. Whereas naturism is only practised occasionally when the weather is warm enough, many people go to the sauna regularly for large parts of the year. Sauna-goers in central and northern Europe do not wrap themselves in towels, and in between the sessions, they walk with free skin in the fresh air, which is very healthy with regard to the uptake of oxygen[23] and strengthening the body's robustness against temperature changes. So, these people are accustomed to social nudity, anyway. Therefore, if you have been with your colleagues to the sauna regularly, or if you know them from naturism for sufficient long time, that you can be certain about their integrity, then you can skip those time-consuming and cumbersome practical parts of the field training. However, it is well known in Europe that there are other parts of the globalised society who have meanwhile internalised their distance from nature, which is a severe obstacle for correct conduct in indigenous contexts. For this reason, these aspects have been pointed out in this book with due emphasis, as it would be irresponsible to make any mistakes, which could be to the detriment of indigenous peoples.

4.4.1 Learning How to Prepare Research in Indigenous Contexts

Whereas the previous section was primarily directed to instructors, this section here is predominantly directed to those who have already gone successfully through such a course with education and training for field research in indigenous contexts and who are now in between the seminar and their first excursion to a traditional indigenous community. But of course, it is also directed to experienced researchers, who have long mastered the challenges of the fields and who have full competence and skills with regard to culturally sustainable behaviour and also rescue work, when they are with indigenous peoples.

When you make preparations for a field research to an indigenous community, you will first have to do some online search for relevant literature and sources pertaining to the indigenous people, as well as investigations, enquiries and research in archives. Much of this material, which you will compile, has not been authored by persons, who have tried to minimise any sources of error. Some of them might not even have reflected about their own role and their influence on the cultural context. Such lack of reflecting determines certain ways of perceiving, interpreting and evaluating things. And other authors might even have knowingly and intentionally distorted data, because they were not in line with their own norms and standards.

I remember having seen an American anthropology book a while ago, with pictures of the Yali people of West Papua. I have done field research in that region

---

[23] The upper skin layers rely almost exclusively on external oxygen supply from the atmosphere, not on oxygen transported by blood (Stücker et al. 2002).

myself, and as I am a man, I have also worn a koteka there, which is a penis sheath made from a dried gourd. There are three tribes in and around the Baliem Valley: the Dani, the Lani and the Yali. As long as they have their traditional appearance, you can easily distinguish them from the way they have their penis gourd. The Dani one is slim and straight upward, held close to the body with a thin string. The one of the Lani is wide and thick. It is also worn upward, but it is open at the top, so that the Lani at the same time use it to keep some of their belongings in there. The Yali wear a whole array of bands around their belly, with the penis gourd standing out beneath these bands and away from the body. This sight must have seemed somewhat indecent to the American anthropologists. If they had ever worn it themselves, they would have known that a koteka has nothing to do with sexual arousal, as it in fact suppresses any arousal. Anyway, in this American anthropology book, the penis gourds of the Yali were spotted away with graphical editing, which you could still see when you took a closer look. Such a procedure is actually a severe violation of scientific standards. Apparently, there are cultural standards in America that are valued higher than scientific standards. But a picture like that one is actually lying. The excuse might have been that they were afraid that some children might have a look at this book and they did not want them to see what they thought it was. But it really wasn't what they probably thought, whereas their manipulation of the picture was really an infringement of ethical norms.

While in this case, you only needed to take a closer look to detect the manipulation, the authors' standards become manifest in most other cases in rather subtle ways. When you see pictures of indigenous persons wearing loincloths, or even sheets wrapped around their bodies, it is often questionable that this is really these persons' authentic look. Those who take such pictures, including filmmakers, might have brought the material and told the indigenous persons to wear it. In other cases, other dominant visitors might have done so a while ago, so that the indigenous people put these things on obediently when there are visitors, while behind the scenes and when there are no visitors, they go without. In West Africa, where many people have become accustomed to those colourful cloths, which are actually produced in Europe, it has recently become customary that women, who wear such a cloth around their waists, now pull it up over their breasts when they see strangers. When pictures are taken there, they eventually depict the external influence, which has been exerted on these peoples, both the regulation of covering the loin, which has been imposed decades ago, and also the more recent explicit or implicit instruction to cover the breast. Laypersons, however, do not "read" such pictures semiotically, but they just take them as pictures of West Africans.

Whereas photographies and films can distort reality in the sense that details are chosen or prevented to be shown or that they are cut, in order to show particular sections or sequences only, distortions can be undertaken in written text much more easily. Indigenous cultures are often just described the way the authors want them to be. Interestingly, though sadly, these manipulated descriptions can have a repercussion on the indigenous peoples concerned. As we can see by systemic analysis, the industrial culture's dominance has the effect that indigenous peoples actually become what the dominant culture wants them to be.

All the more you have to reflect about your own role, which is already relevant when you prepare an excursion. You need to know how to interpret reports, records and pictures that you find during your preparation. For this, it is necessary to understand the situations in which the reports came about but also the mechanisms of cultural dominance and the biases within the mutual influences. From the complex intra- and intercultural processes, misconceptions can emerge, either in the form of selective perceptions and depictions, due to cognitive patterns that have been internalised during the dominant person's socialisation, or also in the form of modifications and manipulations, which are done consciously by certain authors in disrespect and refusal of other cultures' standards.

To avoid any misunderstanding, it has to be pointed out here that not all other cultural standards have to be appreciated. There are practices in indigenous cultures, too, which violate human rights. From a human rights perspective, cultural standards have their limits when they make persons suffer, when they are directed against human life or when they are otherwise detrimental. This can also pertain to the natural environment. There are some negative examples from the past about indigenous peoples' customs that have led to desertification, which we have already addressed in the first chapter of this book. There is also a discussion going on with regard to the role of pastoralists. Other than hunter-gatherers, they have a severe impact on the environment, as their herds prevent whole regions to be forested. However, all inter- and transcultural critique needs to be argued out by addressing and discussing the problems openly and with full transparency.

When you seek information from supposed experts in the region, where you want to do the research, you cannot always rely on their expertise. I once had an argument with an American volunteer in Uganda, who was working there for the "Batwa Development Program" in the context of the "Peace Corps Master's International program". He maintained that the Batwa had traditionally worn bark clothing or animal skin, whereas any local will tell you that the Batwa went nude until they were told to put on clothes, which happened relatively recently, so that even middle-aged persons remember them as stark naked. But this graduate student was apparently determined to believe what he had been taught, rather than what locals say. I recommended him to look up the serious anthropological literature, but I do not know if that was of any help. By the way, after that argument, three men with mirrored sunglasses like in a B-movie followed our research team with a four-wheel drive deep into the mountains and disturbed our fieldwork with the indigenous community. They said they were from a big American aid agency.

When you have composed the team, it is always good to have one more workshop, where you go through all relevant theoretical and practical aspects, similar to the workshop described in the previous section but in a condensed form, as all team members should be well trained already. However, if their training had taken place more than a year ago, a freshening up would be recommendable anyway. The head of the excursion should again monitor all team members with scrutiny, as people can change over time.

In the course of the preparation for the excursion, during which the field research is going to be done in the indigenous context, the team members should also be equipped with the knowledge of how to handle some practical aspects that are addressed in the following sections. This is especially necessary for those who are about to do such field research for the first time.

4.5   Culturally Sustainable Field Research

As for the composition of the team, the head of the excursion should make sure that all members have already proven successfully their capacity for teamwork. They should know each other and cooperate very well. If they had just gone through education and training in the sense of the seminar described above, this does not automatically mean that they have passed it successfully. Ideally, the head of the excursion should also have been the instructor and lecturer of the seminar, so that he or she should be able to assess the eligibility. If someone, who has gone through the seminar, wants to join the excursion, but there is some doubt about the integrity of that person, then zero tolerance should be exercised, as we should never run any risk at the expense of the indigenous peoples.

Of course, it is not always possible to compose a team in the sense of a group. In indigenous communities, my wife and I have made the experience that the fact of being a traditional couple is confidence-building. And it is even more confidence-building, when the indigenous hosts learn that you have children. Usually, it is methodologically and ethically sound to show pictures of one's children, if the indigenous persons are acquainted with photography, and any cultural destabilisation is not to be feared. As it is common for toddlers in Europe to play naked outdoor in summer, cultural elements that could be critical, such as clothing, can be avoided to be shown on these pictures, and indigenous persons notice that apart from ethnic features, there is not much difference from their own children. If you want to take your children to an indigenous community, instead of only showing pictures of them, think about your responsibility and calculate the health risks in the area, where you want to do the visit. In this connection, also see the section below on tropical health. Nevertheless, if you are certain that you can take this responsibility, then you, as a family, might find the indigenous doors even more open than if you would only go there as a couple.

While being a traditional couple can be door opening, single visitors are more likely to be met with distrust. Indigenous peoples often fear that men from outside want to take their women. This is even much more the case when two or more men arrive at an indigenous village. The indigenous peoples' fear certainly has its reasons rooted in negative experience that they have made.

Female visitors, never mind if they arrive single, by two or in a group, can be somewhat irritating to indigenous peoples, because for most of them, the idea of women, who are travelling without men, is outside the options of their cultural standards.

The rule of thumb for the composition of a team for an excursion to do field research in indigenous contexts is:

$$f \geq m$$

which means that the number of female members should be equal to or larger than the number of male members. This is owing to the fact that indigenous peoples are generally scared that strange men might take their women. They certainly have their reason from negative experience. We should understand this fear and take it seriously, and we should also do our best to prevent such fears. When there are more men than women in the team, then the indigenous people could assume that there are some couples in the team plus some superfluous men, and therefore, they might be suspicious. With an equal number of men and women in the team, there would not be such suspicion, nor would it be a problem if there were more women than men. This is for two reasons. Firstly, it is not feared from women that they might take their men, and even if a strange woman would take an indigenous man, then this would usually be accepted in traditional societies as the man's decision. And secondly, there are more polygamous than monogamous traditional societies, and thus, more women than men in the group would be considered normal.

However, I can tell you from my own experience that balanced teams are much better to handle than unbalanced ones. I can strongly recommend against one male head with the rest of the team being women. The stronger the mismatch, the worse. From a certain size, there should be at least a second man.

It follows from the sections and chapters above that you should obey to the rules of the indigenous community, once you have arrived in their place. The lines of decency are often drawn much stricter than in the globalised society. I remember the report of a member of a group of men – sailors, if I remember correctly – who happened to end up in a traditional indigenous village, where the people were nude. I think it was in South America. The one, who reported this insisted that they had only made eyes at the ladies, nothing else. Nevertheless, the indigenous people there became very enraged and threw the foreign men out of the village. So, reflect everything you do, even the automatisms. Behaviour patterns that you know from your habitual contexts may not work in indigenous cultures.

Principally, you can already derive many guidelines as how to do culturally sustainable fieldwork, from what has been said so far in this book. I have tried to insert a number of anecdotes, examples and details from my field research in indigenous contexts during the past three decades, which hopefully complement theory with practice. As all theory should have its foundation in practice, and should also be related to practice, the last two sections of this book are dedicated to practical aspects, some of which might be answers to questions that you have not dared to ask so far.

4.5.1   Practical Aspects

Many practical aspects regarding conduct in indigenous contexts have already been made clear in this book. Regarding self-presentation and the abandonment of clothing, it might be mentioned that one should also refrain from wearing a watch in traditional indigenous contexts. If you need to wear glasses, please try to use contact lenses instead. Perhaps your dioptres are not that high, so that you can even go without any vision aid.

If you need to hire a tour guide to reach the indigenous place, make sure that he (guides usually are men) is really well acquainted with the people and the terrain and that he speaks the indigenous language. You need to make sure beforehand that the guide complies with, and that he participates in, all the minimally invasive techniques, total immersion and rescue work. The tour guide will know how to announce your arrival, which is done in New Guinea, for example, with yodelling already in some distance of the settlement. Immediately before arriving at the indigenous village, pause and let the guide go ahead to tell the people that you are there and to ask for permission that you enter. As indigenous people often notice that you are approaching long before you actually arrive, they might have put on some cover, as described above (Sect. 4.3), in order to appear more "civilised" and less "backward". Therefore, tell the guide that he shall explain to the people that you appreciate their culture, and to encourage them to be in their traditional way, and that you try your best to also be that way. Before the guide comes back to pick you up from the spot where you have been waiting, and to take you into the village, you should have taken off your clothes at the latest.[24]

Before you start to do any field research in indigenous contexts, it is necessary to equip yourself at least with the knowledge of how to handle some very basic practical aspects, which we shall look at now.

Eating

Let us begin with the question what to eat during the time that you spend with indigenous peoples in their contexts. In case that you are accompanied by a tour guide, he will have taken care of this question and probably cook for you, depending on the length of your stay. But if you are without a guide, you need to be prepared regarding the food issue. Minimising one's invasiveness also means to keep the stay relatively short, so that in many cases, the question won't be relevant. You can eat enough before you arrive there, so that you can manage for the hours of your stay. But if you spend some more time in the indigenous context, then the question becomes somewhat complex indeed. On the one hand, eating with the indigenous would be quite an integrative behaviour. And it is interesting, too, to learn what they eat and to become acquainted with food that one has neither seen nor tasted before. But there are several other aspects to consider. Food might be scarce, and you don't want to eat from what they have and take the risk that they or maybe even their children go hungry. Even if they invite you and offer the food to you, this might be out of their etiquette. Traditions sometimes require that the host insists that you accept something, but it might likewise be traditional practice that you refuse. Yet, rejection could also be seen as being unfriendly, which could then lead to tensions that you certainly don't want, either. A reasonable way to handle this is not to

---

[24] Interestingly, after leaving the indigenous village and on their way back to globalised contexts, research teams sometimes try to avoid as long as possible to put on clothes again.

demand anything, unless you know that there is sufficient supply and that you can reward it. If you are invited, be polite and only try a little bit, unless there is plenty of food and all are eating. If you have a good reason not to eat it, explain that you have stomach problems, which you can even do with gestures. I have always found understanding in such situations, as indigenous peoples generally are aware that strangers cannot always cope with their food. It is important that you don't communicate in a negative way, but rather do it in a friendly manner. In particular, you should be cautious with anything that has not been freshly and sufficiently cooked or fried or which you don't peel yourself. Otherwise, your carelessness could set an abrupt end to your activities, as you might catch some severe infection. Because you have a globalised cultural background, your body is neither used to the quantity nor to the quality of germs that you typically find in indigenous contexts, and so your immune system does not know the right answers when confronted with them. Since you don't know beforehand if any food will be offered to you and if so, what will be offered, you should always carry some food with you. But when can you eat it? If they had offered something, which you could not take, referring to stomach problems, the further options of how you deal with the situation depend on their knowledge of strangers. If they know that people from the globalised culture have sensitive stomachs with regard to food that they are not used to, then they will understand. You may want to retreat a bit, since you do not want to give a show by eating in front of them. We have never been molested in such situations. There might be some curious kids, but that is what you can find in non-indigenous places, too. If you are uncertain about the situation, then eat your energy bar when you are alone or when nobody sees it. Nightfall is around 7 p.m. in the tropics, and night is almost as long as day, so you have plenty of time before sunrise.

Sleeping

This brings us to the next point – where and how to sleep? Well, in cases where there is a longhouse that accommodates several families anyway, and in which there is still space, chances are good that you will be invited to stay overnight in there as well. Make sure that you don't occupy more space than it is allocated to you and to respect the spots of other families or persons when you pass by. Don't stare at other persons. Even when they stay together in a longhouse, they have their privacy. When someone of a tribe that is not fully nude, but has loincloths, turns his or her back on you while changing the loincloth, it means that he or she does not want to be seen. So, don't even look in that direction. In those cultures, people can rely on each other that they respect the virtual walls, and you should do your best to do the same. Don't try to fool them; they are not stupid. Rather, they sometimes unfold a practical intelligence that makes us feel ashamed.

Of course, not all indigenous cultures live in longhouses. Those who have big community houses for men and for women will probably allocate you accordingly. You might then be expected to bring your own hammock, which should be no problem, as in those South American regions where hammocks are common, those that you can buy for reasonable prices on the market are of indigenous design, anyway. Again other cultures have smaller huts but one bigger hut for gatherings, as well as for hosting guests. It could also happen that a hut is not in use, so that you are offered to stay overnight there. But still, among the thousands of indigenous cultures, you might run into situations where the indigenous simply don't have any extra space. This once happened to us in a Bambuti settlement in the eastern Congo basin. It actually was a double settlement, one consisting of five and the other of only two huts, the first run by the "grand chef" ("great chief") and the second headed by the "petit chef" ("little chief"), as those Bambuti said humorously, since they don't have a very strict social hierarchy. The Bambuti huts were in traditional Pygmy style: cupola-shaped, made of bent branches and a layer of big leaves. We happened to have a tent of very similar colour, shape and size with us. When pitched, it consisted of bent thin fibre poles, covered with an olive coloured layer. The Bambuti themselves confirmed that it resembled their huts very much. Therefore, I can give the advice to carry such a tent with you when you are uncertain with regard to your overnight stays. Also from a perspective of cultural theory, the use of such a tent can be approved. If you think of the cultural spectrum from "cold" to "hot", as outlined in Chap. 1 of this book, and factors of heating up, then you are on the safe side if you use cultural elements from the cooler part of the spectrum than from parts that are warmer or even hotter than the present state of a culture. We can find the cupola as the shape of the housing in archaic cultures – in the Talayot culture, it was made from stone, the Inuit made (and occasionally still make) it from blocks of snow and various Pygmy cultures make it from branches and leaves.

You might even be lucky that your hosts build such a hut especially for you. The Batwa in southwest Uganda did that once for us. It was amazing how fast they could build the hut. Many hands make light work. It did not take much more than 10 min until the hut was finished. Admittedly, it was quite a small one. But it was good to have it; as immediately after it was finished, the rain set in.

Nights in the jungle can be quite noisy. Often, there are much more sounds at night than during the day. If you are not used to it and cannot sleep, you might want to put in some earplugs. But only do so in places where you are safe. Otherwise, it would be prudent to remain in a vigilant state, so that although you are sleeping, you can instantly become fully alert. The indigenous can discern between safe and dangerous sounds. Some sounds are annoying, like some bugs that make an ototoxic noise like an amplified electric shaver; other sounds are scary but harmless, like some antelope's bugling; and again other sounds are really impressive. I vividly remember how I was once aroused at daybreak in an Indian village in Panama. A cacique had provided me with an empty hut next to his. These huts there only consist of a platform on poles, open all around and usually with a grass roof above. At dawn, there suddenly was a giant choir of howler monkeys in the surrounding forest, it sounded like thousands. Like in a big stadium, the roaring moved around in waves. You certainly do not need an alarm clock there!

Mosquito Nets
How about mosquito nets, you might ask now. And you are right. Without such protection, we risk to catch life-threatening illnesses. In fact, some indigenous peoples use mosquito nets, because governmental or NGO initiatives that promote

mosquito nets have reached them. They have these nets inside their huts, while they pursue their everyday life. Apparently, their identity is not noticeably influenced by those mosquito nets.

Interestingly, Pygmies seem to be immune to malaria and similar diseases, as long as they live their traditional life in the jungle, but they become affected, once they have been forced out of the forest.[25] Even the seroprevalence of antibodies against Ebola and Marburg viruses is relatively high in Pygmies (Gonzalez et al. 2000). However, this is a privilege of specific populations, and we, as representatives of the globalised culture, need to take precautions. Now, you might add for consideration that the sight of a mosquito net could have some destabilising effect, and we should take such concerns seriously, weighing the pros and cons.

As this is part of a complex issue, we have to make a little digression into theoretical aspects. In Chap. 2 of this book, we have pondered over the protection of culture (Sect. 2.4). Cultural elements are of different relevance to a person's cultural identity. The closer something is to the self, the more relevant it is. Therefore, the way the body is presented is of crucial importance. Also, the more permanently perceivable over time a person-related cultural element is, the more identity relevant it is to that individual. From a communication perspective, one can say that what counts is the intensity of the linkage between the cultural element and a person, as it is perceived by others. If others perceive a particular cultural element as linked to a high degree with a person, then that person is usually aware of that. Consequently, this cultural element has a constitutional value regarding that person's cultural identity. When indigenous persons receive dominant input from globalised role models, who do not minimise their invasiveness and present themselves with clothing, so that the indigenous persons, once they have obtained such clothing, also show up with their bodies covered in a globalised style, then this implies several cognitions. These indigenous persons communicate how they want to be seen. The others – fellow indigenous persons, as well as anyone else, who perceives them – attribute, accordingly, their affinity towards the global culture. As each perceivable behaviour is an act of communication and as there is an interplay of mutual influences with transference and countertransference, at least when both sides are aware of the behaviour, the person has thus modified his or her cultural identity. Transference and countertransference, by the way, are of course also active between the globalised visitor and the indigenous person. The globalised person sees that person who now presents him- or herself in a not-so-indigenous-any-more way. For the worst, the globalised person takes this as an excuse to further exert his or her dominance by saying, "oh, this indigenous person seems to like it", without considering the socio-cognitive determinants, especially the effect of dominance, that have led to that "liking" and maybe, in further infringements of several articles of the UN declaration, even give some more pieces of clothing as presents. For the best, globalised persons see the effect of their behaviour and reflect it in a self-critical way, realising that without this influence, the system would have remained stable, as now

---

[25] Personal communication by the filmmaker Hans-Jürgen Steinfurth (cf. Steinfurth 2001).

that influence is highly probable to propagate within the indigenous community, leading to an imbalance and then to the destabilisation of the social system.

An example of less relevance to cultural identity would be an indigenous person's knowledge of a European language. As long as there is no European or other speaker of such a language around, this person would speak the indigenous mother tongue with the other members of that cultural group. And as long as no further dominant cultural elements are used by that person, he or she would just be seen as a fellow member of the group, who happens to be able to communicate with those strangers.

The use of a global-style mosquito net is something in between. Other than language, it is permanently present. But it is not permanently linked to the person who uses it. If in that culture, families have separate, closed huts, then those who do not belong to this person's family won't even see it. In that case, the use of the mosquito net would not even be an act of communication towards the other villagers. The degree to which the mosquito net would be identity relevant would be correspondingly small. Even if the people of an indigenous culture live in longhouses or in open huts, so that each one sees how the others sleep, and one of them would start to use a mosquito net, which would then spread and become a habit, as all somehow managed to obtain a mosquito net, how identity relevant would that be? The nets would probably be rolled away in the morning and be out of the people's mind during the day. And at night, they would sleep and not see them, anyway. Under health aspects, benefits would prevail.

We have discussed this question so far under the premise that mosquito nets are an achievement of the dominant European, industrial culture and that those nets do not genuinely belong to indigenous peoples' cultures. Yet, I had to reconsider this assumption recently. When I stayed with the Wounaan people in the Darién, I happened to find some evidence that mosquito nets are not so new in indigenous contexts. According to what I saw there, they are not an invention by Europeans, but they probably are a traditional element of indigenous cultures. I found this out by chance, and usually, external visitors won't see that. I had come to that place on my own and participated in a session of the village council. After nightfall, the elders showed me a place in the assembly hut, where I could sleep, but warned me that youngsters might try at night to steal some of my belongings. I did not have too much with me, as I was travelling on foot, but I was not very thrilled with the prospect of having to be alert all night long. Therefore, I asked one of the elders if I could stay with him in his hut. He hesitated for a moment, then he said that was all right and took me to the hut, where he lived with his wife. It consisted of one big room that hosted him and his wife. Their kids were grown up, had left the village and went to live in town, from where they only came to visit their parents occasionally. To my surprise, the old folks had a large bed in their hut, but they said they never used it. It was only there for their kids, who were acquainted to a more globalised lifestyle in town and used to sleep in a bed now. Therefore, the parents had that bed in their hut for those occasions, when their children came to pay them a visit. So, there was this bed for them in the room, with a plastic cover above the bedding. In fact, the old folks seemed to treat the bed like an alien object, which they did not use themselves, but they told me to sleep there. First, I was not too sure if they had offered me that bed only out of politeness and said no, I did not want to occupy their bed, and I could just as well sleep on my mat on the floor. But the elderly couple insisted very firmly that they did not sleep in the bed. I finally accepted, thanked them and made myself comfortable for the night on top of the plastic cover. There also was a relatively large hammock in the room, and if I had only seen that place during the day, I would have assumed that this was the old couple's sleeping place. But to my astonishment, they did not use it, either. In fact, hammocks are not common among Wounaan and Emberá people, who have united to form a joint group that was then able to claim a common territory. Either of them would have been too small for such a claim, but together, they have managed. Anyway, the old lady used the hammock only during the day.

During my overnight stay in that hut, I witnessed for the first time how these indigenous people actually sleep – not in the hammock, as I had first taken for granted. At night, those indigenous folks sleep on the bare planks of the hut. But now comes the most interesting part: before they lay down, the Wounaan built a cuboid out of sticks and gauze on the floor and disappeared inside of it. The cuboid had the size of approximately $70 \times 70 \times 150$ cm. The people of that particular group are quite small, adults are about 1.5 m. In the darkness of the night, I had the impression that even a third person arrived and also went to sleep inside the gauze cuboid. The Wounaan rose very early, before daylight, and took down the cuboid. Then, there was no trace left on the floor that the cuboid had ever been there.

Although the material used for the cuboid seemed to be an industrial product, resembling to old-fashioned swaddling clothes, the design of the cuboid is different from the usual style of mosquito nets. The cuboid is apparently a traditional element, with industrial material now being used for the walls. Nevertheless, the indigenous peoples of that region, like in other parts of the world, know how to produce textile-like fabrics from tissues underneath the barks of certain trees. When the first whites arrived and told them to cover certain parts of their bodies, these were the only fabrics they had. So, when they were urged to put on loincloths, they had to use these fabrics, unless they were given textiles by the whites. The loincloths from bark fabrics were then claimed to be the indigenous "traditional dress", although without the pressure from the invaders that material would hardly have been used for covering the loin. But it is well suited for keeping mosquitos out of sleeping cuboids.

The way the Wounaan sleep reminds me, somehow, of the medieval sleeping cubicles that one can see in European museum villages. In the half-timbered farm houses, the peasants slept in cupboard-like places with sliding wooden doors that were positioned between two rooms. Not only one of them slept in there, but five or more squeezed it. But other than the Wounaan, they were frightened to lie down, so they slept sitting.

Anopheles mosquitos, the vectors of malaria, sting between sunset and sunrise. But there are many other stinging insects that can transmit diseases. The Wounaan, as well as the Emberá and other Latin American indigenous peoples, claim that their body paintings are not only for decoration purposes but that they also work as insect repellents. The paintings are done with the juice of the jagua fruit. The colour does not show very strong when it is freshly put on. You have to let it dry for about an hour and then go to the river to wash it off. What is left on your skin then oxidises over several hours, so that the next day, the painting is really strong like ink. When you are at such an indigenous village, where the people use that body painting, you will hardly overlook it. There is usually one artist lady, who is specialised in doing these paintings. If you ask them to paint your body, they are very proud. The other indigenous people there appreciate very much if you do that, as this is, in turn, an appreciation of their culture. And if you go to other indigenous villages later on, they will welcome you in a particularly appreciating way. You don't have to be afraid that the painting remains for too long. Depending on the concentration of the juice, it will be gone after a couple of days or after a couple of weeks. If you arrive with a large team with everybody asking to be painted, the artist will probably thin down the juice to serve you all, but this diluted paint won't last very long, but fade out quickly.

Indigenous Body Painting

In connection with being painted by the Emberá (cf. Sect. 4.2), I made a discovery similar to the key insight during our first Punan expedition (see above, Sect. 4.3). And also similar to that one, this was found out, too, only due to strict orientation towards the reconstruction of the indigenous traditions. Again, we need to do a little digression due to the complexity of the subject. From the historical data, we can reconstruct that the indigenous peoples of Latin America, similar to those of other regions, did not veil their bodies prior to the European influences. Even the indigenous peoples of Tierra del Fuego were naked, despite the almost Antarctic climate. They were systematically extinct by the Europeans. Almost all of the remaining few died from infections, after they had been forced into clothing. Anything similar to European clothing was only found in the advanced civilisations of Central America, where similar factors of progress were at work as in Europe. The indigenous population of the climatically cool Altiplano was as naked as those of the other zones, before they were clothed by the Incas. This is what these indigenous people reported to Pedro de Cieza de Leon (1553 etc.), who travelled that region shortly after Pizarro had conquered what is now Peru. When I visited the *Museo de Culturas Indígenas Amazónicas* in Iquitos in 2015, there was an information board that explained the origin of alleged traditional costumes of different indigenous peoples. In all cases, they had been naked in their everyday life. But they had clothing-like accessories for special festivities. This is comparable to, for example, the red Santa Claus dress known in the industrial culture. The indigenous peoples were then told that this was their traditional dress and that they have to wear it always now. Usually, the indigenous peoples are very obedient, having little choice due to the power constellation, and do what they are told. But not all indigenous peoples had such festive attire. What happened under the pressure of the introduced standards is interesting, on the one hand, from the perspective of cultural semiotics. But it is, on the other hand, also sad to see the loss of culture that is going along with the changes. The Ngäbe-Buglé of Panama have a similar role now in some urban areas as the Romani or so-called Gypsies in Europe. Having lost their traditional life, the Ngäbe-Buglé seem frozen in the time when the clothing was imposed on them, as they still wear the old-fashioned costumes, lingering in the streets and alleys. The Kuna people, who do not live too far away, apparently did not want to lose the body painting altogether. They make themselves clothing now with the design of the former body painting. The women wear skin-tight fabrics on their lower legs, almost as if the design was painted on the skin. Yet, their culture underwent rapid changes. Many are trying to make their living by selling souvenirs to tourists in Panama City, and despite attempts to blandish, it is somewhat humiliating. In the case of the Emberá, the indigenous were told, during the time of US presence at the Panama Canal, to cover their loins with fabric from a particular factory. This happened in the middle of the twentieth century and thus before the breast taboo became very pronounced in the USA at the end of the twentieth century. The Emberá women were ordered to wear skirts with floral design, and the men were prescribed plain-coloured cloths. Meanwhile, these fabrics are imported from Asia. As they are not allowed to hunt and gather any more, some of this indigenous people might also try to sell you things. Such situations can be quite whimsical. An elderly Emberá man once tried to sell me such an industrial cloth as their "traditional dress", but he affirmed, when I mentioned that it was produced in Asia.

We have to bear this course of history in mind, when we go into the fields, in order to find the best possible solution with regard to our own behaviour. Especially, we want to observe the UN Declaration on the Rights of Indigenous Peoples. This includes that we find ways not to impede, but rather facilitate the indigenous peoples' right to revitalise traditions. Having said all this, I can now continue to explain what I discovered in connection with the body painting.

Globalised visitors generally gain the impression that what they see in those indigenous villages really represents these peoples' daily lives. They think, "nowadays, they wear loincloths with this design, and they paint their visible body parts". But we have to revise that. At my first visit to an Emberá village, my wife and I only had one overnight stay, and we then left the next morning. In the evening, I had realised from a distance that people took their bath in the river, and before leaving, in the mist of dawn, I vaguely saw someone go to the river as well. I did not have the time to scrutinise in more detail their use of identity-relevant cultural elements. But I agreed with one of the village's heads that I would come again and that I would bring a larger team then. That is what I did, and we took the chance to investigate their culture systematically and in more detail then. If clothing was imposed on them, the question was how much had that already changed their identity? Did they still identify with their traditional way of life before the interference? And if so, how could they exercise their right of choosing the option of revitalising those traditions with the same freedom and the same chances as choosing the way towards globalisation?

How to Gain Access to Look Behind the Façade

To test this step by step, the first thing our team did was to take a bath in the river in full nudity. At arrival, we all, including the female team members, had uncovered our tops, to be equal to the indigenous peoples. Both of their sexes only had their loins covered with the said fabrics. And we could also assume that they would take them off when taking a bath. When we took the naked bath, there was no particular reaction from the indigenous side. Communication went on as normal as before. The next step was to return to the village without covering the loin. Still, they did not pay any attention to that. Another step further: we asked the body-painting artists, naked as we were, to paint our bodies. And eventually, there was a reaction! With a mixture of relief, approval and grinning about the slow-witted whites, they proudly explained: "We always paint the whole bodies of our people".

That was surprising. On the surface, it seems like the Emberá had resigned themselves to what has been imposed on them. The question was if they had internalised it. In fact, they have not. This is very positive with regard to the option of not only maintaining but revitalising their culture. We would not have found that out if we had not applied the minimally invasive research technique that was oriented towards the presumed authentic tradition. So here it turned out that the partial body paintings that some tourists requested from the Emberá artists were only done by them out of politeness, in order to please these tourists. But such partial body paintings are non-authentic, and probably the Emberá artists are amused about these tourists, who keep some clothing on even when being painted. But indigenous peoples, throughout their painful history, have learnt not to criticise, to question or to contradict the dominant.

However, this finding in that particular situation should not be taken by anyone as an excuse not to do rescue work, by saying something like "They have not quite lost their original way, they still practice it among themselves, so we don't need to support it". The situation is only a snapshot out of a process. And the process of dominant, globalised influences deleting indigenous culture is proceeding. In countless indigenous villages, it is long beyond that point. Along the way of cultural loss, loin cover and breast taboo seem to be markers; especially, once the latter is established and the cultural system collapses, it is then closely aligned with the dominant culture, and the transgenerational passing on ceases. But it is our ethical obligation to prevent the destabilisation of indigenous culture.

Going to the Toilet

One little problem all researchers have to solve, if they stay more than a few hours with indigenous peoples, is going to the toilet in a context-appropriate way. Theoretical treatises usually don't even mention this. But perceivable behaviour cannot be separated from methodology during a researcher's stay in the field. Whatever you do and however you do it can have an influence on those who perceive it. Therefore, any action should be carried out in a way that the potential influence is least destabilising or otherwise detrimental – in our case, to the indigenous culture. As we have elaborated already, we are on the safe side if we orient ourselves towards the respective tradition and towards the way it was before the external dominant influence.

It is true that we find many non-hygienic situations nowadays in indigenous contexts, especially with regard to defecation, urination and the disposal of waste that in the industrial culture either goes down the drain or into the bathroom's litter bin.

But if we take a closer look to the lack of hygiene mentioned, we can see that these are often hybrid constellations of culture, in which the respective indigenous people have abandoned or partly abandoned a traditional behaviour pattern and then tried to adopt the corresponding pattern of the dominant culture, but did not fully manage to do so. In that situation, they have lost their previously functioning cultural element, while a non- or only partially functioning element has been put in that place. With regard to toilets, any globalised person, who has travelled through regions like Ethiopia, knows what is meant.

Other contexts with still-functioning traditional toilets cannot be blamed of being non-hygienic. The villages of the Congo basin usually have toilets that consist of deep, dug caverns that are 2–3 metres in diameter. These caverns have then been covered with a roof of branches and clay, so that they almost look like even soil, only slightly arched and a bit elevated. A little opening is left in the centre, about 20 cm wide and covered with some lid while not in use. A rush mat might serve as privacy shield. So, you squat over the hole, take aim and make sure you hit. It is also common to spread some chalk powder over the mass down in the hole. Interestingly, those toilets hardly smell. By all means, it is a quite hygienic solution. You are not in touch with any excrements; you do not have to wade through any leaking or droppings, and the pit is usually deep enough that nothing splashes up to hit you. Once such a pit is filled, it is a perfect spot for planting a tree.

Hunter-gatherers in tropical rainforests usually have their camps, settlements or villages near a stream or river. This can even be reflected in the language. Some indigenous people do not give directions with terms like right or left, ahead or behind, but rather take orientation with regard to the nearest flowing water. Instead of saying, for example, my right foot or my left foot, they say, my foot that is directed towards the nearest flowing water or my foot that is directed away from the nearest flowing water. Access to water is something vital. And the particular stream of such a dwelling is divided into zones. Of the zones used, the one that is furthest upstream is used for fetching water for drinking or cooking. If there is a cataract, that spot might be just below it. It is then followed by the further zones downstream, such as the zone for taking a bath and then the one for washing objects, and the last one below is reserved for going to the toilet. Depending on the type of running waters, those who are excreting do so in full immersion into the water or in squatting. If the stream is shallow and flows between rocks, you place each foot on a rock and aim right into the flowing water. But there are a couple of aspects you should bear in mind. In case that it has not been fully taken away by the waters, you have to mark the place where you left something, in order to prevent others of stepping into it. Choose a twig with green leaves that you can turn upside down and place it like a tripod over that spot. By the way, such signal twigs are also used outside indigenous contexts on the roads of tropical countries as a warning, when a car has broken down or when there is an extraordinary pothole. I have also seen such twigs tagging a house of mourning.

Another, even more important aspect concerns privacy, which is very much respected in indigenous cultures. Indigenous peoples can be fully naked because of this high respect of privacy. That respect is the equivalent to the textiles that veil the human bodies in the global culture. Naked indigenous cultures do not need such covers, as no one stares at another person's body. And in those indigenous cultures, where loincloths have been established, someone who changes the loincloth only needs to turn the back towards the others. That is a clear signal that this person does not want to be looked at. It is like a virtual wall separating this person from the others for that moment. There are virtual walls, too, separating families living together in a longhouse. Real walls are not necessary between the spots reserved for each family. They all have their compartments because they respect each other's privacy.

The same is true when people go to the toilet in a stream. They are protected from prying eyes by the very virtual walls. If you happen to pass by within sight of a person in such a situation, you should completely ignore him or her and just keep on walking your way. If you need to go to the toilet as well, go a bit further on and wait until the other person is finished, unless it is common in that particular culture that more than one person can go to the toilet in the respective stretch of the stream. In this case, keep a similar distance from the others, as they do from each other, and refrain from communicating with them (unless they address you or are chatting anyway). Otherwise, wait until it is your turn.

I remember that in my younger years, I made a somewhat embarrassing mistake. I report it here to help you to avoid it if you come across such a situation. We were having a walk in the outskirts of a Dani village near the Baliem Valley. Downhill in the little stream, there was a lady squatting on the rocks. I thought she might be washing something. I tried to be kind, so I waved and shouted some hello, and so did my wife. The Dani lady's reaction seemed a bit ashamed. Today, I would say that, compared to our culture, the situation was as if you were on a public toilet and some stranger would lean over the partition wall from the neighbouring toilet cabin to say hi and ask you how you were doing.

In indigenous villages that are occasionally visited by tourists, the local people might have installed something that is supposed to be a toilet for the visitors. This has certainly been done with the best intentions, but from a hygienic perspective, the traditional way might often be the better choice. If you happen to be in a place, where you find neither any of the traditional solutions nor an installed surrogate and your enquiries where to go for your purpose do not yield the desired result, then go and find a place in the nature that is protected from sights. If there is a natural hole in the ground, then make sure that there are no snakes or other unwanted creatures. Afterwards, cover what you have left.

Drinking Water

We have already addressed water as something vital for human life. This is not only true for indigenous peoples but just as well for the globalised researchers. The main particularity about the latter is their relatively low resistance against pathogenic germs. We have the choice either to find ways of coping or to give up research right away. Drinking the same water as the indigenous peoples would, in many cases, strike us with severe, if not fatal, illnesses.

Wherever there is some globalised infrastructure, we can nowadays find bottled water around the globe, even deep inside Africa and other less industrialised regions. Indigenous peoples, who do not live too far away from this infrastructure, know that globalised persons have problems with germ-infested water. They are used to the fact that visitors carry their water. The risk of inducing an identity-relevant behaviour pattern of drinking water from plastic bottles is low, as that would involve permanent expenditures. In fact, I have never met traditionally living indigenous peoples, who have become avid drinkers of bottled water. But I have seen many old plastic bottles in indigenous contexts that have been given a new utilisation, either in whole or after parts had been cut off. The question, do these plastic objects have any destabilising function, is difficult to answer. Generally, we can derive from theoretical models (cf. previous chapters) that objects, which are not close to the body, which are not frequently used and which are not communicated to others as being in special connection with a person, do not have much relevance to this person's identity. Yet, we do not have enough data to certainly rule out the eventuality of any detrimental effect of plastic bottles left in indigenous communities. Therefore, to be on the safe side, keep those bottles with you and take them with you when you leave the indigenous setting.

However, you will need different strategies when you leave the globalised infrastructure further behind, as the time for which you can carry your water supply is very limited. Beyond that, what will you do? Well, as indigenous peoples in rainforests usually stay close to running water, find out which is the zone that is reserved for taking drinking water. Apart from that, larger communities usually have water reservoirs. It is clear that humans permanently need water and therefore sure that they always have some, except in times of extraordinary drought. In Central African villages, it is quite easy to find this water. Do not make it more complicated than necessary! Be aware of the social structure and the hierarchies in traditional societies. No one will call into question that you, as a human being, need water, and if there is a public water reservoir, no one will deny you a moderate share. So, you do not have to go top-down by asking the elders for help. Rather, you can go bottom-up in this case. Children will be proud to show you the water. To avoid any bustle of countless children gathered around you, ask a local boy personally by showing him your empty flask. It never happened to us that the boy did not understand – they all did. He will then guide you to the water storage, which might be some kind of basin or a big barrel, always covered and usually under a roof. Fill your flask modestly, don't spill it and don't use it other than for drinking or eating purposes. Don't pour it over your head, even if you feel hot, because that water might be precious to the people.

Now that you have some drinking water, you should still be cautious. Refrain from drinking it right away. It is very likely that there are still some germs dwelling in it. For globalised persons, it is usually still necessary to sterilise it. You might have heard of the method of just exposing water, filled into clear plastic bottles, to the full sun for a few hours. This reduces germs to a minimum that is supposed to be harmless for local people. But you might also have heard of the method of growing algae in plastic pipes, which are exposed to the sun. Therefore, do not rely on the sun in this case. The intake of algae might cause some unexpected problems. There are different additives for water purification. Iodine-based products have an austere taste and so do tablets based on silver salt. But silver salt-based solutions are relatively tasteless. You just add the necessary number of drops and leave it for a while to allow the substance to take effect.

Outside human settlements, or when you are with smaller communities without a water reservoir, it is good to have a ceramic filter. It is actually a little pump, and you press the water through the ceramic cylinder. Bacteria and parasites cannot pass through that material. But the water to be filtered should be as clear as possible, otherwise the filter will be blocked quickly. Depending on the trip you are planning, it could also be wise to carry a straw with a built-in iodine filter. It is very small and light of weight, and in case of emergency, you could drink with this device straight from almost any water you have found. But once you have tasted it, you will certainly reserve the use of this tool to real emergency cases. Another type of filters, ion exchangers, have a limited scope. They are primarily meant to soften tap water, but parasites would not care and pass through them.

Make sure you also use purified water for brushing your teeth. Indigenous peoples have their ways of cleaning their teeth, too. Some split the end of a piece of a stem of a liquorice plant, so that they have a little brush. Even if they see you using a different type of brush, that would be acceptable, as long as you don't use an electric toothbrush. Different tribes have different toothbrushes, and your unobtrusive toothbrush should be in line with that.

Taking a Bath
Above, we have considered the different zones of water use in a stream, such as the most upward zone for taking drinking water or the most downward zone for going to the toilet. The zone for taking a bath will most likely be found between them, probably right below the one for taking drinking water, followed by the one for washing objects, such as calabashes or other containers. For reasons explained above, you should refrain from washing clothing there and all the more from putting it on a line, even if you see indigenous women do so with pieces of clothing that have reached that particular context. You need to be aware that everything you do, as long as the indigenous persons are aware of it, has a potential of influencing their culture. Since you are perceived as representative of the dominant global culture, you are a role model. Also, taking into consideration the United Nations Declaration on the Rights of Indigenous Peoples, anything has to be avoided that could potentially have any destabilising effect on an indigenous culture. Washing your clothing in a traditional indigenous context would be an act of communication that could be understood as promoting clothing. As an effect of the existing bias of cultural dominance, it is not only likely but most probably that this perceptual and cognitive association would trigger the wish of the perceiving indigenous person to have clothes as well. This wish would not originate out of a rational decision that wearing clothes in tropical climate would be beneficial, but it would modify the indigenous person's identity away from indigeneity and towards globalisation. Since cultures consist of persons, each deletion of an indigenous identity contributes to the

respective culture's destabilisation and, eventually, deterioration. Indigenous cultures can be stable over long periods of time, as long as there are no destabilising external influences. But they become very fragile, when they are confronted with a dominant culture that introduces identity-relevant elements. This is so because the cognitions and motivations linked to the persons' identities are the core mechanisms of the culture's functioning. The destabilisation of a culture due to the introduction of something that causes a structural change within the persons' cognitions, which then has a destabilising effect on the culture as a whole, can, by all means, be compared to a viral infection. Viruses first have a cytopathic effect on the host cell, and the reproduction of the virus and its spreading to other cells lead to the destabilisation of the organism. It cannot be emphasised enough that anything has to be avoided that could possibly trigger destabilising mechanisms. We, as researchers, are morally obliged to look at the changes over time, to analyse historical and contemporary processes, in order to understand the mechanisms of cultural input and its effects, to avoid destabilisations and to counteract further detriments. With regard to our own activities in the fields, we need to link the theory derived from this analysis to the reality of our concrete work, including such minor action units like washing objects or washing ourselves in the indigenous setting.

As for washing ourselves, it is not enough to look how the indigenous take a bath and then do it likewise. Our presence is generally a major source of behaviour modification. We are not invisible, and we are members of the dominant culture. Especially with regard to self-presentation, many indigenous peoples' behaviour is very much determined by the fear of being rejected and of receiving repressions if it does not conform to the dominant culture's standards. Sometimes, one can see odd things, such as indigenous persons wrapping in large sheets for taking a bath in the river. It is clear that this cannot be a traditional behaviour pattern, as textiles, let alone of such a size, are not a part of the respective culture. If you happen to see something like this in a predominantly traditional indigenous context, then the most probable explanation for that behaviour is your own presence. Persons of the indigenous culture concerned have had previous encounters with globalised persons, which have exerted some social pressure on them. As a result, these indigenous persons want to avoid further sanctions. Thus, their behaviour is based on fear, and it would not be justified if we would fuel that fear. But we would actually do so by accepting their fearful behaviour and joining them by acting likewise. The solution in such a situation is to orientate oneself towards the most probable behaviour before the external influence. In simple terms, you cannot do much wrong if you do not introduce your cultural elements, whereas if you do introduce them, you would contribute to the destabilisation of the indigenous culture. In this case of taking a bath in the indigenous context, the self-presentation is concerned, which is of particular importance to identity. Traditionally living indigenous peoples, especially in tropical contexts, fuse with their natural environment. They don't separate themselves from the air or from the water. Introducing textiles to wrap their bodies would lead to a break with this harmony. From an autonomous indigenous perspective, it would be quite irrational to put on clothes when it is warm and, especially, when taking a bath. The bodily state has a backlash on a person's affect and cognition (West 2017; Gallagher 2005; Niedenthal et al. 2005). Introducing standards of covering oneself terminates the indigenous identity of being an integral part of nature. This modification of indigenous identity is the core mechanism of destabilising, and finally disintegrating, indigenous culture (Groh 2006). Bearing in mind the effects of cultural dominance with its imbalance of mutual influence, then it is clear that the traditional social system is stabilised or restabilised, when researchers or other guests take the bath without clothing, because doing that with clothing would have a destabilising impact. This approach has always worked well. We have applied it over the years in different cultures. Eventual fears on behalf of the researchers have always proven to be unfounded; it rather became evident that they were merely caused due to the behaviour patterns, which the globalised researchers had internalised in their own socialisation. Projecting these standards on indigenous cultures would be destructive. It is obvious that the causal connections apply not only to the situation of taking a bath but to the entire stay in the indigenous context.

Sun Cream and Insect Repellent
As our skin is exposed, we are faced with the questions of how to protect it from the sun, as well as from aggressive insects. If we would ignore this, then we might soon be impaired to such an extent that we could not carry out our research any more. Therefore, we have no choice. We have to protect our skin, but not by veiling it. We need to apply a protective sun lotion. There are sun blockers with a protection factor of 60. You probably won't find them on the usual sun cream shelf of a drugstore, but rather in the children's department. They have the advantage of being especially skin-friendly, waterproof and even sand-proof. But how does the application of sun cream and insect repellent on our skin comply with the minimising of our invasiveness?

The major aspect here is that there are hardly any alternatives. As for sun protection, yes, you could accustom your skin to the sun in other places, outside any indigenous context, but that might be too time-consuming and thus not feasible. Yet, there are situations where you won't need any sun lotion. If the rainforest is intact and not hilly, then it is very shady and almost dark on the ground. If it is hilly, then you might often come to spots where you are fully hit by the sun. Anyway, you will have to travel to and from that place. When you travel by boat, it might be the indigenous people who are transporting you. To show respect for and acceptance of their traditions, clothing should be taken off already during the trip or even before departure, as soon as one is in the company of the indigenous people. Even if you travel on your own or with a guide (who always should be involved in your methodological procedure), you might be met by the indigenous people at the riverbank when you arrive. The situation is quite similar when you travel by road. So, you should be prepared for situations, in which you need sun cream. Likewise, it would be too risky to forego any repellent, if there are insects that transmit diseases. Malaria is only one of them. Thus, taking malaria prophylaxis would not be sufficient, as the vectors usually carry several types of parasites.

To assess the effects, let us have a semiotic look at the use of such creams, lotions or sprays in indigenous contexts. One thing you can do is to reduce the perception of their application. Put them on when the indigenous people do not see you. The sun blocker mentioned above with the high protection factor lasts for the whole day, so you can put it on in the early morning or before you depart to the indigenous place on the last stage of the trip to it. However, perception does not only take place through the visual channel. The indigenous people will smell what you have put on. But they take that as a curiosity, just like some others of our features that seem funny to them. Generally, these are features that cannot be copied (or if so, then only in a temporary and very limited way) and therefore cannot function as identity modifiers. We once met a gentleman of the Bagyeli Pygmies in the jungle near the Lobé River, and he was so kind to participate in our olfactory study. The stimuli consist of standardised smells, each of which is stored in something that looks like a marker pen. After explaining and obtaining consent, the smells are presented one by one by taking off the cap and holding the tip of the pen about 2 cm under the nose of the participant for 2 s. This is followed by some questions about perceived intensity, descriptions, associations, etc. for each scent. Of all the hundreds of participants in that study, this Bagyeli gentleman was probably the quickest to understand and respond. He answered so fast that my wife, who was filling the questionnaire, could only follow with difficulty, although the responses took more time due to the translation by one of the tour guides. One of the descriptions the Bagyeli participant gave was that a particular smell was like that of a body lotion of a white woman. We can see from this example that indigenous persons perceive and remember such things. These perceptions are associated with members of the industrial culture. But the lotions and sprays as cultural elements are not made use of as constituents of identity, the more so as they are not available. They are seen as something distinct and inapplicable, such as different colours of skin or hair. Generally, the indigenous peoples are sympathetic and understanding with regard to the higher sensitivity of the visitors' skin. When your skin is very pale, as perhaps you come from the winter of your home region, or if the textiles, which you have worn in summer, have left pale stripes on your body, then you might want to receive some tan from the solarium before you go to the indigenous context.

Tattoos and Piercings
Other than hair and skin colour, tattoos and piercings are not naturally given, but they are manipulations that are intentionally done to the body. Seen from a semiotic perspective, it is clear to anyone, who sees the tattoo or piercing, that something is supposed to be expressed with it. Although it is often not quite clear what exactly is to be expressed, it is a sign and a relatively permanent act of communication. Due to the manipulation, it is immediately linked to the body and thus an expression of the person's identity. Since anything, that could possibly influence an indigenous people's identity, researchers should refrain from presenting tattoos or piercing in indigenous contexts. How to proceed in practice, if there is a tattooed or pierced team member? Well, the removal of piercing is easy, and as for tattoos, there is

so-called camouflage makeup, which can totally cover them. Camouflage makeup is also used for patients after facial operations and certain skin problems. The exact tone of the skin colour can be mixed, so that it appears very natural. I once went with a group of students to a Batwa group in eastern Uganda, and one of the students had a big skull tattoo near his collar bone. I told him that he could not take part in visiting the Batwa unless he would cover it with that particular makeup. He then did so, and I can assure you that it worked quite well. Exceptions might be possible in cultures, where body painting is practised. But since the indigenous persons might see the difference, I am cautious to give an advice here.

Presents for the Host

Finally, indigenous peoples often expect that visitors bring some gifts. Even when you do not know if this is expected, it would be a sign of politeness to bring a present. For obvious reasons, we have to ask here, what is non- or at least minimally invasive to a traditional culture, what does not pave the road towards dependencies and what does not interfere with the indigenous peoples' autonomy? – Well, fruit is all right and other food that the people of the respective community hunt, gather or produce themselves or that they customarily obtain from neighbouring communities or from the market. In West Papua, we stayed in a Dani village about 2 h walking distance from a local market that was used by many surrounding indigenous communities, who therefore not only consumed food that originated from their immediate environment but also what others brought to the market. So, we bought some salt at that local market and gave it to the Dani as a present, which they were very happy about.[26] All around the globe, the human body needs salt. There are a few, especially marine, sources of food with a relatively high salt content. But indigenous peoples have different ways of producing salt. Some particular leaves leave ashes, when they have been burnt, with high NaCl content. I think I remember that also in West Papua, we saw a tiny salt mine, less than half a metre in diameter, at the slope of a hill. Salt is something that is always welcome by traditionally living indigenous peoples.

Whatever you bring should be scrutinised for its invasiveness. Clothing is a no-go, as it is immediately linked to self-presentation and has a direct impact on a person's identity. But not everything from the industrial culture automatically unfolds destructive effects. Some items vanish quickly, such as balloons, which make children happy and then burst and disintegrate without receiving much notice. Like balloons, soap bubbles help to break the ice. They even burst sooner and are not seen any more.

---

[26] It so happened that we also carried out our gesture study in that village, and when the Dani women sat together to have some sweet potatoes with the salt that we had brought, they made a gesture of happiness, which led to very interesting insights in the framework of historical cultural studies, as described in Groh (2002), and which might be of particular interest to feminist studies.

4.5.2   Being Prepared for Tropical Diseases

To a large extent, indigenous peoples live in tropical areas, where particular illnesses are prevalent. Many of these illnesses are treated as so-called "orphan diseases" in the industrialised world. They are neglected, because they are considered unimportant, as it is thought that only very few people are affected by them. But a closer look unveils quickly that this label is not justified with regard to many of those tropical diseases. The negligence dates back to times when travelling to the tropics was not very popular. But times have changed a lot. Tourism is the world's largest public business sector. Increased mobility is now causing the spread of illnesses that previously were confined only to particular areas.

Unfortunately, doctors in the non-tropical industrial nations are generally not trained very well in detecting tropical diseases, so that wrong diagnoses are quite common. Patients are subjected to erroneous medical treatments, which do not cure the disease and cause unnecessary suffering. This is reason enough to attach particular importance to prophylaxis and infection prevention when educating and training people for field research in indigenous contexts.

However, this is not the place to treat tropical diseases exhaustively. But we shall have a look at some, at which chances are high that most doctors, as well as lecturers and field trainers, will fail to warn researchers-to-be. Once infected, it might be too late. Some tropical infections are hardly curable after a certain time. Therefore, we should be aware of the risks well in advance and do our best to prevent the infections.

Many of the tropical diseases are parasitical infections. One good aspect, if we can call it that way, about parasites is that they generally are not up to kill you. They want to dwell inside your body and produce offspring. They weaken you and cause many kinds of suffering, with diarrhoea being among the most harmless symptoms, and skin diseases, joint problems, limb swelling and blindness being the more severe ones. If they push it too much, so that the host is dead, their game is over, too.

It is not really necessary to mention malaria, as this is a well-known illness, and any diligent general practitioner would advise someone, who is planning for a trip to the tropics, to take appropriate precautionary measures. There are different types of malaria, which, taken all together, form the largest group of tropical diseases, with worldwide approximately 600 million people being affected. But even the second largest group of tropical diseases, with estimated 200 million people affected, is largely unknown. These are the various types of filarial infections.

Like the different forms of malaria, filariae are also transmitted by insects. These insects, which are the intermediate hosts of the parasites, are called vectors, as they transport the intermediate forms of the parasites to the definite hosts, where the transmitted intermediate forms develop into the final parasites. Once mature, the parasites mate, and the offspring, which they produce, are intermediate forms again, which then hope to be picked up by a vector with its blood meal and transported to another final hosts. Those parasites living in a particular species are called a reservoir.

Some of the intermediate parasite forms are very picky and only accept a certain type of insect to travel with. Others accept to be transported by more than one insect species. Those which are specialised have adapted to the insect's behaviour. If it is a nocturnal insect, which comes to sting people around midnight, then the intermediate parasite form indeed waits in the host's peripheral blood around that time, and chances to detect it in probes from peripheral blood, for example, in blood smear taken from the finger pad, are highest around midnight. But if the intermediate parasite form is specialised to be transported by a diurnal insect that comes to sting around midday, then that is the time when it waits in the peripheral blood. This is important to know, and not to rely on repellents or mosquito nets only between sunset and sunrise, when the anopheles mosquitos bite, the vectors of malaria.

Anopheles mosquitos not only transmit malaria but also lymphatic filariasis. Various species of insects can transmit various diseases. The tsetse fly, for example, does not only transmit the sleeping illness. A colleague[27] from the University of Buea, Cameroon, told me that he found 1000 microfilariae in the head of a tsetse fly. Loa loa filariasis is transmitted by deer flies (*Chrysops* spp.) but are probably not too picky about that, as loa loa seems to be spreading all around the tropical belt since several years. Onchocerciasis, another subform of filariasis, is transmitted by black flies (Simuliidae), and mansonelliasis, yet another subform, is transmitted by tiny midges (*Culicoides*), which are only 1.5 mm in size. Therefore, make sure that your mosquito net has at least 1000 mesh per square inch. The filarial larvae of mansonelliasis are not very picky as well, as they are also transmitted by black flies and probably by further insect species, too, because a mansonelliasis infection is generally associated with other filariasis subtypes. As the name of the nematode *Mansonella perstans* says, the illness is persisting, and there is no known effective cure.

There are other tropical parasites that you can catch when you are in touch with water. The intermediate hosts of bilharziosis are freshwater snails, and dracunculiasis is transmitted by copepods, which are 2–4 mm in size and also live in water. The parasites of filariasis and dracunculiasis are all worms, residing in various parts of the human body. They differ in length, some are a few centimetres long, and the dracunculiasis parasites can be up to 90 cm long. The bilharziosis parasites are leeches, and there are several other parasitic leeches, the intermediate hosts of which are freshwater snails. Many of these leeches prefer to reside within the human liver, such as *Fasciola hepatica*, *Fasciola gigantica*, *Clonorchis sinensis*, *Opisthorchis felineus* and *Dicrocoelium dendriticum*. While the common treatment for both of the *Fasciola* types is triclabendazole, cure for the other three is praziquantel.

The bilharziosis leeches are flatworms that are called schistosoma, from Greek "split body", but they actually do not consist of single split bodies. Rather, each of them is a pair of trematodes that copulate permanently, and the female can produce up to 300,000 eggs per day. This causes inflammations of the intestinal and bladder walls, which can then be penetrated by the eggs (in the long run, the risk of cancer

---

[27] Samuel Wanji, see, e.g. Poole et al. (2017).

is increased at these locations). Then, the eggs make their way out of the body with the excrements, where the life cycle goes on with the infection of snails as intermediate hosts and so forth. Schistosoma are also called blood flukes, and a typical symptom is blood in the urine. There are regions in Africa, where it is thought that children's urine is normally red. These children spend much time every day in the water. But there are many other symptoms of bilharziosis, such as dermatitis; fever; shivers; cough; headache; enlargement of lymph nodes, liver and spleen; intestine or problems with bloody diarrhoea; and further organ complications due to vascular obstructions, especially of minor vessels. Praziquantel is the drug of choice. The various schistosoma subtypes are 1–2 cm long. If untreated, they live between 10 and 30 years – provided that the host survives.

Bilharziosis can be contracted by touching any water, in which snails live, which means that activities such as bathing in or wading through tropical freshwater can lead to the infection. Likewise, it can be contracted by touching the water while sitting in a boat or by taking a shower with contaminated water.

Whereas bilharziosis can be caught by touching water, people can become infected with dracunculiasis by drinking contaminated water. The migrations of the large worms through the body can be quite painful. Symptoms of this illness include fever, vertigo, nausea, vomiting, arthritis, inflammations and abscesses. Large blisters on the foot burst open when in contact with water. From there, the female worms release larvae, which then proceed with the life cycle of this parasite. Due to the open wounds, there is a severe risk of superinfections. Therefore, make sure that you only drink water that is filtered, boiled or otherwise sterilised.

Loa loa infections have a wide range of symptoms as well. There can be various allergic reactions that become apparent in dermatological problems and joint inflammations. Patients can become tachycardic, which then is accompanied by sleeplessness and subsequent cognitive problems. Conjunctivitis is common, and in some spectacular cases, worms can be found moving through the sclera. Because of lymphatic oedema due to the blocking of vessels by the microfilariae produced by the adult filariae, there are swellings of the skin and in particular of the extremities. Interestingly, this is often lateralised, so that only one side, either the left or the right arm and leg, is swollen. Loa loa can lead to heart valve disease, to kidney damage and, as long-term complications, to inflammations of the brain and to meningitis. At an early stage, loa loa can be treated with ivermectin and DEC (diethylcarbamazine). Loa loa worms can live for two decades, if the human host makes it that long.

In the tropics, one can often see people with knob-like swellings. These subcutaneous tumours are common symptoms of onchocerciasis, caused by the filariae-subtype Onchocerca volvulus. The female worms have a length of 60 cm. They reside inside the knobs and give birth to up to 3000 microfilariae per day. Symptoms include itches, skin damages, eosinophilia and inflammation of lymph nodes, but the greatly feared result of that infection is river blindness. At an early stage, onchocerciasis can be treated with ivermectin and DEC. At later stages, it can still be treated with doxycycline, but this is only owing to the fact that there are certain bacteria (*Wolbachia*) inside the worm, which needs these bacteria in a similar way as humans have an intestinal flora, which they also need for their digestion.

Doxycycline is a well-tried antibiotic that kills the internal bacteria of the worms, which then die. By the way, doxycycline has another revival as malaria prophylaxis. This has the advantage that several pathogens are covered by it, and several illnesses can be prevented, including filariae that carry endobacteria.

Mansonella perstans filariae also live up to 20 years. Once infected with them, the symptoms include itches, stomach ache, headache, joint swellings, hypereosinophilia, swellings of the extremities, retinal lesions and vision defects. The female worms lay up to 1 million eggs per year. Treatment can be tried with mebendazole plus levamisole or with mebendazole plus DEC, but only with limited success; symptoms can only be reduced, but a fully effective cure is not known.

Lymphatic filariasis is caused by *Wuchereria bancrofti*. During the acute phase, patients have general indisposition, repeated but infrequent fever attacks, an increase of the eosinophil leucocytes (eosinophilia), acute inflammations of lymph nodes and lymph vessels, allergic cough and asthmatic afflictions. In the chronical phase, the obstruction of the lymph fluid drainage in the lymphatic system leads to an extension of the lymphatic vessels, then to lymphatic oedema with massive swellings of the lymph nodes and finally of the extremities, the genitalia and the breast. This clinical syndrome is called elephantiasis. Like in loiasis, the limb swellings usually only or predominantly affect one side of the body. And as the worms that cause lymphatic filariasis also carry *Wolbachia* endobacteria, this illness can be treated like onchocerciasis, namely, at the early stage with ivermectin and DEC and at later stages with doxycycline. Male worms are up to 4 cm; female worms are up to 10 cm long, and they live up to 10 years.

In this selection of tropical illnesses, I presented only a few of them, which are lesser known but which, in fact, should be better known, as their prevalence is quite immense.

One thing that should be mentioned is that indigenous peoples seem to be less affected by such diseases as long as they live in their traditional ways in their natural environment. But once this habitat has been destroyed, or the indigenous peoples have been expelled from it, their resistance vanishes, and they catch malaria and other illnesses.[28] This phenomenon needs some more research, in order to understand the mechanisms behind it. Is it that a particular diet, which includes certain herbs, fruits and other natural products, which are only available in the forest, strengthens the body defences? Or is it an interplay of malnutrition and poor psychological condition that makes the indigenous peoples immunodeficient after the displacement? Whatever the reason is – as researchers – we should use our capabilities to prevent such displacements and urge that expelled indigenous peoples be repatriated. When they are in contact with the industrial culture, they should be able to fully enjoy medical treatment, whenever necessary, like anyone else. Their natural environments need to be protected from destruction, as the indigenous cultures need to be protected likewise. Therefore, as researchers, we shall do our best to apply minimally invasive techniques with truly participatory immersion, to

---

[28] The filmmaker Hans-Jürgen Steinfurth, who spent some time with the Baka pygmies, confirmed this to me in personal communication.

do rescue work where damage has been done, to support indigenous peoples to implement their rights according to the United Nations declaration and to ensure their right to revitalise indigenous culture. But to be able to function and to do our best, we have to take the necessary precautions regarding illnesses. Do it in time and don't wait until it is too late. Stay healthy!

References

Asch, S. E. (1951). Effects of group pressure upon the modification and distortion of judgement. In: H. S. Guetzkow (Ed.), *Groups, leadership, and men. Research in human relations.* Reports on research sponsored by the Human Relations and Morale Branch of the Office of Naval Research, 1945–1950. Papers derived from the United States Navy's conference of its Human Relations Advisory Panel and research contractors at Dearborn, Michigan, September, 1950. Reissued (pp. 177–190). Pittsburgh: Carnegie Press.

Assmann, J. (1992). *Das kulturelle Gedächtnis. Schrift, Erinnerung und politische Identität in frühen Hochkulturen.* Munich: C. H. Beck (Engl.: *Cultural memory and early civilization: Writing, remembrance, and political imagination.* Cambridge: University Press, 2011).

Baddeley, A. D. (1976). *The psychology of memory.* New York: Basic Books.

Baddeley, A. D. (2004). *Your memory: A user's guide.* New York: Firefly Books.

Bartlett, F. C. (1932). *Remembering. A study in experimental and social psychology.* Cambridge: Cambridge University Press.

Baudrillard, J. (1986). *Subjekt und Objekt: fraktal.* Bern: Benteli.

Braun, O. L. (1990). Selbsteinschätzung der Fähigkeit: Realistisch oder kompensatorisch? *Zeitschrift für Experimentelle und Angewandte Psychologie, 37*(2), 208–217.

Brown, J. D. (2007). *The self.* New York: Routledge.

Chartier, D. (2003). «Au–delà, il n'y a plus rien, plus rien que l'immensité désolée.» Problématiques de l'histoire de la représentation des Inuits, des récits des premiers explorateurs aux oeuvres cinématographiques. *International Journal of Canadian Studies / Revue internationale d'études canadiennes, 31*(2005), 177–196.

Cieza de Leon, P. (1553 etc.). *The Incas.* Edited, with an introd., by von Hagen, V. W. Translation of the Crónicas del Perú, Vol. I (Sevilla, 1553) and Vol. II,[29] by de Onis, H. (The Civilization of the American Indian series, no. 53). Norman: University of Oklahoma Press, 1959.

Cohen, C. E. (1981). Person categories and social perception: Testing some boundaries of the processing effect of prior knowledge. *Journal of Personality and Social Psychology, 40*(3), 441–452.

Dijksterhuis, A., Aarts, H., & Smith, P. K. (2005). The power of the subliminal: On subliminal persuasion and other potential applications. In R. R. Hassin, J. S. Uleman, & J. A. Bargh (Eds.), *The new unconscious* (pp. 77–106). Oxford: Oxford University Press.

Dixon, N. F. (1971). *Subliminal perception; the nature of a controversy.* London: McGraw-Hill.

Erdheim, M. (1988). *Die Psychoanalyse und das Unbewußte in der Kultur.* Frankfurt/M: Suhrkamp.

Even-Zohar, I. (1990). Polysystem studies. *Poetics Today*, special issue, *11*, 1.

Farah, M. J., Péronnet, F., Gonon, M. A., & Giard, M. H. (1988). Electrophysiological evidence for a shared representational medium for visual images and visual percepts. *Journal of Experimental Psychology: General, 117*(3), 248–257.

Fonagy, P. (1999). Attachment, the development of the self, and its pathology in personality disorders. In J. Derksen, C. Maffei, & H. Groen (Eds.), *Treatment of personality disorders*

---

[29] No year given for the second volume because to my knowledge, the oldest version of *La historia de los incas o Segunda parte de la Crónica del Perú* is the London edition of 1871.

(pp. 53–68). New York: Plenum Press. Available online at: http://mentalizacion.com.ar/images/notas/Attachment,%20the%20development%20of%20the%20self%20and%20its%20pathology.pdf. Accessed 2 Aug 2017.

Fonagy, P., & Target, M. (2006). The Mentalization-focused approach to self pathology. *Journal of Personality Disorders, 20*(6), 544–576.

Freeman, D. (1983). *Margaret Mead and Samoa. The making and unmaking of an anthropological myth.* Cambridge/MA & London: Harvard University Press.

Frey, D. (1981). *Informationssuche und Informationsbewertung bei Entscheidungen.* Bern: Huber.

Gallagher, S. (2005). *How the body shapes the mind.* Oxford: Oxford University Press.

Goffman, E. (1959). *The presentation of self in everyday life.* New York: Doubleday.

Gollwitzer, P. M., & Wicklund, R. A. (1985). Self–symbolizing and the neglect of others' perspectives. *Journal of Personality and Social Psychology, 48*(3), 702–715.

Gonzalez, J. P., Nakoune, E., Slenczka, W., Vidal, P., & Morvan, J. M. (2000). Ebola and Marburg virus antibody prevalence in selected populations of the Central African Republic. *Microbes and Infection, 2*(1), 39–44.

Groh, A. (1997). *Kultureller Verlust: Mechanismen und Interventionsmöglichkeiten.* PhD thesis, University of Bielefeld, Dept. of Psychology, Bielefeld.

Groh, A. (2002). Humanontogenese in kulturelen Kontexten – Gesteninterpretation in Südostasien. *Zeitschrift für Humanontogenetik, 5*(1), 66–83.

Groh, A. (2006). Globalisation and indigenous identity. *Psychopathologie africaine, 33*(1), 33–47.

Groh, A. (2008). *Marketing & manipulation.* Aachen: Shaker.

Groh, A. (2016). Culture, language, and thought: Field studies on colour concepts. *Journal of Cognition and Culture, 16*(1–2), 83–106. https://doi.org/10.1163/15685373-12342169.

Gweon, H., & Saxe, R. (2013). Developmental cognitive neuroscience of theory of mind. In P. Rakic & J. Rubenstein (Eds.), *Neural circuit development and function in the brain: Comprehensive developmental neuroscience* (Vol. 3, pp. 367–377). New York: Elsevier. Available online at: https://sll.stanford.edu/docs/2013_Gweon_Saxe.pdf. Accessed 2 Aug 2017; https://doi.org/10.1016/B978-0-12-397267-5.0005.

Happé, F. (2003). Theory of mind and the self. *Annals of the New York Academy of Sciences, 1001*, 134–144. https://doi.org/10.1196/annals.1279.008.

Heine, B. (1987). Das Bergvolk: Einige Bemerkungen zu den Ik im Nordosten Ugandas. In H. P. Duerr (Ed.), *Authentizität und Betrug in der Ethnologie* (pp. 63–86). Frankfurt am Main: Suhrkamp.

Heine, S. J. (2012). *Cultural psychology* (2nd ed.). New York/London: W. W. Norton.

Herman, E. S., & Chomsky, N. (1988). *Manufacturing consent. The political economy of the mass media.* New York: Pantheon Books.

Hill, T. L. (1996). The problem with non-nudists. *Society / Société: Newsletter of the Canadian Sociology and Anthropology Association, 20*, 23–25.

Husserl, E. (1948), *Erfahrung und Urteil. Untersuchungen zur Genealogie der Logik.* (Ed.), L. Landgrebe (2nd unchanged ed., 1954). Hamburg: Claassen & Goverts.

Ingarden, R. (1985). *Selected papers in aesthetics.* (Ed.), P. J. McCormick. Munich: Philosophia & Washington, D.C.: Catholic University of America Press.

Khadilkar, A., Khadilkar, V., Chinnappa, J., Rathi, N., Khadgawat, R., Balasubramanian, S., Parekh, B., & Jog, P. (2017). Prevention and treatment of vitamin D and calcium deficiency in children and adolescents: Indian Academy of Pediatrics (IAP) Guidelines. *Indian Pediatrics, 54*, 567–573.

Knorr-Cetina, K. (1981). *The manufacture of knowledge. An essay on the constructivist and contextual nature of science.* Oxford: Pergamon Press.

Kohonen, T. (1988). *Self-organisation and associative memory.* Berlin/Heidelberg: Springer.

Kuhn, T. S. (1962). *The structure of scientific revolutions* (2nd ed., 1970). Chicago: University of Chicago Press.

Lévi-Strauss, C. (1962). *La pensée sauvage.* Paris: Librairie Plon (Engl.: *The savage mind.* Chicago: The University of Chicago Press, 1966).

Lewin, K. (1951). *Field theory in social science: Selected theoretical papers*. New York: Harper & Brothers.

Liedloff, J. (1975). The continuum-concept. In *Search of lost happiness*. London: Duckworth.

Mau, S. (2017). *Das metrische Wir. Über die Quantifizierung des Sozialen*. Berlin: Edition Suhrkamp.

McCauley, R. N., & Henrich, J. (2006). Susceptibility to the Müller-Lyer illusion, theory-neutral observation, and the diachronic penetrability of the visual input system. *Philosophical Psychology, 19*(1), 79–101.

Mead, G. H. (1934). *Mind, self, and society*. (Ed.), C. W. Morris. Chicago: University of Chicago Press.

Mead, M. (1977). *Letters from the field, 1925–1975*. New York: Harper & Row.

Meier, A. C. (2013). Minik and the meteor. http://narrative.ly/minik–and–the–meteor/. Accessed 19 May 2016.

Meltzoff, A. N. (1999). Origins of theory of mind, cognition and communication. *Journal of Communication Disorders, 32*, 251–269.

Mesman, J., van IJzendoorn, M. H., & Sagi-Schwartz, A. (2016). Cross-cultural patterns of attachment. Universal and contextual dimensions. In J. Cassidy & P. Shaver (Eds.), *Handbook of attachment. Theory, research, and clinical applications* (3rd ed., pp. 852–877). New York: Guilford.

Milgram, S. (1963). Behavioral study of obedience. *Journal of Abnormal and Social Psychology, 67*(4), 371–378.

Milgram, S. (1974). *Obedience to authority; an experimental view*. New York: Harper & Row.

Miltenberger, R. G. (2012). *Behavior modification: Principles and procedures* (5th ed.). Wadsworth: Cengage.

Moray, N. (2017). *Attention. Selective processes in vision and hearing, Psychology Library Editions: Perception* (Vol. 23). London: Routledge.

Niedenthal, P. M., Barsalou, L. W., Winkielman, P., Krauth-Gruber, S., & Ric, F. (2005). Embodiment in attitudes, social perception, and emotion. *Personality and Social Psychology Review, 9*(3), 184–211.

Othieno-Abinya, N. A., Wanzala, P., Omollo, R., Kalebi, A., Baraza, R., Nyongesa, C. N., Muthoni-Musibi, A., Maina, M. D., Waweru, A., & Githaiga, J. (2015). Comparative study of breast cancer risk factors at Kenyatta National Hospital and the Nairobi Hospital. *Journal Africain du Cancer / African Journal of Cancer, 7*, 41–46, doi: https://doi.org/10.1007/s12558-014-0358-1.

Paasche, H. (1921). *Die Forschungsreise des Afrikaners Lukanga Mukara ins innerste Deutschland*. Hamburg: Goldmann Verlag.

Palm, G. (1982). *Neural assemblies. An alternative approach to artificial intelligence*. Berlin/Heidelberg: Springer.

Papaleontiou-Louca, E. (2008). *Metacognition and theory of mind*. Newcastle: Cambridge Scholars Publishing.

Pearson, J. C., & Child, J. T. (2007). A cross-cultural comparison of parental and peer attachment styles among adult children from the United States, Puerto Rico, and India. *Journal of Intercultural Communication Research, 36*(1), 15–32.

Penfield, W. (1952). Memory mechanisms. *American Medical Association Archives of Neurology and Psychiatry, 67*(2), 178–198.

Pfotenhauer, K. M., & Shubrook, J. H. (2017). Vitamin D deficiency, its role in health and disease, and current supplementation. *The Journal of the American Osteopathic Association, 117*, 301–305. https://doi.org/10.7556/jaoa.2017.055.

Plarre, R. (2005). Wegskizzen und andere Mitteilungen. Zeichnungen und spontane Kartographie in Neuguinea. In A. Groh (Ed.), *"beWEGung". Akademische Perspektiven auf Reisen und Ortswechsel* (pp. 173–208). Berlin: Weidler.

Plous, S. (1993). *The psychology of judgment and decision making*. New York: McGraw-Hill.

Poole, C. B., Li, Z., Alhassan, A., Guelig, D., Diesburg, S., Tanner, N. A., Zhang, Y., Evans, T. C., Jr., LaBarre, P., Wanji, S., Burton, R. A., & Carlow, C. K. S. (2017). Colorimetric tests for diagnosis of filarial infection and vector surveillance using non–instrumented nucleic acid loop–mediated isothermal amplification (NINA–LAMP). *PLoS One, 12*(2), e0169011. Published: February 15, 2017. https://doi.org/10.1371/journal.pone.0169011, downloaded 8 June 2017 from http://journals.plos.org/plosone/article?id=10.1371/journal.pone.0169011.

Posner, R. (1989). What is culture? Toward a semiotic explication of anthropological concepts. In W. A. Koch (Ed.), *The nature of culture: Proceedings of the international and interdisciplinary symposium, October 7–11, 1986 in Bochum* (pp. 240–295). Brockmeyer: Bochum.

Rutter, M. (2006). Implications of resilience concepts for scientific understanding. *Annals of the New York Academy of Sciences, 1094*, 1–12. https://doi.org/10.1196/annals.1376.002.

Silva Rios, S., Rios Chen, A. C., Rios Chen, J., Calvano Filho, C. M., Santos Amorim, N. T., Lin, C. W., & Fátima Brito Vogt, M. (2016). Wearing a tight bra for many hours a day is associated with increased risk of breast cancer. *Advances in Oncology Research and Treatments, 1*(1), 105. https://doi.org/10.4172/2572-5025.1000105.

Solomon, C. (2003). Transactional analysis theory: The basics. *Transactional Analysis Journal, 33*(1), 15–22.

Steinfurth, H.-J. (2001). *The pygmies*. VHS video, Films Incorporated.

Stücker, M., Struk, A., Altmeyer, P., Herde, M., Baumgärtl, H., & Lübbers, D. W. (2002). The cutaneous uptake of atmospheric oxygen contributes significantly to the oxygen supply of human dermis and epidermis. *Journal of Physiology, 538*(3), 985–994. https://doi.org/10.1013/jphysiol.2001.013067.

Svane, M. S., Gergerich, E., & Boje, D. (2016). Fractal Change Management and Counter-Narrative in Cross-Cultural Change. In S. Frandsen, T. Kuhn, & M. Wolff Lundholt (Eds.), *Counter-narratives and organization*, Chapter 6 (pp. 129–154). New York: Taylor & Francis. Available online at: http://davidboje.com/vita/paper_pdfs/CHAPTER_Fractal%20change%20management%20and%20counternarrative%20in%20crosscultural.pdf. Accessed 28 Aug 2017.

United Nations Conference on Freedom of Information. Held at Geneva 23 March – 21 April 1948. Final Act. Lake success, New York: UN.

United Nations General Assembly (1948). Universal Declaration of Human Rights. [Part A of General Assembly resolution 217 (III). International Bill of Human Rights].

Vanhove, A. J., Herian, M. N., Perez, A. L. U., Harms, P. D., & Lester, P. B. (2015). Can resilience be developed at work? A meta-analytic review of resilience-building programme effectiveness. *Journal of Occupational and Organizational Psychology*. https://doi.org/10.1111/joop.12123. Available online at: http://digitalcommons.unl.edu/cgi/viewcontent.cgi?article=1010&context=pdharms. Accessed 4 Aug 2017.

Watzlawick, P., Beavin, J. H., & Jackson, D. D. (1967). *Pragmatics of human communication. A study of Interctional patterns, pathologies, and paradoxes*. New York: Norton.

West, K. (2017). Naked and unashamed: Investigations and applications of the effects of naturist activities on body image, self-esteem, and life satisfaction. *Journal of Happiness Studies, 17*, 1–21. https://doi.org/10.1007/s10902-017-9846-1.

Wicklund, R. A. (1990). *Zero-variable theories and the psychology of the explainer*. New York: Springer.

Epilogue

This is an application-oriented book. Therefore, you probably have read it because you intend to do field research in indigenous contexts, and perhaps you are even preparing for a concrete excursion.

When you have done your research in indigenous contexts, you will, ideally, return to your own culture with a widened horizon. It does not necessarily involve a transitional phase that is characterised by a disorienting dilemma, as described by Taylor (1994a, b), before you have an enriched worldview. And it will certainly not be enough to experience only one such particular field setting to take comparative perspectives that are sufficient for the differentiated dealing with trans- and intercultural phenomena. However, minimally invasive research in those traditional indigenous contexts, which are infrastructurally not attached to globalised culture, is the only way of obtaining truly comparative data, as such a setting really contrasts industrial culture. Stay alert with regard to claimed cross-cultural studies, which often only measure different degrees of manifestations within interconnected structures of the global culture.

Over the years, I have made the experience that our society is not just heterogeneous, but rather polarised with contrasting attitudes. Accordingly, for one part of the readership, many of the detailed explanations in this book regarding the meticulous bodily integration into indigenous contexts might seem superfluous – I apologise for that – whereas the other part of the readership might find these passages embarrassing at first sight. This is of course owed to the respective socialisation that a person has gone through within a particular subculture of the globalised society. It would have been unpractical, though, to write one shorter book and one longer book, in order to meet the requirements of both sides. Therefore, the audience more turned towards nature might want to skip those explanations, while the other will hopefully find it useful for overcoming unnecessary obstacles.

229
A. Groh, *Research Methods in Indigenous Contexts*,
https://doi.org/10.1007/978-3-319-72776-9

The focus on very traditional indigenous cultures is owed to a number of circumstances that are related to each other. As it was once put by the United Nations Environment Programme, vital and indispensable knowledge is enshrined in indigenous cultures.[1] Paradoxically, they remain largely ignored, although we could learn so much from them, and they could prevent scientists from some misconceptions. But much worse is the fact that due to the dominant culture's ignorance, severe violations of their rights can happen unnoticed. When doing research in indigenous contexts, you will have to face much human suffering. From this perspective, the focus is directed on very traditional indigenous cultures because they need it most.

You will find that not everyone is willing to understand that particular consideration is necessary with regard to research in indigenous contexts. But these are usually persons, who are not fully familiar with the issue, and especially those who have never experienced immersion in a traditional indigenous setting themselves. Ask them, what would be the alternatives? Carrying out field research in a destructive manner, against one's conscience and better judgement? Or ignoring indigenous peoples, their cultures and their problems altogether?

Furthermore, you might encounter persons who might not appreciate the strict interpretation of the United Nations Declaration on the Rights of Indigenous Peoples and who continue to pledge, explicitly or implicitly, for indigenous peoples to give up their lifestyles and become part of the global culture. This deletion of social systems is usually euphemistically called "transformation" or "process of adapting". The problems of the loss of thousands of cultural systems, aiming for the reduction to one instable global culture which, in an apocalyptic way, is devouring the whole earth, treading it down and breaking it in pieces,[2] are often deliberately overlooked. When you find such complacency, it might be useless to waste your time, energy and nerves. Don't cast pearls before swine.

References

Taylor, E. W. (1994a). Intercultural competency: A transformative learning process. *Adult Education Quarterly, 44*(3), 154–174.

Taylor, E. W. (1994b). A learning model for becoming interculturally competent. *International Journal of Intercultural Relations, 18*(3), 389–408.

---

[1] UNEP news release, Nairobi, 8. Feb. 2001.

[2] Cf. Dan. 7:23.

Index

© Springer International Publishing AG 2018
A. Groh, *Research Methods in Indigenous Contexts*,
https://doi.org/10.1007/978-3-319-72776-9

PGSTL